The Gospel among Religions

The Gospel among Religions

Christian Ministry, Theology, and Spirituality in a Multifaith World

David R. Brockman

and

Ruben L. F. Habito,

Editors

ORBIS BOOKS

Maryknoll, New York 10545

Founded in 1970, Orbis Books endeavors to publish works that enlighten the mind, nourish the spirit, and challenge the conscience. The publishing arm of the Maryknoll Fathers and Brothers, Orbis seeks to explore the global dimensions of the Christian faith and mission, to invite dialogue with diverse cultures and religious traditions, and to serve the cause of reconciliation and peace. The books published reflect the views of their authors and do not represent the official position of the Maryknoll Society. To learn more about Maryknoll and Orbis Books, please visit our website at www.maryknollsociety.org.

Library of Congress Cataloging-in-Publication Data

The Gospel among Religions : Christian ministry, theology, and spirituality in a multifaith world / David R. Brockman and Ruben L. F. Habito, editors.
    p. cm.
  Includes bibliographical references (p.   ).
  ISBN 978-1-57075-899-7 (pbk.)
  1. Missions—Theory. I. Brockman, David R. II. Habito, Ruben L. F., 1947-
  BV2063.G67 2010
  266.001—dc22

                                            2010009881

Contents

Part II
CHRISTIAN MINISTRY, THEOLOGY, AND SPIRITUALITY
IN INTERFAITH DIALOGUE

Preface

RUBEN L. F. HABITO

THIS VOLUME IS OFFERED FOR PASTORS, MINISTERS, CHRISTIAN educators, religious leaders, theological students, and general readers interested in the question "How can Christians, as individuals and communities, live in fidelity to and as effective witnesses of the gospel of Jesus Christ in the context of a multireligious contemporary global society?" It is intended as a sequel to an earlier volume, entitled *Ministry and Theology in Global Perspective: Contemporary Challenges for the Church*, edited by Don Pittman, Ruben L. F. Habito, and Terry Muck (Grand Rapids: Eerdmans, 1996). This latter collection was the outcome of an interseminary course participated in by students from several theological schools in the southwestern region of the United States, team taught by the three editors, who at the time were faculty members at Brite Divinity School, Perkins School of Theology, and Austin Presbyterian Theological Seminary, respectively. Since publication, it had been used over many years as a textbook and reader for classes taught by the editors at their respective institutions. (Don Pittman is now vice president for Academic Affairs and dean at Phillips Theological Seminary in Tulsa, Oklahoma, and Terry Muck is dean of the E. Stanley Jones School of World Mission and Evangelism at Asbury Theological Seminary.) In my case, it remained a staple for a course entitled "World Religions and Christianity: A Global Perspective," required for all Master of Divinity students at Perkins School of Theology, Southern Methodist University, for a good number of years, until it went out of print some years ago.

At that point, conversations began with Kenneth Cracknell, who was then teaching at Brite Divinity School, and Robert Hunt, a colleague at Perkins, to collaborate on a collection that would include more recent developments in the field of theology of religions, comparative theology, and global studies. With his retirement, Kenneth handed over the baton to David Brockman, who had just completed his Ph.D. at Southern Methodist University with a dissertation on recent developments in theology of religions, and who had had several years of experience in teaching courses in world religions to undergraduates, as well as the required course noted above at Perkins School of Theology. As his contribution to the projected volume, Robert Hunt had compiled a collection of material that depicts the panorama of how Christians have interacted with religious others in history. But upon consultation with Bill Burrows and the Orbis editorial staff, it was agreed that it would be best to publish his section as a separate book. (As of June 2010 it is available in print as *The Gospel Among the Nations: A Documentary History of Inculturation*.) Encouraged by Bill Burrows, David Brockman and I thus continued work on a volume focusing on theological issues in relating to the religious other to serve as a handy guide for pastors, Christian educators, seminary students, and general readers. This book is the outcome of this cooperative venture.

A Parliament of the World's Religions held in Melbourne, Australia, in early December 2009 gathered together about six thousand people from all over the world. Among them were roughly a hundred students from fifteen theological schools in North America, who, along with faculty coordinators from these schools, were supported by a grant from the Henry Luce II Foundation to participate in a five-day workshop on the theme "Educating Religious Leaders in a Multifaith World." The workshop built up a consensus among participants of a sense of the urgent need for and a deeper appreciation of the intricacies of a multifaith dimension in the formative education of those who are called to be leaders in their respective religious communities. My own participation in the workshop confirmed for me that a volume like this could be among the resources for the tasks that lay ahead.

Acknowledgments

AMONG THE MANY WHO DESERVE MY THANKS, MY CHIEF DEBT IS TO Kenneth Cracknell, without whom I would not have had the pleasure of collaborating on this project. Kenneth was originally to have played the role I play here. When he decided to step aside, he kindly recommended me—a brand new, unpublished Ph.D.—as his replacement. Yet my debt to Kenneth runs deeper than that. As my instructor at Brite Divinity School in the 1990s, he awakened my interest in the theology of religions and encouraged my initial efforts to make theological sense of my experience as a Christian exploring the profound truths of the Buddhist tradition.

I am also grateful to Kenneth's original collaborators in this project, Ruben L. F. Habito and Robert A. Hunt. Besides serving as my partner in this volume, Ruben was one of my instructors in my Ph.D. work at Southern Methodist University. In addition to his fine work as a scholar of Buddhist thought and practice, he models authentically Christian openness to religious others. Robert Hunt was originally to be our third co-editor; however, his contribution has been published separately by Orbis Books, under the title *The Gospel among the Nations: A Documentary History of Inculturation*. I am grateful to Robert for his valuable input in the planning phase for the present volume.

Two doctoral students at Southern Methodist University deserve special thanks: Cheryl Strimple, who assisted with the initial preparation of sources; and Sarah Bloesch, who helped in formatting the manuscript and obtaining publisher permissions.

I also want to thank my students at the Perkins School of Theology and at Brite Divinity School who "road-tested" parts of this manuscript over the past three years. Their feedback and suggestions have strengthened the book considerably.

I would be remiss if I did not acknowledge the support of the staff at Panera Bread in Fort Worth, who provided the "clean, well-lighted place" where I did much of my work on this book.

Finally, words cannot express the depth of my debt to my spouse, Eleanor Forfang-Brockman. She embarked on the journey of interreligious dialogue many years before I, and she remains my principal source of inspiration. For her support, patience, and love, I am truly grateful.

David R. Brockman
Last Sunday of Epiphany, 2010

* * *

I continue to be thankful to Don Pittman and to Terry Muck, my co-editors of the volume *Ministry and Theology in Global Perspective,* for the collaborative efforts that occasioned enriching conversations and led to ongoing friendships through the years.

Deep gratitude goes to Kenneth Cracknell, who "conspired" with me in planning a new volume that would update *Ministry and Theology,* and who, as he moved up to greener pastures in Vermont, passed the baton to David Brockman and to Robert Hunt, who happily completed his share of work for the project that Orbis subsequently agreed to publish as a separate volume (*The Gospel among the Nations*).

The task of putting this volume together was undertaken as I was serving as Associate Dean for Academic Affairs at Perkins School of Theology, Southern Methodist University. I thank Stephanie Carroll, assistant to the associate dean, for doing her work very well so I could do mine. Special thanks to Lucy Cobbe, who came to the rescue a number of times in response to my calls for help as I got lost in the intricacies of the new versions of Microsoft Word; and to Carolyn Douglas, administrative assistant to the faculty at Perkins, who has accomplished many tasks I requested of her related to this and other projects with a cheerful smile. Much of the meticulous work of seeking permissions to reprint was also undertaken by Peter Jones, Kenneth Loyer, and Sarah Bloesch, Ph.D. students who helped me as research assistants, and I am truly grateful to each of them for their share in the work that went into putting this volume together.

I thank all my colleagues at Perkins for bearing with me in many different ways through the years. Deep gratitude to our dean, William B. Lawrence, for his astute leadership and for the inspiring way he carries on his tasks on behalf of all of us at Perkins. I am grateful to all the students of Perkins School of Theology whom I have met and/or taught over these twenty-some years. I have learned so much from them that goes beyond what I can express here. When some of them who have graduated and are now serving in various capacities in Christian ministry drop in on occasion and tell me they learned something from me too, that is truly unequalled joy, and a source of gratitude as well.

David Brockman and I would like to dedicate this volume to all who have been, are, and will be students at Perkins School of Theology. In particular I would like to acknowledge and express deep thanks to Dodee Frost Crockett (Perkins MTS, 2003) and Billy Crockett (SMU, 2005), for a major donation to the school honoring my work.

Bill Burrows, while he was with Orbis Books, continued to encourage us to keep this project going, and so we did. When the time came for him to move on to newer horizons, Susan Perry kindly took on the editorial tasks in the preparation of this volume. For this, deep gratitude to Sue, and to Robert Ellsberg and our friends at Orbis, for being willing to take the risk involved in seeing this volume published.

And lastly, David Brockman and I thank all the authors, deceased and living, of the essays included in full or excerpted for purposes of the collection, and the publishers who kindly gave permission for these to be reprinted in this volume. The list of authors' names and the publication data of the items included can be found at the end of the volume.

Ruben L. F. Habito
February 22, 2010

Introduction

Christian Ministry and Theological Education in a Multireligious World

"For God so loved the world. . . ."

—John 3:16

A CHRISTIAN IS SOMEONE WHO HAS HEARD THE GOOD NEWS, AND, having welcomed and accepted it as a guiding beacon for one's life, seeks to share this Good News with everyone in the world.

It all began around two thousand years ago in Palestine with a small band of men and women who followed a carpenter's son, one Jesus of Nazareth, who had a short-lived career as an itinerant preacher among the Jewish populace of the time. This man announced the coming of God's reign among the people, and, in proclaiming his message, said and did things that upset people in authority at the time; so they put him to death among criminals. Very soon afterward, his followers went around proclaiming that this Jesus was God's Anointed One (Christ) who was now raised from the dead, and that this was a salvific event for the entire world for all time. The message they sought to convey was that God, unknown and unknowable yet also Creator of heaven and earth, relates to us as a loving Father to his children, and out of love for us and for all creation, chose to be fully manifest in this human being Jesus, who lived and walked among us, died on the cross, and was risen from the dead by the power of God's own Spirit. The Good News of Jesus Christ, in very short form, is that God's reign is in our midst, and that all people are called to enter into God's *kindom*.[1] This One God, loving Father, obedient Son, and vivifying Spirit, loves each of us unconditionally, and is with us even now, calling us to an ever-deeper life of communion in the Divine Life and with one another, for always.

Those who welcome this Good News in faith are commissioned by Jesus himself to go and convey the message to the entire world: "Go therefore and make disciples of all nations, baptizing them in the name of the Father and of the Son and of the Holy Spirit, teaching them to observe all that I have commanded you; and lo, I am with you always, to the close of the age" (Matthew 28:18). The early assembly (*ekklesia* = church) of believers did precisely that, and now,

1

twenty-one centuries later, the followers of Jesus Christ number around one-and-one-half billion, roughly one-fifth of the world's entire population, found in every part of this inhabited world we call planet Earth. Throughout their history, Christians have undertaken this mission that defines their very identity as Christians: living out, witnessing to, and sharing the Good News of Jesus Christ with all. This very word "mission," which comes from the Latin *mitto*, "to send," is about being sent to convey this Good News to all.

How are Christians to relate to people of other religious traditions or to those who reject religion entirely in a way that is faithful to and truly embodies the Good News of unconditional divine love for all of creation? This question comes to us in our twenty-first-century global society with particular urgency, in our world marked by an ever-increasing gap between rich and poor, a growing sense of insecurity due to violence and conflict on different levels, and an impending ecological crisis of global proportions, and in a world wherein exist a wide variety of religious traditions that present differing or even conflicting absolute claims. Sad to say, religion has often served as a source of tension, conflict, and violence in our human history: in short, our religious differences can be counted among the causes of the problems facing us as a global community today.

These are underlying questions posed in this volume: How can we Christians, grounded in our commitment to our own faith tradition to convey the message of God's kindom and God's love for all, relate to and engage "religious others" in constructive ways, that we may live fully in the light of our faith in the Triune God, and offer resources toward healing our Earth community, deeply wounded on many levels? Further, in terms of our mission and ministry to the world, in our own theological understanding, and in the conduct of our spiritual life as Christians, what may we learn in our engagement with those religious others that may shed light on our own tasks? As we endeavor to faithfully live out the Good News and share it with others in the best way we can, we are at the same time called to listen to, understand, and cooperate with people from other religious traditions as we attend to our shared tasks in our global community. In doing so, we may thereby broaden and deepen our own understanding and appreciation of our own Christian faith tradition, and enable it to become more firmly rooted in our own lives and inform the way we relate to the people around us.

The World as My Parish: Cultivating Global Awareness

The term "global village" is often used to describe our contemporary world. This comes from an awareness that all of us who live on this Earth are connected with and interdependent with one another, no matter where we may be. This awareness of our being in a global community came to the fore during the age of space exploration from around the second half of the twentieth century, as the astronauts and cosmonauts beheld this Earth from their rocket ships, and experienced something profoundly holy.[2] The following are some of their remarks reporting their experience.

> As I looked down, I saw a large river meandering slowly along for miles, passing from one country to another without stopping. I also saw huge forests, extending across several borders. And I watched the extent of one ocean touch the shores of separate continents. Two words leaped to mind as I looked down on all this: commonality and interdependence. We are one world." (John-David Bartoe, USA)

> During the eight days I spent in space, I realized that [hu]mankind needs height primarily to better know our long-suffering Earth, to see what cannot be seen close-up. Not just to love her beauty, but also to ensure that we do not bring even the slightest harm to the natural world. (Pham Tuan, Vietnam)

> From space I saw Earth—indescribably beautiful, with the scars of national boundaries gone. (Muhammad Ahmad Faris, Syria)

> The Earth was small, light blue, and so touchingly alone, our home that must be defended like a holy relic. (Aleksei Leonov, USSR)

> My view of our planet was a glimpse of divinity. (Edgar Mitchell, USA)

Only very few select individuals may have had this privilege of seeing our Earth from a rocket ship, but this experience of interconnectedness with our fellow inhabitants of this Earth community, our fellow "earthlings," is now widely shared, approached from different angles and expressed in different ways.

Whether we live in a metropolitan area of the industrialized world, such as Chicago or Paris or Tokyo, or in a barrio in Chiapas, Mexico, or a mining town in South Africa, or a village in Afghanistan, or on a farm ranch deep in the heart of Texas, whatever happens on any part of our globe affects each and every one of us, and conversely, what we do and how we live our lives affect everyone else.

As we celebrate this heightened global awareness in ourselves and among our contemporaries, we are also invited to take a straight look at the grim realities of the world we live in.[3]

Data from UNICEF (United Nations Children's Fund) and other sources indicate that roughly eleven million children under the age of five die from hunger-related causes each year, or around 30,000 on a daily basis.[4] This means one child starves to death every few seconds, in this same world wherein large quantities of food are produced and available to a point of surplus in many places. In other words, millions die of hunger and malnutrition in our world today not because there is not enough food to go around, but because there is a blatantly lopsided maldistribution of resources and means of production between the haves and the have-nots of the world.

This stark inequality that marks our global situation can be seen from different angles. For example, the combined wealth of roughly 500 billionaires is greater than the combined incomes of the poorest half of the world's population. There are other statistical figures that call our attention to the lopsided nature of our priorities on a global scale. Based on a recent study, the estimated additional costs in developing countries to provide water and sanitation for all per year would have been US$9 billion; basic health and nutrition for all, $13 billion; reproductive health for all women, $12 billion; basic education for all, $6 billion. In the same year, the amount spent in cosmetics in the United States amounted to US$8 billion; for ice cream in Europe, $11 billion; for perfumes in Europe and the United States, $12 billion; for pet foods in Europe and the United States, $17 billion. In this same year, total military spending in the world was estimated at $780 billion, and this figure climbed up to $956 billion in 2003.[5]

In other words, while roughly one-sixth of the world's population is consigned to situations of chronic hunger and subhuman conditions, and up to about half continue to live in poverty, a great part of the world's resources are spent, not on those things that would alleviate such poverty and need, but on luxury items, and on weaponry.

The hunger and poverty that are part of the lives of millions of our fellow human beings on earth today are not unrelated to the growing sense of insecurity felt by more and more people in different areas of the world, now making itself felt on a global scale. This sense of insecurity is a key factor for increased military spending in many countries today. Expense for military purposes has increased even more dramatically especially in the past few years, with the escalation of the actual armed conflicts in particularly volatile areas of the world.

It is significant to note that industrialized, high-income countries with 16 percent of the world's population take up 75 percent of world's military expenses. The United States, as the world's superpower, stands out all the more in this regard, with the U.S. military budget for 2006 at $441.6 billion. This includes Defense Department and Department of Energy budgets, the latter of which includes funding for nuclear weaponry. This figure does not include combat figures for the Afghan and Iraq wars, with an extra $70 billion for fiscal year 2006 earmarked over and above the $50 billion approved by Congress. In proportionate terms, U.S. military spending amounts to around 40 percent of the total, 7 times larger than second place China, and 29 times as large as the combined expenses of those labeled as "rogue states" (Cuba, Iran, North Korea, Sudan, Syria, Libya), which total $14.65 billion.

Armed conflicts stemming from various factors, in addition to famines and economic, social, and political crises in different parts of the world, have forced large numbers of peoples to become refugees, uprooted from their ancestral homes and seeking more secure living conditions elsewhere. In 2005, estimates by various international agencies place the number of refugees at over 40 million throughout the world. The majority of these are in Africa and Asia, comprised mostly of women and children.

Expanding on the definition of refugee given by the United Nations Convention of 1951 (Geneva), Catholic social teaching understands "refugees" as referring to "all persons persecuted because of race, religion, membership in particular social or political groups; to the victims of armed conflicts, erroneous economic policy or natural disasters; and . . . to internally displaced persons." These latter are those forcibly uprooted from their homes for various reasons, but who do not cross national frontiers.[6] The fact that large numbers of peoples are seeking places to settle and to call a home becomes a cause of concern, and even alarm, for others, especially in the so-called more affluent countries such as the United States and Western Europe, driving people in these countries to call upon their leaders to tighten their borders and prevent or at least restrict the influx of such "strangers and outsiders" into their own territory. Xenophobia and attitudes of discrimination bring about tensions between segments of the population, and lead to recurrent incidents of violence among different groups. Such a situation in turn serves to heighten the sense of insecurity felt in society.

Every year, over thirty million acres of tropical forests are destroyed, mostly through the activities of corporations that seek timber for commercial use. As a related figure, over 50,000 species of living beings whose natural habitat is found in these forests become extinct.[7] The loss of forests also contributes to the increase in the volume of carbon dioxide piling up in the Earth's atmosphere. Together with emissions from coal-burning power plants and from automobiles, the increase in carbon dioxide is contributing to the widely noted phenomenon of global warming, which is causing and will continue to cause damage to Earth's inhabitants in various ways.

How are Christians called to respond to this dire situation of our global family? A saying attributed to John Wesley is pertinent in this regard: "I look upon all the world as my parish."[8] Setting aside the original context in which Wesley uttered it in the eighteenth century, we can take it as an invitation to widen our horizons, to embrace the entire global community in our own heart as a field of concern. In short, we are called to look at all the Earth and all that fills it (Psalm 24)[9] with the eyes of the One who so loved the world as to send the Only Begotten, that the world may be saved (John 1:16).

The Multireligious Arena of Our Global Community

Our world is an arena of diverse religious beliefs, practices, and traditions. Faced with our finitude and our mortality, we human beings have always been confronted with the big questions that inevitably come to us at some point of our journey through life: What is the point of it all? Who am I? Where do I come from? Where am I going? Is there life after death? What ought I to do? What is ultimate reality? How can we know it? What is my ultimate purpose in life (if any)? Human beings have grappled with these questions in different forms, and thinkers throughout the ages have proposed various answers to those questions.

The many religious traditions of the world, with their differing origins and trajectories of historical development throughout the widely diverse societies and cultures of the world, offer their differing answers to these questions, giving their adherents a sense of meaning, of belonging, of comfort, of some kind of cosmic affirmation. Sociologist Peter Berger describes this role of religion as a "sacred canopy" that contains human beings and shields them from the onslaught of uncertainty in the face of Mystery and also provides a buttress for the fragility of our mortal existence.

Religion also has the capacity to draw out the creative energies in human beings, giving its adherents a sense of belonging, absolute purpose, and a clearly defined direction in life. The downside of this, however, is that members of a given religious group, with its shared vision and values and sense of cohesion as a community, tend to draw a sharp line of distinction between themselves and those outside the group. This distinction easily turns to an attitude of "us" versus "them," and consequently, the denigration or even demonization of "those others" who don't belong to "us." Conflict and violence between individuals and groups can easily arise in the name of religion, and throughout our human history have often in fact arisen.

Given the double-edged nature of the role religion can play in our human society, people of good will belonging to different religious traditions have taken initiatives to foster interreligious understanding, interaction, and cooperation throughout various stages of history. In those regions of the world wherein multiple religious traditions and communities coexist within a given geographical area, such cooperative and mutually beneficial modes of interaction have been devised in those local contexts, if only to protect the members of the different religious communities against threats to their own survival and to their distinctive way of life.

In our twenty-first-century multireligious global society, wherein we live and interact on different levels with people of different religious backgrounds and beliefs wherever we may be located geographically, it is imperative that we all seek to understand our differences, as well as to discern and highlight the common ground we share. Since the last century, initiatives in interreligious dialogue and cooperation have been launched on many fronts, and we are beginning to see the fruits of these various initiatives.

One notable step in this regard was the convening of a Parliament of World Religions in Chicago in 1993, as a commemoration of the World's Parliament of Religions held in conjunction with a World's Fair in Chicago one hundred years before. This earlier Parliament is regarded as the first initiative for a global dialogue of faiths, involving representatives from Eastern as well as Western religious traditions. The 1993 event, attended by more than eight thousand participants from the world's major religious traditions as well as members of indigenous traditions, called for all members of the many different religions to cooperate in the tasks of healing the wounds of our global community based on the resources found within their respective traditions.

One of the highlights of this 1993 Parliament was the document *Towards a Global Ethic: An Initial Declaration*, drafted by Roman Catholic theologian Hans Küng, and endorsed by the religious leaders and participants gathered at the Parliament Assembly. A statement from this document has served as a rallying cry of those who have taken interreligious dialogue as a vital task of our day: "There will be no peace among the nations without peace among religions. There will be no peace among religions without dialogue among the religions."

The 1993 Parliament in Chicago was followed by subsequent gatherings held in Cape Town, South Africa, in 1999; in Barcelona, Spain, in 2004; in Monterrey, Mexico, in 2006; and in Melbourne, Australia, in 2009. These gatherings with participants from all over the world representing the many living religious communities and traditions active in our global society have served to bring representatives of various faith communities together to discuss issues of mutual interest and concern, and share resources in meeting the tasks and challenges of our global community.[10]

Christians are among those who have taken initiatives in interreligious dialogue and cooperation since the latter part of the twentieth century. The promulgation of the document *Nostra Aetate* by the Second Vatican Council of the Roman Catholic Church at its closing session in 1965 opened new horizons for Catholic Christians to engage members of other faith traditions in constructive dialogical efforts and cooperative ventures. The World Council of Churches, in a series of assemblies and conferences, followed suit and issued documents encouraging its member churches to open themselves to interreligious endeavors. The Catholic Federation of Asian Bishops' Conferences, in a joint statement with the World Council of Churches–based Christian Conference of Asia, issued guidelines in 1987 encouraging Christians in the Asian subcontinent to carry on multilevel dialogues of life and faith with their many brothers and sisters of the various religious and spiritual traditions of Asia as a vital aspect of their own Christian life and mission. Mainline and other Christian denominations have also issued official statements encouraging their members in different parts of the world to reach out to their neighbors who belong to other religious communities and traditions in the spirit of Christian love and hospitality.[11]

The papacy of John Paul II was characterized by bold initiatives in interreligious cooperation and dialogue. Among notable examples, Pope John Paul II convened religious leaders of the world's faith traditions to gather together in a World Day of Prayer for Peace in Assisi in 1986, and again in 2002, and also convened Jewish, Christian, and Muslim leaders to gather together for a Day of Prayer for ending the war in Bosnia in 1993.[12]

Theological Grounding for Interreligious Dialogue and Cooperation

In the spirit of the gospel, and as proclaimed by the many official documents of the churches since *Nostra Aetate*, it is incumbent upon Christians, moved by love of God and love of neighbor, to take on the crucial task of working toward greater understanding and cooperation with our neighbors from different faith traditions.[13] Those who are entrusted with the guidance of Christian communities, as pastors and ministers, priests, professional religious, educators, community leaders, and others, are especially called to take the lead in this regard.

For Christians to be able to wholeheartedly engage in the tasks called for in a multireligious world, some theological considerations need to be brought to the fore. In this regard, Karl Barth, one of the highly influential figures of twentieth-century Christian theology, has presented a widely acclaimed theological argument distinguishing "religion" from "revelation." In Barth's framework, religion is about the human attempts to seek and know and grasp the Divine, whereas revelation is about the Divine reaching out in Grace and conveying the authoritative Word that saves human beings from sin and misery. Barth identifies the locus of Divine revelation with Christian faith in Jesus Christ, the Word of God, but he also gives due caution to Christians not to rely on their own smug religiosity and thus fall into "unbelief," which he associates with religion.

Many Christians have followed Karl Barth in this view, and assert the supremacy of their Christian belief and practice over and above all those "others" that belong in the category of "religion." Barth himself, while admitting that he had never met a Hindu, summarily dismissed the Hindu religious traditions as "unbelief," a priori, from his theological position. However, an earnest question that even some followers of Barth legitimately ask is this: can we preclude the possibility that in God's own Divine Wisdom, revelation may have been or is also extended, in different and perhaps to us inscrutable ways, to those outside of the Christian fold? Posing this question more strongly, one can ask: (if God so loved the world,) could Divine revelation also have been extended to different peoples in different ways throughout human history? To say no a priori is to make the preposterous claim that we humans can know the inscrutable mind of God and that we can make a decision on God's behalf. The only way to go forward then would be to undertake an inquiry, with an open-minded, open-hearted, and open-handed attitude that engages members of other religious traditions in earnest dialogue.[14]

In our twenty-first-century global society—which not only allows, but necessitates us meeting, interacting, becoming friends and associates on various levels, with people from differing faith traditions—taking a stance that dismisses the religion of others a priori is not only untenable, but also downright unacceptable. If so, how then are Christians, committed to their own faith tradition, to understand and relate to people of other faith traditions? In this question itself the first step is hinted at: *to understand*. To be well informed about basic features of the world's religious traditions can thus be said to be a basic requisite for living in our contemporary global society, in order to be able to relate constructively and cooperate with peoples of differing beliefs in the many difficult tasks of our world today.[15]

In a thoughtful essay reflecting on ways to overcome conflicts based on religious differences, Jacob Neusner, a well-known scholar in Judaic studies, observed that "the single most important problem facing religion for the next hundred years, as for the last, is that single intellectual challenge: how to think through difference, how to account within one's own faith and framework for the outsider, indeed, for many outsiders."[16]

This, then, comes to the fore as a fundamental requisite for those called to serve, minister to, and/or guide their respective religious communities on different levels in our world today: *theological grounding* from within one's own faith tradition that would enable one to relate constructively with the many individuals and groups that belong under the category of "religious other," even from our markedly differing faith perspectives, and to be able to cooperate with them wholeheartedly in shared tasks of healing the wounds of our Earth community. Needless to say, this kind of theological grounding is a must for those educational institutions preparing religious leaders for ministry in their respective communities.

At a Parliament of the World's Religions held in Melbourne, Australia, in December 2009, among the hundreds of presentations and panel discussions on various topics relating to interreligious dialogue and cooperation among participants from the world's many faith traditions, a series of special sessions was conducted on the theme "Educating Religious Leaders for a Multireligious Society." Undertaken with support from the Association of Theological Schools (of North America) and funded by the Henry Luce II Foundation, this five-day seminar was open to the general public and attended by over one hundred theological students from fifteen selected Christian, Jewish, and Muslim educational institutions in North America. The seminar addressed questions such as the following: Why is there a need for a multireligious education of religious leaders (inclusive of all traditions and communities) in our contemporary world, and what does this education consist in? What are the resources for and the obstacles to multireligious education in one's own religious community or tradition? What are the virtues and skills needed by religious leaders for guiding their respective communities in a multireligious world? In addressing these questions, examples and practical initiatives already taken by various theological schools and religious communities along these lines were also offered and considered.

In response to the "why" of educating religious leaders in a multireligious world, a simple answer that can be given is one that echoes the quip attributed to well-known explorer George Mallory when asked why he wanted to climb Mt. Everest: "Because it's there." There is by now an ever-growing number of possible institutional, professional, bibliographical, and other kinds of resources that provide the stimulus, needed information, and technical expertise in this regard. The Association of Theological Schools has been heralding multicultural, and, by consequence, multireligious formation as an important feature of theological education among its current and prospective members. This is especially vital for those preparing to guide religious communities of different traditions and denominations as they course through the crucial tasks facing all of us in our global society.

Virtues and Skills for Ministry in Interreligious Settings

In addition to adequate theological grounding on how to situate the religious other within the framework of one's faith tradition, there are certain attitudes, virtues, and skills that would appear to be crucially needed in being able to creatively relate to, engage, and cooperate with religious others. In an excellent volume specifically addressing the subject, Catherine Cornille has laid out humility, commitment, interconnection, empathy, and hospitality as five such key elements to be nourished and cultivated in this regard.[17]

Humility, to be distinguished from "modesty" that entails a reluctance to acknowledge a due honor or rightful claim, is an attitude and virtue that ensures an openness and capacity for growth in our search for truth. If we look at members of other religious traditions with an attitude that we hold *the* truth, that they either do not or have only a partial grasp of it, and that we have nothing to learn from them, we are not only closing off all doors for a veritable heart-to-heart communication with others, we are also depriving ourselves of the possibility of seeing new horizons, and obstructing growth and deepening in our very own understanding and appreciation of what is true, both in the worldly as well as in the religious sense.

Yet genuine humility is not to be equated with an attitude of religious relativism, but can and should come hand in hand with a firm *commitment* to one's own faith tradition. Such a commitment on the one hand may be seen by some to be an obstacle to interreligious dialogue and cooperation with members of other faith traditions. Quite the contrary: without such a commitment, interreligious interaction on different dimensions will remain on the level of bland cocktail party discourse. It is only as I remain committed to my own Christian faith and engage with others also committed to their own respective religious communities and traditions that true learning and broadening of horizons can result on all sides, as we challenge one another grounded on mutual trust and friendship.[18]

A sense of *interconnection* between members of different religious communities comes home to us as we consider what we do have in common as persons committed to a faith tradition, with loyalties to something bigger than our own individual self-serving interests, with a shared openness to Mystery even if we may relate, and understand and interpret it in diverging or contrasting ways, and in our contemporary global society, especially with the manifold challenges of healing our global society faced by all of us as inhabitants of Planet Earth.

This interconnection that undergirds our solidarity with peoples of differing faith traditions is further enhanced by an attitude of *empathy*, the human capacity to "stand in another's shoes," to put oneself in the place of another, and see, think, and feel from the perspective of the other. The activation of such a capacity in our interactions with religious others can effectively and definitively broaden our own horizons, and not only enable us to see through own biases and overcome our prejudices, but also broaden and deepen our own understanding, appreciation, and theological articulation of our own faith tradition.[19]

Hospitality, understood as a virtue that welcomes and embraces the other as one's own in a spirit of kinship, also involves an acceptance of the other *as other* in the face of religious differences, and in this context of interreligious encounter and dialogue, implies "an attitude of openness and receptivity to those very differences as a possible source of truth."[20] Recognizing those differences, with earnest attempts at sorting them out with all the intellectual and other tools at one's disposal, but with the honesty to acknowledge where differences remain as differences, that is, with a willingness to "agree to disagree," keeps the relationship within a spirit of mutual respect, without engulfing the other unwarrantedly into one's own self-defined and determined theological framework or worldview. In other words, while welcoming the other into one's own circle, allowing space for Mystery to be an active element paves the way for continuing growth and dynamism and mutual challenge in the relationship.

The virtues and attitudes outlined above issue forth from a basic spiritual attitude, that of an openness to listening to the voice of the Holy Spirit as she speaks in the depths of our hearts. It is the work of Holy Spirit that will open to us new horizons in understanding, and will assure us, as we go about our tasks of healing the wounds of our global family in cooperation with our brothers and sisters of the different faith traditions, that the kindom is in our midst.

Our Approach

The introductory essay above has presented a bird's-eye view of our twenty-first-century world as the context in which the Good News is to be conveyed and shared with all, noting various features that bring home to us the brokenness and serious dysfunction of our global family. Highlighting the multireligious character of our global society and the need for interreligious understanding and cooperation, it has also offered a brief outline of virtues and attitudes to be cultivated for taking on the tasks and challenges of living in a multireligious world.[21]

The first part of the book, introduced by an essay that surveys attitudes Christians have taken toward religious others and summarizes recent developments in Christian theologies of religions, consists in a collection of readings representing the different ways Christians have thought theologically about other religious traditions, from New Testament texts to more recent theologians. The last segment of this first part includes excerpts from significant church documents that address the question of relating to religious others constructively in the light of Christian self-understanding, mission, and ministry.

The second part is a collection of essays exploring and describing new horizons in Christian ministry, theology, and spirituality by various authors who have engaged with and continue to learn from members of other religious traditions, while reflecting on the implications of these interreligious encounters for one's own Christian faith.

Intended to serve as a handy guide and collection of resources for those who serve Christian communities as pastors and ministers, as Christian educators and in other service roles, as well as for the general reader seeking to navigate through the issues involved in living in our multireligious global society, this volume is also offered for use as a reference or as a textbook for courses in seminaries or theological schools preparing students for various forms of Christian ministry and leadership.[22]

Notes

1. The Greek term *basileia tou theou*, translated as "kingdom of God" or "reign of God," has been rendered as *kindom of God* by theologian Ana María Isasi-Díaz. The term highlights the kinship and communion of all created beings with God our source of life.

2. See Kevin W. Kelley, ed., for the Association of Space Explorers, *The Home Planet* (Reading, MA: Addison-Wesley, 1988). The citations in the following text are from this volume, which also presents photographs of Earth taken from space.

3. The Worldwatch Institute publishes an annual *State of the World* report, which details aspects of the global scenario. A cursory look at the issues of the past several years would suffice to indicate the serious condition of our global woundedness on many levels.

4. State of the World's Children, 2005, UNICEF.

5. Poverty Facts and Statistics, in http://www.globalissues.org/article/26/poverty-facts-and-stats.

6. Pontifical Council Cor Unum, and Pontifical Council for the Pastoral Care of Migrants and Itinerant Peoples, *Refugees: A Challenge to Solidarity* (Rome: Editrice Vaticana, 1992).

7. www.rainforest-alliance.org.

8. In a letter to James Hervey, March 20, 1739. In Albert Outler, ed., *John Wesley* (New York: Oxford University Press, 1964), 72.

9. From a translation of Psalm 24 by Norman Fischer, *Opening to You: Zen-Inspired Translations of the Psalms* (New York: Penguin Compass, 2002), 36.

10. Detailed descriptions of the themes and accomplishments of the Parliaments of the World's Religions held so far can be accessed at the Web page of the Council for the Parliament of the World's Religions, with its head office located in Chicago: www.parliamentofreligions.org.

11. Excerpts of these documents are included in part I of this volume, with references for accessing their full texts.

12. See Byron L. Sherwin and Harold Kasimov, eds., *John Paul II and Interreligious Dialogue* (Maryknoll, NY: Orbis Books, 1999). His successor, Benedict XVI, appears to have stepped back from taking such initiatives. The latter, as Josef Cardinal Ratzinger, head of the Vatican Congregation of Faith and Doctrine, is known for having drafted *Dominus Iesus*, promulgated by the Congregation in 2000, which reemphasized the supremacy of Christian revelation as handed down in the Roman Catholic Church. This was a document widely viewed as dampening the spirit of interreligious understanding and cooperation that *Nostra Aetate* had opened up and that had been followed up by further Roman Catholic initiatives up to this time. See Pontifical Council for Interreligious Dialogue, *Interreligious Dialogue: The Official Teaching of the Catholic Church (1963-1995)*, ed. Francesco Gioia (Boston: Pauline Books, 1997).

13. See also Scott Jones, *Evangelistic Love of God and Neighbor: A Theology of Witness and Discipleship* (Nashville: Abingdon, 2003), which offers convincing theological grounding from an Evangelical Christian perspective for reaching out to those from other religious traditions, seeking fellowship through mutual understanding and cooperation, based on the Christian mandate to love God and our neighbor.

14. David Lochhead, a "neo-Barthian," offers helpful criteria for Christians in pursuing this matter, in his *The Dialogical Imperative: A Christian Reflection on Interfaith Encounter* (Maryknoll, NY: Orbis Books, 1989).

15. A survey of the basic features of the world's religious traditions is recommended as a component for those using this volume in classroom contexts.

16. Don Alvin Pittman, Ruben L. F. Habito, and Terry C. Muck, eds., *Ministry and Theology in Global Perspective: Contemporary Challenges for the Church* (Grand Rapids, MI: Eerdmans, 1996), 465-66.

17. Catherine Cornille, *The Im-possibility of Interreligious Dialogue* (New York: Crossroad, 2008).

18. James Fredericks discusses the fruits of interreligious friendship in an essay in the second part of this volume, pp. 218-24.

19. Examples of how Christian theological horizons can be radically expanded in considering perspectives and ideas from other religious traditions are also offered in this volume. See articles in the second part, in the section on Theology in Interfaith Dialogue.

20. Cornille, *The Im-possibility of Interreligious Dialogue*, 177.

21. See ibid. for a detailed treatment.

22. See also *Changing the Way Seminaries Teach: Pedagogies for Interfaith Dialogue*, ed. David Roozen and Heidi Hadsell (Hartford Seminary Series on Innovation in Theological Education, 2009), as a valuable resource containing case studies from six different theological schools on theological education in a multireligious context.

PART I

Christian Attitudes toward Religious Others

Introduction

Thinking Theologically about Religious Others: Christian Theologies of Religions

DAVID R. BROCKMAN

We explain the fact that the Milky Way is there by the doctrine of creation, but how do we explain the fact that the Bhagavad Gita is there?[1]

WILFRED CANTWELL SMITH'S QUESTION CRYSTALLIZES A CENTRAL concern of the Christian theology of religions. It is a question of origins: How do we as Christians account theologically for the existence of religions other than Christianity? If God is one, why are there so many religions?[2]

However, Christian theologies of religions rarely, if ever, stop at this etiological problem. They also wrestle with two other questions (or, more accurately, two constellations of questions). First, what is the relation of other religions to the Christian "thing"? Commonly—though by no means exclusively—this question is framed in *soteriological* terms: Are religious others[3] in any sense "saved"? Does the fact that they do not believe in Christ place them beyond the scope of his saving work?[4] The question of relations can also be framed in terms of *validity*: Does the fact that other religions differ in important respects from Christianity make them invalid? Does difference amount to idolatry, pure and simple? Or is it more complicated than that? Is it possible that the God to whom Christians witness is active in and through other religions, and if so, how?

Second, what implications (if any) do the beliefs and practices of religious others have for Christian theology? Are they irrelevant to Christian theology simply because they are not Christian? Or can Christian theologians learn from them, and if so, what is the relation of such beliefs and practices to the sources and norms of Christian theology?[5]

Pulling together these different strands of inquiry, we can formulate the following provisional definition of the Christian theology of religions: it is *Christian theological reflection about the existence and significance of religious others, and about their relation to Christianity and that which it proclaims (e.g., salvation, knowledge of God).*[6]

Despite this broad commonality of subject matter, there is no single, universally accepted Christian theology of religions. Quite the contrary: Christians have developed many different approaches to theological reflection about religious others.[7] Furthermore, as in other areas of Christian theology, the theology of religions has undergone significant development over the last two thousand years. The following sections of this chapter examine the diversity and development of the Christian theology of religions. The first section looks at the Christian theology of religions diachronically, tracing its history and development. The second section offers a synchronic view, identifying commonalities of orientation across time. We conclude with suggestions for future development in the theology of religions.

Continuity and Change: The History and Development of Christian Attitudes toward the Religious Other[8]

The story of Christian theological reflection about religious others can be broken into three parts, which together inscribe a broad circle, from diversity to monopoly and back to diversity. In its early days, Christianity was one religious community among many, jostling for space in a diverse religious environment. Christians differed about its relationship to other religious traditions and about the soteriological status of religious others. This changed during the second period, that of Western Christendom, when Christianity was the official religion first of the Roman imperial state and then of the medieval European states. Christian theologians displayed little concern with religious others, and the few comments about them were largely negative. Then, beginning with the "discoveries" of the navigators sailing under the flags of Portugal and Spain, Christianity once again found itself as one religion among many. This third period is marked by increasing awareness of religious diversity around the globe and, more recently, within Western societies themselves. In struggling to cope with this situation, Christian theologians, as they did in the early period, have adopted various approaches. Let us examine these three periods in greater detail.

The Early Period (to ca. 400 C.E.)

Due to the particular circumstances in which Christianity had its origins, its adherents have been thinking theologically about other religions from the beginning. Much as Buddhism and Jainism arose within the Indian religious context commonly called Hinduism, Christianity began as a messianic reform movement within the Judaism(s) of Palestine in the first century C.E. Since the new movement did not succeed in replacing other forms of Judaism, Christians had to come to terms with the fact that many of their former co-religionists did not convert to Christianity.[9] As the New Testament texts indicate, Christians early on recognized a need to establish their own identity in relation to the continuing Jewish traditions and communities. Complicating this process of identity formation was the fact that Christians and Jews shared not only a body of texts—the Hebrew Bible, or Old Testament—but also basic notions about God, an emphasis on salvation, a concern for the poor and the outsider, a wisdom tradition, and belief in the fundamental goodness of the divinely created cosmos.

Given the fact that Christianity asserted both its distinctiveness *from* Judaism and its shared heritage *with* Judaism, Christian thought about Judaism—and, as we will see, other religious traditions as well—was from the beginning characterized by what Lucien Legrand terms the two axes of continuity and discontinuity.[10] These two axes reflected the affirmations Christians made about Jesus Christ himself. On the one hand, Christians held that Christ is the culmination of the whole salvation history from Adam's fall through the election of the people of Israel (e.g., Jesus says that he comes not to abolish but to fulfill the Law and the prophets [Matt 5:17-18]). On the other hand, Christians held that in the Christ-event God has done something unique and decisive. Christ is the new Adam (1 Cor 15:40-50); he is the mediator of a new covenant between God and humanity (Heb 8:6-13).

The tensions between continuity and discontinuity raised a number of questions about Christians' relationship to Judaism, questions that form the foundation of the Christian theology of religions. In what respects does the Christian message preserve and carry on the preceding (and continuing) Jewish tradition? And in what respects does the gospel represent a break with that tradition? Given the new circumstances of the coming of God in Jesus Christ, what are Christians to make of God's historical promises to Israel? Are Jews still the "chosen people," in light of their non-acceptance of the Christian message?[11] Given the fact that Christians share a body of sacred scripture with the Jews, what accounts for the significant difference between Christian and Jewish interpretations of those texts?

There also arose a number of soteriological questions. If Christ is the one and only savior, what was the soteriological status of those Jews who lived and died before "the Word became flesh and lived among us" (John 1:14), such as Moses, David, and the prophets? Did Christ's salvific work operate retroactively, and if so, how, and under what conditions? If not, how can God be called just and loving?

Similar questions characterized Christian thought about religions other than Judaism, the so-called pagan religions of the Gentiles. Although the Gentiles seem to have been no more than a marginal concern of Jesus himself (see the readings under "New Testament Texts," below), they grew increasingly important as Christianity spread beyond Palestine and eventually became a predominantly Gentile community. In this broader context, Christianity found itself as one religion among many. Besides the Roman imperial cult and the mystery religions (such as the cults of Isis/Osiris and Mithras), Christianity ran up against the various philosophical schools, which concerned themselves with questions we would today associate with "religion": the nature of ultimate reality, the nature and destiny of the human soul, how one lives a virtuous life, how one distinguishes good from evil, and so forth. As was the case with Judaism, Christianity had to formulate its own identity over against these other religious (or religio-philosophical) traditions.

Once again, Christian thought was concerned with the two axes of continuity and discontinuity. Is the Christian message an utterly "new thing" for the Greeks? Or is there some continuity between the Gospel and the venerable tradition of Greek thought and religiosity? Paul's speech in Athens (see readings below) manifests both tendencies. The axis of discontinuity appears in his clear opposition to what he considers the idolatry of the Greeks, and in his declaration that God "commands all people everywhere to repent." However, Paul also quotes from pre-Christian Greek writers—that is, "pagan" testimony—in support of his Christian message. In doing so, he appeals to a kind of divine witness already present among the Greeks—in other words, to an underlying continuity between the Christian message and the Greek tradition (or at least aspects thereof).

From the second century on, these two approaches characterized Christian theological reflection about the "pagan" religions. While insisting on the distinctiveness of the gospel, Justin Martyr and Clement of Alexandria stressed the gospel's continuity with whatever is good and true in the Greek religio-philosophical tradition. Tertullian and Cyprian, on the other hand, stressed discontinuity, holding that only Christian teaching is salvific, or, in a phrase that would be associated with Cyprian, *extra ecclesiam nulla salus* ("There is no salvation outside the church").

The soteriological questions that were raised in regard to Judaism also arose in theological reflection about the "pagans." If Christ is the one and only savior, what was the soteriological status of those Gentiles who lived and died before the incarnation, particularly such worthies as Socrates and Pythagoras? Did Christ's salvific work operate retroactively, and if so, how, and under what conditions? If such admirable persons were excluded from salvation, how can God be called just and loving?

Christendom (400s to ca. 1500)

After centuries of intermittent but at times devastating persecution, Christianity suddenly "made it." It was adopted by the emperor Constantine, and within a generation, it was established as the official religion—and as the only officially *tolerated* religion—of the Roman Empire.

As Joseph Kitagawa notes, this new relationship between church and state was a quid pro quo arrangement. For his part, Constantine "envisaged a new religious-cultural-social-political synthesis," under his own supreme authority, "which was to be given its cosmic legitimation by Christianity." For its part, "The Christian community . . . eager to be on the main stage in the empire, coveted the opportunity to serve Constantine, even though it had to be subservient to his will." As a result of this new alliance, Christianity "began to be reshaped, patterning itself after the prototype of the *imperium*."[12]

Under this new "religious-cultural-social-political synthesis"—which I will call the "Christendom synthesis"—allegiance to the church came to be conflated with allegiance to the imperial state. Christianity was threatened when the state was threatened. And vice versa: disloyalty to the church came to be seen as treason to the state. Heretics and non-Christians were not simply a theological problem: they were seen to threaten the religious-political order, the Christendom synthesis, itself.

After 380, when the emperor Theodosius I established Christianity as the official religion of the Roman imperial state, non-Christians began to suffer persecution as intense and sustained as that which Christians had endured before Constantine. Theodosius "promulgated harsh anti-pagan laws and ordered the destruction of the huge, world-famous Serapis temple in Alexandria."[13] Presaging the Nazis's book-burning spectacles two millennia later, Christian officials organized the destruction of non-Christian writings "in great bonfires at the center of the town square," and discouraged copyists "from replacing them by the threat of having their hands cut off."[14] The very instruments of coercive state power which had been used to punish Christians were now used by Christian authorities against non-Christians and those Christians who deviated from orthodoxy.

The Christendom synthesis inevitably affected Christian theology. Augustine, bishop of the North African city of Hippo, employed the parable of the banquet (Luke 14:22-23) to justify the use of state force against those who deviated from what he perceived as orthodoxy. Thomas Aquinas later used Augustine's argument to support forcibly compelling heretics (though not Jews or other non-Christians) to return to the official Catholic faith.[15]

Beginning in the fifth century, various Germanic peoples, some non-Christian, overran the Western empire in successive waves. By 1000, however, most of Europe had been (at least nominally) Christianized, and the Christendom synthesis re-emerged.[16] Although there was persistent tension—and sometimes outright conflict—between church and state, the Christendom synthesis remained the ideal, if not always the actuality, throughout the medieval period. Illustrative of this alliance between the power of the church and the power of the state were the successive Crusades, beginning in 1095, in which the church authorized the use of "Christian" military force to retake the Holy Land from the Muslims.

Theologically, this was a period of great confidence in the rightness of the Western European Christian perspective and institutions. Until the late fifteenth century, there was a general belief that the gospel message had reached all parts of the world; those who were not Christian had willingly rejected the gospel message and were thus justifiably outside the realm of salvation. Accordingly, in 1215 the Fourth Lateran Council gave the doctrine *extra ecclesiam nulla salus* a new, extreme form: "There is one Universal Church of the faithful, outside of which there is *absolutely* no salvation."[17]

Due in part to this ecclesiocentric orientation, but also to Western European ignorance about the rest of the world, this period saw few works of systematic theological reflection about religious others. As illustrated by the excerpt from Thomas Aquinas (see the readings below), Christian theological reflection about religious others in this period was confined to scattered passages embedded in discussions of other topics. Ironically, Thomas himself borrowed philosophical concepts from the "pagan" philosopher Aristotle, mediated through Muslim scholars, who had preserved the Greek philosophical tradition that Western Christianity had largely forgotten.

One of the few works from this period devoted to the consideration of religious others is Nicholas of Cusa's *De Pace Fidei* ("The Peace of Faith," excerpted below). Nicholas meditates on the problem of interreligious violence (he has in mind the recent Muslim conquest of Byzantium), and envisions an irenic solution. True to the time, the supreme confidence of Christendom resurfaces in the fact that the solution Nicholas imagines is a single religion with Christ as the center, recognized as the true God by the representatives of Judaism, Islam, and Hinduism.

Modernity and After (since ca. 1500)

In the late 1400s, the European "discovery" of the rest of the world (the Americas, sub-Saharan Africa, east Asia, and the Pacific) gradually stirred Christian thinkers from their theological slumber regarding religious others. They awoke to two disconcerting realizations. First, not only were most of the world's inhabitants non-Christians, but, contrary to the governing assumption of the medieval period, most had never encountered the gospel. Second, alongside Christianity, Judaism, and Islam, there existed venerable and highly sophisticated religious systems, which envisioned the Ultimate, the cosmos, and humanity in ways that were both radically different from Christianity and surprisingly similar. For the first time since the beginning of Christendom, Western Christians became conscious of themselves as one religious community among many. We are still dealing today with the issues raised by these realizations of the early Modern period. Indeed, these issues have become all the more pressing given the continual "shrinking" of the world that began with the so-called voyages of discovery.[18]

For much of the modern period, the dominant Christian theological approach to religious others asserted the supremacy of Christianity and the necessity of the church (the Catholic view) or explicit faith in Christ (the principal Protestant view) to salvation. With some notable exceptions (discussed below), religious difference was regarded as a sign of deficiency at best, of idolatry at worst. Yet European theologians often made such claims without substantial, direct knowledge of the religious traditions they were condemning.[19]

Nevertheless, the "discovery" of vast numbers of religious others raised difficult soteriological questions that had largely been on the back burner during the Christendom period. If Christ was the one and only savior, what was the soteriological status of the innumerable peoples in the newly discovered lands who lived and died without ever hearing the gospel? Given the fact that they never (explicitly) believed in Christ or were baptized, did Christ's salvific work also apply to them? If so, how were they saved, and under what conditions; and what does the answer say about the status of the church and its sacraments? On the other hand, if Christ's salvific work did *not* apply to these non-Christian peoples, how can God be called just and loving?

In light of these troubling questions (as the editors of *Ministry and Theology in Global Perspective* write), "A growing number of Christians, especially Roman Catholics, judged it no longer appropriate to try to maintain the rhetoric of the traditional doctrine of no salvation outside the church in view of the overwhelming number of innocent persons, past and present, involved."[20] The theological problem lay in reconciling belief in the centrality and necessity of the church with the belief that a just and loving God would not condemn those who had not encountered the gospel.

For Roman Catholic thinkers, Thomas Aquinas's notion of baptism by desire offered one way to reconcile these two notions: "If pagans could not be baptized with water (*in re*), they could 'through desire' (*in voto*). If they followed their conscience and lived morally, they were implicitly expressing a desire to join the church and could thus get through the doorway of salvation."[21] Another reconciliation for Catholic thinkers involved the *inculpability* of non-Christians: "If a [non-Christian] person were truly open to the mysterious inward workings of divine grace within the interiority of his or her own soul, such a person might be *oriented toward* the church even if he or she had never heard of it and thus, from God's perspective, inculpable."[22] In 1854, Pope Pius IX gave voice to this compromise between the necessity of the church and the possibility of salvation beyond its boundaries:

> Certainly we must hold it as of faith that no one can be saved outside the apostolic Roman Church, that this is the only ark of salvation. . . . But nevertheless, we must likewise hold it as certain that those who labor in ignorance of the true religion, if that ignorance be invincible, will never be charged with any guilt on this account before the eyes of the Lord. Now who is there who would arrogate to himself the power to point out the extent of such ignorance according to the nature and variety of peoples, regions, talents, and so many other things.[23]

This relatively charitable perspective opened the way for the work of Karl Rahner in the twentieth century.

For many Protestants, however, such solutions were not available, since they seemed to run counter to Protestantism's strong assertion of the radical discontinuity between Christianity and other religions, of the need for explicit faith in Christ, and of the centrality of the Bible over reason and tradition. Consequently, for much of this period, Protestant discourse about religious others was largely negative.[24] Rather than allowing for the possibility of divine presence among non-Christians, Protestants (especially in the nineteenth century) tended to stress the need for conversionary mission.

Ironically, a more open and nuanced attitude toward religious others came from some of the very Christians, Catholic and Protestant alike, who were sent to convert them, and who thereby gained first-hand knowledge of their perspective, beliefs, and practices. For example, the Dominican priest Bartolomé de Las

Casas (1484-1566), the first bishop of the southern Mexican region of Chiapas, developed a deep respect for the indigenous peoples of the Americas. He argued that they not only were nobler and more rational than the ancient Greeks, but also held a superior notion of God.[25] Appalled by the gross mistreatment of the Indians at the hands of their "Christian" conquerors and overlords, Las Casas even envisioned a Day of Judgment in which Christians, because of their oppression of the Indians and because of the latter's own good works, will be outnumbered by unbelievers at the right hand of God.[26]

Equally important was the contribution of Jesuit missionaries to Asia, most notably Robert de Nobili (1577-1656) and Matteo Ricci (1552-1610). Much as Justin Martyr and Clement of Alexandria had found much to admire (and to claim as proto-Christian) in the Greek philosophical tradition, so de Nobili developed deep respect for Hinduism, as did Ricci for Confucianism.[27] These missionaries, as J. J. Clarke writes, "sent back to Europe detailed and sympathetic accounts of the beliefs and practices of the people they sought to convert," and produced some of the first translations of the Asian religious classics into Latin.[28] In many cases, this was the first time the texts of Hinduism, Buddhism, Confucianism, and Daoism were available in the West, and they had a significant effect on Western thought. Clarke writes that the Jesuit missionaries' reports and translations of Asian texts

> were widely read in Europe in the latter part of the seventeenth century, and the ideas they transmitted to the West were to have a profound influence on the European mind of that era, entering deeply into the ideological debates of the Enlightenment period, and playing a part in the formation of some of the major ideas of the time in ways which are often not adequately acknowledged.[29]

As Clarke suggests, the European encounter with religious others coincided with the beginnings of modernity, a true sea change in Western culture. Wearied by decades of intra-Christian violence and buoyed by recent advances in science and technology, prophets of modernity such as Voltaire, Kant, and Hegel promoted faith in human reason as the basis of knowledge, rather than revelation or religious authority. Modernity also saw the rise of democratic thought, a new emphasis on the individual, advocacy of individual human rights, and the rise of free-market capitalism and the middle class. In the dominant cultural circles in the West, a new, secular confidence in human progress along European lines replaced the religious confidence of Christendom. As Steven Best notes, the advocates of modernity depicted the flow of human history in terms of an overarching teleological narrative:

> Under the secularizing influences of modern rationality, Enlightenment philosophers interpreted historical events in terms of improvement in the human condition rather than the realization of a divine plan. History was thereafter understood in terms of progress, rather than providence, where progress signified cumulative advances in human learning, morals, happi-

ness, and freedom. . . . History is seen to be the process of the civilization and education of the human species, of the realization of universal norms such as freedom, equality, and reason. This process is motivated and defined by cumulative advances in science, economics, morality, and politics, which occur through the gradual rationalization of social and personal existence. . . . Each era advances the progressive movement of history more than the preceding one and the whole process culminates in European modernity with the moral improvement or perfection of human beings.[30]

Another result of the European encounter with religious others was the rise of the discourse of "comparative religion" or "history of religions." This new discipline, which arose in part from the translations and reports of the missionaries, grew apace in the nineteenth and twentieth centuries and rapidly branched into numerous approaches (including anthropological, sociological, phenomenological, and philosophical). Working with the sacred texts of other religions (as well as reports from the new disciplines of ethnography and anthropology), Western scholars such as Max Müller, William James, Rudolf Otto, and Emile Durkheim detected fundamental similarities between what came to be called the "world religions." This essentially modern (and essentially European) category was usually thought to include Christianity, Judaism, Islam, Hinduism, Buddhism, Confucianism, Daoism, and sometimes Zoroastrianism.[31] The world religions were held to differ from "primitive" religions by having certain characteristics in common. These included a set of moral teachings (often remarkably similar from one "world religion" to the next), a corpus of sacred texts, a movement from polytheism to ethical monotheism, a sense of the holy or sacred, some sense of transcendence and immanence, and a criticism of crude idolatry.

In this period, there also surfaced the notion that understanding one's own religious tradition entails learning about other religious traditions. For instance, Paul Carus, in his *Buddhism and Its Christian Critics* (1897), "expressed the belief that 'Mankind does not want Buddhism, nor Islam, nor Christianity; mankind wants the truth, and the truth is best brought out by an impartial comparison', and urged that 'every religious man should study other religions in order to understand his own.'"[32] This insight would later resurface as a key argument in support of comparative theology (discussed below).

By the early nineteenth century, as Western scholars grew more knowledgeable about the sophistication and complexity of other religions, as well as the common ground between Christianity and religious others, it became more difficult for Christian theologians to make unqualified assertions about their inferiority, or to insist that they were totally without truth or the presence of the divine. This had a dramatic impact on Christian theological reflection. Indeed, the German Protestant theologian and philosopher of history Ernst Troeltsch (1865-1923) noted in 1897 that "the rise of a comparative history of religion has shaken the Christian more deeply than anything else."[33]

In the nineteenth and early twentieth centuries, this disturbance was particularly evident in the Protestant community. A common strategy in this period was to define religion in a particular way (usually drawing on features of Christianity) and then show how Christianity represents its ultimate or most complete manifestation: that is, as Troeltsch puts it, to argue that Christianity "is not a *particular* religion, it is *religion*."[34] For Friedrich Schleiermacher (1768-1834), the essence of religion lies in a universal "feeling of absolute dependence" that Christianity alone (and Protestantism in particular) expresses fully. It should be noted, however, that Schleiermacher derives this universal experience not from data from the religions themselves, but from his own Pietist Christian background.[35] By contrast, one of Schleiermacher's successors, Rudolf Otto (1869-1937), looked both within Christianity and in other religions (predominantly Hinduism) for a common essence. In his *The Idea of the Holy* (*Das Heilige*, 1917), Otto argues that what characterizes all religion is the essentially non-rational experience of the numinous, the "Wholly Other," which he called the *mysterium tremendum et fascinans*, the awe-inspiring and enthralling mystery. Yet while Otto finds common ground between Christianity and other religions, he, like Schleiermacher, also asserts the superiority of the former.[36]

In the mid-twentieth century, the Swiss theologian Karl Barth (1886-1968) gave this approach a novel twist by first setting up a dichotomy between divinely originated "revelation" and human-originated "religion" (which he equated with "unbelief"), and then arguing that Christianity is the only religion that, thanks to divine revelation, recognizes its own character as unbelief, and can therefore be considered the true religion. Like Schleiermacher, however, Barth decides on Christianity's supremacy a priori, not as a result of first-hand investigation into the actual beliefs and practices of religious others.[37]

While sharing with Schleiermacher the modern metanarrative of human progress with Christianity at the apex, the Anglican theologian Frederick Denison Maurice (1805-1872) developed a more nuanced and positive view of religious others. Echoing John's Gospel, Maurice stressed that the kingdom of Christ is not simply a future hope, but has always been vitally present, and continues to be so today. This had important implications for his view of religious others. Since for Maurice, "There was not and could not have been any place or time when Christ was not present," he must have been present in non-Christian religions as well, making them a preparation for the gospel.[38] The religions of the world were not mere human inventions, but were "integral to the working out of God's purposes in the world."[39] Maurice even anticipated the notion of some contemporary theologians of religions that dialogue with other religions can serve as a corrective to Christianity's own errors—allowing, for example, the rediscovery of doctrines which Christians "might have forgotten, understated or distorted."[40]

Other Christian theologians—particularly those who endeavored to study other religions in depth—found the task of establishing the unqualified supremacy of their own religion far more difficult. A case in point is Ernst Troeltsch, who dedicated much of his theological career to this task. In his 1902 work, *The Absolute Validity of Christianity*, he argued that Christianity's understanding of revelation made it independent of any particular culture and thus uniquely universal. Nonetheless, his growing knowledge of the historical development of

Christianity and other religions made him increasingly aware of fundamental problems with such an argument. First, the modern historical sensibility challenged notions that Christianity transcends history; by revealing "the mutability of Christianity," Troeltsch wrote, historical research "destroyed the Catholic fiction that the church simply represented the continuation of original Christianity, as well as the Protestant fiction that the Reformation represented its restoration." Christianity was revealed to be just as much "the culmination of complicated historical developments" as Islam or Buddhism.[41] Troeltsch also found, as John B. Cobb, Jr., writes,

> that the religions of Asia were far more capable of transcending particular cultural contexts than he had supposed. Hence he finally acknowledged the relativity of the higher religions, including Christianity, as varied expressions of one Divine Life. Christianity is best for the heirs of Western civilization, but Hinduism and Buddhism best meet the needs of the cultures they have shaped.[42]

Near the end of his life, Troeltsch wrote that Christians must rethink the missionary project, foreshadowing the contemporary emphasis on interreligious dialogue:

> In relation to the great world religions [Christians] need to recognize that they are expressions of the religious consciousness corresponding to certain definite types of culture, and that it is their duty to increase in depth and purity by means of their own interior impulses, a task in which the contact with Christianity may prove helpful, to them as to us, in such processes of development from within. . . . There can be no conversion or transformation of one into the other, but only a measure of agreement and of mutual understanding.[43]

As Troeltsch's comments indicate, there was a growing realization in the nineteenth and twentieth centuries of the need for dialogue among religions. An early sign of this move toward dialogue was the World's Parliament of Religions, held in Chicago in 1893, which offered many North Americans their first opportunity to encounter Buddhists, Hindus, and Muslims.[44] The interfaith dialogue movement, however, began in earnest in the period after World War II. The new interest in dialogue was triggered in part by the horror of the Nazis' attempt to obliterate the Jews of Europe, as well as by increasing interreligious violence in formerly colonized countries in the Middle East and on the Indian subcontinent. Religious leaders increasingly realized that mutual tolerance and understanding were required if people were to combat not only interreligious violence but also a host of other social, political, economic, and ecological problems.[45]

By the 1960s, this realization had reached the highest levels of mainline denominational leadership. A milestone was the Vatican's 1965 "Declaration on the Relation of the Church to Non-Christian Religions," known as *Nostra Aetate*.[46] This document recognizes an authentic sense of the Divine in the religions of "various peoples." Referring specifically to Hinduism and Buddhism, the declaration states: "The Catholic Church rejects nothing that is true and holy in these religions. She regards with sincere reverence those ways of conduct and of life, those precepts and teachings which, though differing in many aspects from the ones she holds and sets forth, nonetheless often reflect a ray of that Truth which enlightens all men." Finally, the declaration exhorts Catholics to engage in "dialogue and collaboration with the followers of other religions, carried out with prudence and love and in witness to the Christian faith and life," so as to "recognize, preserve and promote the good things, spiritual and moral, as well as the socio-cultural values found among these men [i.e., non-Christians]."[47] While the main Protestant and Orthodox ecumenical body, the World Council of Churches, was slower to formulate a clear statement on the need for interreligious dialogue, it has recently moved decisively in that direction.[48]

Another shift in contemporary theological thinking has been triggered by (or at least is associated with) recent developments in thought—including postmodernism, postcolonialism, poststructuralism—which, for lack of a better term, I will call the "post-isms." As evidenced in the works of such varied thinkers as Ludwig Wittgenstein, Jacques Lacan, Jean-François Lyotard, Michel Foucault, Gilles Deleuze, Jacques Derrida, Luce Irigaray, Edward Said, Gayatri Spivak, and Homi Bhabha, these post-isms currents in contemporary thought

- critique the "metanarratives" of modernity;[49]
- question the possibility of universal principles, and the Eurocentric motives behind their construction;[50]
- interrogate how meaning is constructed, and stress the critical role of language and/or discourse; and
- reject the modernist notion of objectivity, asserting instead the fundamental cultural and historical situatedness of all thought.

Before we turn to the impact of "post-ist" perspectives on contemporary Christian theology of religions, it should be noted that some contemporary Christian discourse about religious others proceeds more or less as if postmodernity—or, for that matter, many of the developments of the modern period—had never happened. However, such instances of Christian thought often demonstrate little or no familiarity with the actual beliefs and practices of religious others. They argue primarily from a priori claims about Christianity and religious others (often stressing the particularistic strain of the biblical witness to the exclusion of the universalistic strain).[51]

That said, the insights of post-ist thought have decisively influenced many other contemporary Christian thinkers, particularly those involved in theological reflection about religious others. In his *Dialogue with the Other*, Catholic theologian David Tracy pulls no punches in asserting the critical importance of post-ist thinking to contemporary Christian theology:

The assumption of [the] cultural superiority of Western modernity is finished. Any thinker who continues to think and write (as many in the modern Western academy still do) as if other cultures either do not exist or exist only as stepping-stones to or pale copies of Western modernity is self-deluding. . . . [T]he Enlightenment notion of rationality is in grave danger of becoming part of the problem, not the solution. . . . The acknowledgement of the role of language (and thereby history) in all understanding united to the acknowledgement of the large role of unconscious factors in all conscious rationality have made . . . theologically necessary transcendental forms of reflection not impossible, but far, far more difficult to formulate adequately than modern theology (including my own) once believed.[52]

One mark of this post-ist consciousness is a concern for otherness and difference generally. Since the 1960s, liberation-oriented Christian theologians have drawn attention to those whose voices have been suppressed in traditional Christian discourse—including women, people of color, gay and lesbian persons, the poor, and the oppressed—and the ways in which this exclusion has tainted Christian thought and practice.

More recently, this concern for the marginalized has been extended to religious others. Paul Knitter, for example, highlights the essential link between religious marginalization and social-political-economic marginalization when he holds that "concern for the suffering Other" cannot be separated from "dialogue with the religious Other."[53] Similarly, Rita M. Gross criticizes Christian feminist theologians for tending "to equate 'religion' with 'Christianity,'" and argues that a feminist theology that is true to its own principles will also be open to religious diversity.[54] Indeed, the very presence of Gross, a Buddhist, in the feminist theological conversation indicates the degree to which religious others are beginning to be heard in what once was a purely intra-Christian discussion.[55]

The post-ist stress on the inevitable situatedness of experience and thought pervades much recent theological reflection about religious others. Carrying on the insights of Troeltsch, John Hick stresses the influence of culture on religion. Rather than viewing difference as a mark of error, Hick interprets it as a natural result of the situatedness of all religious experience.[56] George A. Lindbeck pushes this notion even farther. Reflecting the general post-ist stress on language and discourse, Lindbeck contends that religions are language-like entities that determine the experiences and beliefs of adherents. Where Schleiermacher and Otto argued that religions are "about" a universal core experience, Lindbeck argues that adherents of different religions

have different experiences. Buddhist compassion, Christian love and—if I may cite a quasi-religious phenomenon—French Revolutionary *fraternité* are not diverse modifications of a single fundamental human awareness, emotion, attitude, or sentiment, but are a radically (i.e., from the root) distinct way of experiencing and being oriented toward self, neighbor, and cosmos.[57]

Indeed, Lindbeck argues, just as it makes no sense to say that Japanese is a "better" or "truer" language than French, so it makes equally no sense to compare religions, to claim that Christian teaching is superior to Buddhist teaching: they are simply—and radically—different. More recently, S. Mark Heim has extended the notion of radical difference into the realm of soteriology. He argues that there are many religions because there are many "religious ends": "religious paths in fact lead persons to the distinctively varied states they advertise and on which they set such transcendent value."[58] As Knitter describes Heim's stance, "Buddhists arrive at Nirvana, Christians arrive at union with God. And both are happy."[59]

Another mark of the increasing concern for difference is the development of comparative theology, including the work of theologians such as James L. Fredericks, Francis X. Clooney, and John P. Keenan.[60] Reflecting the post-ist distrust of a priori universals and grand narratives, comparative theology (as Fredericks writes) "does not start with a grand theory of religion in general that claims to account for all religions," nor does it "look for some abstract lowest common denominator or essence that all religions, including Christianity, share."[61] Indeed, comparative theology holds that a complete and satisfactory theology of religions is not possible prior to in-depth dialogue with other religions. Instead, it is "a theology that arises *through* dialogue," "a Christian theology done by means of dialogue with those who follow other religious paths."[62] Indeed, comparative theology can be regarded as a move to move beyond the theology of religions paradigm altogether, to bring dialogue with religious others to the center of Christian theological reflection.[63]

Among the more interesting recent developments in recent theology of religions are contributions from Christians working in the formerly colonized world, in contexts that are (or have until recently been) predominantly non-Christian or that have large and flourishing non-Christian communities. For Christians in Asia and Africa, interreligious dialogue is not a theological option, but a fact of life, one to be welcomed, as the Indian theologian Michael Amaladoss, S.J., makes clear:

> For us Asian Christians, Hindus, Buddhists, Muslims, and others are part of our life. We share a common culture and way of life. We belong to a common economic and political system. We have a common history. Our religious differences have cultural, political, and even economic implications. In this ongoing dialogue of life we have begun to appreciate the believers of other religions. We respect and read with profit their scriptures and other sacred writings. We learn from their *sadhana*, methods of prayer, and religious experience. We regard positively their moral conduct. We collaborate with them in the promotion of common human and spiritual values like freedom and justice, love and service. We do not feel superior to them. . . . At least for some of us, interreligious dialogue is also an interior, personal search for our own religious roots, which we want to rediscover and integrate.[64]

In a series of conference statements, the Roman Catholic Federation of Asian Bishops' Conferences echoes Amaladoss's sensitivity to the Asian context, the need for Christians to work in solidarity with Asian religions, and even the possibility of finding within them resources for Christian theological reflection:

> We are keenly aware that the struggle for a full human life is not confined to the Christian community. We acknowledge that there are many great religious traditions in Asia which form the basis of the establishment, growth and development of the many cultures and nations in this great continent. In solidarity with them, we seek the full flowering of the human person and the transformation of the world of Asia into that which pleases the Creator (cf. Gen 1).[65]

> In the rich diversity of ancient Asian cultures and faiths is a vision of unity in diversity, a communion of life among diverse peoples. In this context we seek to become persons of dialogue.[66]

As early theologians such as Justin Martyr contextualized Christian teaching to the Greek religio-philosophical tradition, so present-day Christians in Asia, Africa, and the Pacific are developing ways in which the message of Christ can both find expression in and be illuminated by contexts shaped by Asian religions such as Hinduism, Buddhism, Daoism, and Confucianism. This process is sometimes referred to as *inculturation*, which Pope John Paul II described as "the incarnation of the Gospel in native cultures and also the introduction of these cultures into the life of the Church."[67] Inculturation is not, strictly speaking, a species of the theology of religions. Given the close relationship between religion and culture, however, the actual praxis of inculturating the gospel frequently assumes and/or implies a theological stance regarding the value of non-Christian religions to the Christian message, and often results, not merely in a "translation" of the Christian message, but also in the incorporation of non-Christian insights into Christian theology.

Take, for instance, two South Korean Protestants, Jung Young Lee and Heup Young Kim.[68] Both theologians unashamedly "own up to" (the phrase is Kim's) not only their Christian faith but also the fact that Confucianism, Daoism, Buddhism, and Shamanism have decisively shaped Korean culture. As Kim writes, these religious traditions "are important parts of our own identity, functioning as native religious languages or spiritual DNA."[69] Lee draws on the yin/yang tradition to develop a theology of the Trinity, while Kim draws on the concept of the Dao ("Way") to retrieve ancient Christian insights about God and the world, insights that have been suppressed by Western dualistic thinking. Similar developments can be found in the work of Christian theologians in dialogue with the religions of the Indian subcontinent, such as Wesley Ariarajah, Lynn de Silva, M. Thomas Thangaraj, Raimundo Panikkar, and Michael Amaladoss.[70] Examples of the inculturation process can be seen in the readings from Chung Hyun Kyung, Engelbert Mveng, and Aloysius Pieris in the section "Modern and Postmodern Voices."

Thematizing Christian Theologies of Religions

As the reader will have noted by this point, Christians have taken a variety of views of religious others. To impose some order on this diversity, several categorical schemes have been proposed. The most commonly used of these are Alan Race's threefold scheme and Paul Knitter's four "models."[71]

Alan Race classifies Christian orientations toward religious others in three main categories. *Exclusivism* holds that salvation is *exclusively* through faith in Jesus Christ; *inclusivism* holds that the salvation recognized by Christians *includes* adherents of other religions; and *pluralism* recognizes many ways of salvation, one of which is the Christian way. Though widely used, Race's schema does have some notable weaknesses. For one thing, since his terms are bound up with attitudes about salvation, which is a major concern for Christians but arguably less so for some other religions (e.g., primal religions, Daoism), these categories cannot be applied easily outside the Christian context. For another thing, Race's schema does not accommodate recent developments such as postliberalism and comparative theology, which do not fit neatly into any of the three slots.

Given these weaknesses, an alternative taxonomy recently suggested by Paul Knitter is gaining increasing acceptance.[72] Knitter identifies four "models": replacement, fulfillment, mutuality, and acceptance. Unlike Race's categories, Knitter's do not presume a concern with salvation, but instead have to do with a given religion's sense of its relation with other religions. Thus, one could theoretically identify, for example, a Hindu replacement theology, or a Daoist acceptance theology. Nonetheless, Knitter's change of terminology masks strong material resemblances to Race's schema. The first three of Knitter's four models map closely to Race's three categories; only Knitter's fourth model (acceptance) constitutes an extension of Race's schema to encompass recent developments.

Race's and Knitter's categories are "ideal types" rather than phenomenological descriptions, and they are not wholly embodied by any single theologian. Yet they are not therefore "straw men." Their usefulness lies in the fact that they represent possible points along a continuum of theological views. They are helpful therefore in situating particular theological positions in relation to one another, and, more importantly, for identifying commonalities among the various theological positions.

Let us then look briefly at each of Race's three categories, incorporating Knitter's models along the way.

Exclusivism/Replacement

According to Race, this orientation "counts the revelation in Jesus Christ as the sole criterion by which all religions, including Christianity, can be understood and evaluated."[73] As Fredericks writes, "Exclusivist theologies of religion claim that Christianity is the only true religion. No other religious path is founded on Jesus Christ, the unique and unsurpassable savior of the world. God's salvation is available to all, but only through Jesus Christ."[74] Knitter classifies this approach as the "Replacement Model," since its adherents see Christianity as "meant to replace all other religions."[75] Prominent representatives of this orientation include Tertullian, Augustine of Hippo, and Karl Barth.

Inclusivism/Fulfillment

Theologies in this category attempt to acknowledge a salvific role for other religions while retaining the uniqueness and ultimacy of Christ and of Christianity.[76] For inclusivists, non-Christian religions may play a positive role in God's salvific plans; God may save religious others by means of the non-Christian religious traditions. Nonetheless, inclusivists generally insist that Jesus Christ is the one and only savior; however, Christ's saving activity extends beyond the bounds of the explicitly Christian community. Furthermore, while other religious traditions may have much that is good and true (and thus from God), only Christianity bears the fullness of divine, saving truth. In the terms of one pioneer of inclusivism, Karl Rahner, non-Christians may be considered "anonymous Christians," Christians who don't yet realize that they are Christians.[77] Another inclusivist, Jacques Dupuis, argues that Jesus Christ is the center toward which all religions strive—that is, the fulfillment of the universal human religious quest.[78] Thus Knitter prefers to speak of inclusivism as the "Fulfillment Model," borrowing the term from the Vatican document *Redemptoris Missio*: "Christ is . . . the fulfillment of the yearning of all the world's religions and, as such, he is their sole and definitive completion."[79]

While Rahner is usually cited as a model of this approach, an inclusivist tendency runs through the theology of Justin Martyr, Clement of Alexandria, Nicholas of Cusa, and Bartolomé de Las Casas. Also, a form of the inclusivism/fulfillment orientation has been the official doctrinal position of the Roman Catholic Church since Vatican II.[80]

Pluralism/Mutuality

There is no single pluralist approach, but instead, as Knitter notes, a "plurality of pluralisms."[81] What these various forms of theological pluralism have in common, however, is that they cast the net of salvific efficacy as widely as possible:

> Thinkers associated with the pluralistic approach, such as John Hick, Paul Knitter, Stanley Samartha and Wilfred Cantwell Smith, each take a different approach to the problem of religious diversity, but generally they are in agreement on this much: within the universe of faiths, there are many ways to salvation. The way of Christ is one path; the way of the Buddha is another.[82]

Fredericks notes that pluralists thereby broaden the understanding of salvation. While "both exclusivists and inclusivists agree that all salvation is in Jesus Christ," pluralists "claim that all religions lead to salvation, but not merely the salvation imagined by Christians."[83] Knitter labels pluralism the "Mutuality Model," because its adherents insist, in various ways and on various grounds, on the need for truly mutual dialogue between religions, "a conversation . . . in which both sides are really talking and listening, in which both sides really open themselves to learning and changing."[84]

Knitter identifies three varieties of the Mutuality Model.[85] The *philosophical-historical* approach, which is exemplified by John Hick, emphasizes "the historical limitations of all religions and the philosophical possibility (or probability) that there is one Divine Reality behind and within them all."[86] The second form of pluralism, which Knitter terms the *religious-mystical*, bases mutual dialogue on the belief that there is a core mystical experience within the religious traditions, and that this fact suggests that "the same Divine Mystery or Reality is being experienced within the many different religions."[87] Knitter cites Raimundo Panikkar as exemplifying this approach. The third type of pluralism, which Knitter calls the *ethical-practical*, seeks common ground, not within or beneath the religions, but "around" them, in the common ethical situations that confront all religious believers in today's world. This approach is exemplified by Knitter himself, particularly in his *One Earth Many Religions*.

The Acceptance Model

Several new approaches have developed since Alan Race posited his threefold schema just twenty-five years ago. Knitter groups these together under what he calls the "Acceptance Model," so called because (according to Knitter) their common feature is that they begin by accepting religious difference as inevitable and do not attempt to reduce all religions to some common denominator. In this category Knitter includes three other approaches discussed above: Lindbeck's postliberal approach, Heim's "many salvations," and the comparative theology of Clooney, Fredericks, Keenan, and others.[88] Excerpts from Heim and Fredericks are included in the readings section, below.

Where next? Christian theological reflection about religious others, like Christian theology generally, is a very dynamic field. Much exciting and significant work is being done today, making important contributions not only to relations with religious others but also to Christian self-understanding. Yet much remains to be done. In closing this survey of the theology of religions, I offer not so much a summary of trends as a *provocation*: a challenge to continue the development of Christian theological reflection about religious others. Some of these points are already being addressed by theologians working on the cutting edge of the field; others have yet to be addressed to the extent they deserve.

First, it is important to recognize that the diversity of perspectives within the Christian community itself cannot be separated from the encounter with religious others. In some ways, Christians have always had religious others in our midst—other Christians whom we have, for whatever reasons, anathematized, excommunicated, dis-fellowshipped, or otherwise excluded. Ironically, Christians sometimes find that they have more in common with members of other religions than they do with other Christians; this insight is ripe with theological implications that should be teased out and explored.

Second, the phenomenon of multiple religious belonging—whereby persons identify themselves as adherents of more than one religious tradition—deserves additional theological investigation. The Abrahamic faiths (Judaism, Christianity, Islam) have traditionally insisted on an either/or relationship among religions—that is, by becoming, say, a Christian one must give up allegiance to all other religious traditions.[89] In other parts of the world, however, this exclusivism does not obtain. For example, many Chinese people are simultaneously Buddhist, Confucianist, and Daoist; many Japanese persons are simultaneously Buddhist and Shinto; and as an old saying goes, Haitians are "80 percent Catholic, 20 percent Protestant, and 100 percent Vodoun." In recent years, this phenomenon has become increasingly common in Western societies, as Christians explore Buddhist practice, Hindu teachings, and so on.[90]

The phenomenon of multiple belonging raises intriguing issues of religious boundary-drawing: Where does "the Christian" stop and "the non-Christian" begin? Is there intersection at those boundaries, or are the traditions mutually exclusive? What relevance do the experiences of Christians in non-Christian practices (such as Zen meditation) have for Christian theological reflection?

Third[91]—and related to the problem of boundary-drawing—it is crucial to examine the ways in which Christianity *discursively constructs* religious others, and the theological implications of that process.[92] Through various discursive practices, Christians mark off the boundaries of the Christian "thing," and in so doing, also mark off, explicitly or implicitly, the "not-Christian," religious others. There is no "Christianity" outside the discourse of those who call themselves "Christians"; correlatively, "non-Christians" only exist as such by means of the discursive practices of "Christians"—in other words, what Christians repress or exclude, explicitly or implicitly. In Christian theological discourse, this boundary-drawing process is evident in the theologian's selection of resources for reflection (such as the Bible, church tradition, experience, reason, the works of other theologians).

While such discursive boundary-drawing is a necessary part of theological reflection (theologians must begin somewhere, and Christian theological reflection naturally begins in and with what is recognizably Christian), it is vital for Christian theologians to undertake this process with full awareness of what voices are being excluded and why. There are two reasons for this. First, if religious others are simply projections or straw men, this undermines the truth value of the resulting theology and calls into question Christian self-understanding.[93] Second, while boundaries delimit certain kinds of truth (the truth revealed in God's incarnation in Christ, as witnessed by the Christian community), they limit or block access to other possible truths outside the Christian community.

Accordingly, Christian theology must recognize that its boundaries are provisional, not fixed and impermeable, and by no means essential, immutable, or worse, divinely appointed. They serve only to mark out a starting point, a field in which to begin Christian theology. As that theology proceeds, it must recognize its limits, and be ready at all times to hear and respond to the truth that lies beyond. That is, Christian theology needs to have a more fluid sense of "inside" and "outside," in order, as Fredericks puts it, to maintain a creative tension between Christian and non-Christian.[94] To do so, Christian theology must be ever mindful of two key questions: What is God saying and doing in and through religious others? What do religious others tell us Christians about ourselves, our witness, the God to whom we witness, and our relationship with that God, with human others, and with other beings? We cannot answer these questions if we do not first listen to religious others—and not just in Christian terms but also in terms of how religious others think and experience the Divine/Ultimate.[95]

Notes

1. Wilfred Cantwell Smith, *Wilfred Cantwell Smith: A Reader*, ed. Kenneth Cracknell (Oxford: Oneworld Publications, 2001), 209. The *Bhagavad Gita* is one of the most beloved of the sacred texts of the Hindu religious tradition.

2. This combines two questions posed by Paul F. Knitter, *Introducing Theologies of Religions* (Maryknoll, NY: Orbis Books, 2002), 1. Similarly, Alan Race defines the theology of religions in terms of the etiological question: "The Christian theology of religions is the attempt, on the part of Christian theologians, to account theologically for the diversity of the world's religious quest and commitment, a diversity which shows all the signs of continuing to exist, in spite of the Christian missions" (Alan Race, *Christians and Religious Pluralism: Patterns in the Christian Theology of Religions* [Maryknoll, NY: Orbis Books, 1983], 2).

3. By this term I mean those persons and communities judged by Christians to fall outside the boundaries of Christianity, however construed. Precisely who is included within this category varies from one theologian to the next. For instance, Karl Rahner's notion of "anonymous Christians" (see readings below) considerably widens the boundaries of Christianity, or at least creates a grey area between explicit Christians and those who are fully non-Christian. Nonetheless, the fact that "anonymous Christians" do not realize their true identity means that they remain religious others from the perspective of explicit believers in Christ.

4. James L. Fredericks stresses this salvific focus in describing the theology of religions as "an interpretation for Christians of the meaning of non-Christian religions and their role, if any, in the salvation of the world" (James L. Fredericks, *Faith among Faiths: Christian Theology and Non-Christian Religions* [Mahwah, NJ: Paulist Press, 1999], 13).

5. In the interests of full disclosure, I should note that this has been the focus of much of my own work to date. See David R. Brockman, "Turning to Religious Others: Visions and Blindspots in Modern Christian Reflection about Non-Christians" (Ph.D. diss., Southern Methodist University, 2006), and Brockman, *No Longer the Same: Religious Others and the Liberation of Christian Theology* (forthcoming from Palgrave Macmillan).

6. I intentionally leave undefined the notion of *theological*, since the various writers to be discussed here have a variety of understandings of the nature and function of theology.

7. One mark of this diversity is the disagreement over the category *religion*. While all Christian theologies of religions by definition assume the validity of this category, different Christian theologians understand it in different ways. Most assume that Christianity is itself a religion, sharing some fundamental characteristics with other religions (although there is widespread disagreement about what those characteristics are). Other Christians consider Christianity to be essentially different from "religion" and/or "the

religions." For example, the Web site for "Christ in You Ministries" insists that Christianity is not a religion: "Christianity has mistakenly been defined and described as a religion. . . . Not true! Christianity is Christ!" (http://www.christinyou.net/pages/notrel. html, accessed May 23, 2007). Straddling these two perspectives, Karl Barth (see readings below) equates "religion" with unbelief (*Unglaube*), and contrasts it with revelation; he contends that Christianity is false insofar as it functions as a religion, but is the only true religion insofar as it recognizes the revelation of the falsehood of all religion (including Christianity-as-religion).

8. In the following remarks, I will focus on European Christianity, and from about the fifth century to the present day, the Western church—Roman Catholicism and the various Protestant groups that arose during and since the Reformation. However, the reader should note that there were other Christianities—the various Orthodox churches (Greek, Coptic, Russian, and others), as well as venerable Christian communities in Asia: the Nestorian community in China dates back to the seventh century, and the Mar Thoma Church in south India is even older. However, these communities lie outside the scope of this discussion.

9. Walter H. Wagner captures the note of anxiety that pervaded Christian thought about Judaism and the Jewish people: "Bluntly, the Jew is the question mark who punctuates every Christian claim. The continued existence of Judaism and the Jewish people are radical criticisms of Christian assertions to be God's people and the bearers of divine truth. If the gospel, even when preached by Jesus, did not succeed in winning over the people to whom it was first proclaimed, then perhaps the messengers and the message were wrong. If God made covenants with Abraham and Sarah, Israel at Sinai, and the House of David, what need was there for another with a carpenter who gave odd interpretations of the Law? If Jesus came to his own and they refused to receive him, maybe they did so for good reasons. And if the descendants of those who rejected Jesus still do not receive his followers, why should anyone else believe in him or his movement?" (Walter H. Wagner, *After the Apostles: Christianity in the Second Century* [Minneapolis, MN: Augsburg Fortress, 1994], 13).

10. Lucien Legrand, cited in Jacques Dupuis, *Toward a Christian Theology of Religious Pluralism* (Maryknoll, NY: Orbis Books, 1997), 50.

11. One strand of Christian thought argued that since it is inconceivable that the unchanging God could have abrogated divine promises to Israel, the fault must lie on the part of the Jews, and the Christians must therefore be the "true Israel." See, for example, Justin, *Dialogue with Trypho*, ch. 135. In such arguments begins the long, painful history of anti-Semitism in Christian thought. For a historical examination of anti-Semitism in the Christian tradition, see Dan Cohn-Sherbok, *The Crucified Jew: Twenty Centuries of Christian Anti-Semitism* (Grand Rapids, MI: Eerdmans, 1997).

12. Joseph Mitsuo Kitagawa, *The Christian Tradition: Beyond Its European Captivity* (Philadelphia, PA: Trinity Press International, 1997), 190-91.

13. Ramsay MacMullen, *Christianity and Paganism in the Fourth to Eighth Centuries* (New Haven, CT: Yale University Press, 1997), 2.

14. Ibid., 4.

15. Augustine's argument is from *The Confessions and Letters of St. Augustin, with a Sketch of His Life and Work,* ed. Philip Schaff (Christian Classics Ethereal Library), http://www.ccel.org./ccel/schaff/npnf101.vii.1.CLXXIII.html. Thomas's argument is in the *Summa Theologica*, II-II, q. 10, art. 8.

16. The Eastern empire managed to hold out for another millennium. However, the armies of a new faith, Islam, captured former Roman territories in the Middle East, Asia Minor, North Africa, and the Iberian Peninsula.

17. The Canons of the Fourth Lateran Council. Emphasis mine. Online at http://www.fordham.edu/halsall/basis/lateran4.html. Accessed 28 May 2007.

18. The term "voyages of discovery" is misleading. Vasco da Gama, Columbus, and their colonizing followers were not purely disinterested explorers. They were motivated in large part by a drive to discover new markets and new resources—spices and gold at first, soon to be followed by other raw materials and human slaves—for exploitation by the European nations.

19. Friederich Schleiermacher's disparaging comments about "fetichism," Judaism, and Islam—which reveal more about his unfamiliarity with these religions than about the religions themselves—are emblematic of this problem (see Friedrich Schleiermacher, *The Christian Faith*, ed. H. R. Macintosh and J. S. Stewart [Edinburgh: T&T Clark, 1999], 37, 319). Similarly, Barth does not ground his theological category "religion" on evidence from empirical study of the religions. He seems to have admitted as much in his oft-cited response to D. P. Niles: "Karl Barth was asked how he knew that Hinduism was a form of unbelief, given the fact that he had never met a Hindu. . . . Hinduism can be known to be unbelief, according to Barth, a priori" (Fredericks, *Faith among Faiths*, 21. The source is D. P. Niles, "Karl Barth—A Personal Memory," *South East Asian Journal of Theology* 11 [1969]: 10-11, cited in Fredericks, *Faith among Faiths*, 34 n.15).

20. Don A. Pittman, Ruben L. F. Habito, and Terry C. Muck, *Ministry and Theology in Global Perspective: Contemporary Challenges for the Church* (Grand Rapids, MI: Eerdmans, 1996), 50.

21. Paul F. Knitter, *No Other Name? A Critical Survey of Christian Attitudes toward the World Religions* (Maryknoll, NY: Orbis Books, 1985), 123.

22. Pittmann et al., *Ministry and Theology in Global Perspective*, 51. The Jesuit Matteo Ricci (discussed below), when asked whether Confucius was in hell, answered: "All those who know God and love Him above all things, and who pass out of this life with such knowledge and love, are saved. If Confucius knew God and loved Him above all things, and passed out of this life with such knowledge and love, without doubt he is saved." Quoted in *Ministry and Theology in Global Perspective*.

23. Quoted in Pittmann et al., *Ministry and Theology in Global Perspective*, 52.

24. Many of the early Reformers regarded religious difference not as a matter of honest disagreement deserving respectful discussion, but as a matter of evil and falsehood in active opposition to the good and the true (in other words, the Protestant Christian). For instance, Martin Luther declared that "the Christian faith is set apart from every other religion and faith of men. It makes all the others false and useless." Among those who are "outside Christianity" and "remain in eternal wrath and perdition," Luther includes not only "heathens, Turks, [and] Jews," but "false Christians," meaning Roman Catholics (quoted in Cracknell, *Towards a New Relationship: Christians and People of Other Faith* [London: Epworth, 1986], 11).

25. "These Indian peoples surpassed the Greeks and Romans in selecting for their gods, not sinful and criminal men noted for their great baseness, but virtuous ones—to the extent that virtue exists among people who lack the knowledge of the true God that is gained by faith. . . . The following argument can be formed for the proof of the above: The Indian nations seem to show themselves to be or to have been of better rational judgment and more prudent and upright in what they considered God to be. For nations which have reached the knowledge that there is a God hold in common the natural concept that God is the best of all things that can be imagined. Therefore the nation which has elected virtuous men as God or gods, though it might have erred in not selecting the true God, has a better concept and estimation of God and more natural purity than one which has selected and accepted for God or gods men known to be sinful and criminal.

The latter was the case of the Greek and Roman states, while the former is that of all these Indian nations . . ." (Las Casas, "Apologetic History of the Indies," online at http://www.columbia.edu/acis/ets/CCREAD/lascasas.htm; accessed June 2, 2007). Las Casas also displays a capacity for empathy with religious others which is unusual in his time and context. Noting that his fellow Spaniards call the Indian peoples "barbarians" because "they do not speak our language well nor understand us," Las Casas also notes that "in this we are as barbarian to them as they to us" (ibid.).

26. "Heathen—those who make no explicit profession of faith in Christ (partly through the fault of Christians)—will perhaps, according to Fray Bartolomé, enter the Reign of God in greater numbers than will the faithful. They will be called to that Reign by the Son of Man, and only because—within their religious world and in their cultural categories—they will have given 'to eat and to drink' to their sibling in need, and in him or her to Christ himself. Works in behalf of one's neighbor are an exigency of salvific grace" (Gustavo Gutiérrez, *Las Casas: In Search of the Poor of Jesus Christ* [Maryknoll, NY: Orbis Books, 1993], 261).

27. Both missionaries practiced *enculturation*, translating the Christian message into the terms of the indigenous religious-cultural context. J. J. Clarke writes: "What Ricci and his successors sought to do . . . was . . . to act not as outsiders seeking to impose on the native Chinese a totally alien set of doctrines and practices, but to infiltrate the very heart and soul of China by first adopting the learning and the habits of a scholar-bureaucrat . . . and then subtly adapting the Catholic rituals to Confucian customs and practices" (J. J. Clarke, *Oriental Enlightenment: The Encounter Between Asian and Western Thought* [New York, NY: Routledge, 1997], 41). Some Protestant missionaries also developed a dialogical approach to mission. These included Bartholomaeus Ziegenbalg (1683-1719) and Thomas Ebenezer Slater (1840-1912). See Kenneth Cracknell, "Dialogue Is Evangelism: Evangelism Is Dialogue," in *Fullness of Life for All: Challenges for Mission in Early 21st Century*, ed. Inus Daneel, Charles Van Engen, and Hendrik Vroom (New York: Editions Rodopi, 2003), 250-54.

28. Clarke, *Oriental Enlightenment*, 40.

29. Ibid.

30. Steven Best, *The Politics of Historical Vision: Marx, Foucault, Habermas* (New York: Guilford, 1995), 3-5. "The theoretical discourses of modernity from Descartes through the Enlightenment and its progeny championed reason as the source of progress in knowledge and society, as well as the privileged locus of truth and the foundation of systematic knowledge. Reason was deemed competent to discover adequate theoretical and practical norms upon which systems of thought and action could be built and society could be restructured. This Enlightenment project is also operative in the American, French, and other democratic revolutions which attempted to overturn the feudal world and to produce a just and egalitarian social order that would embody reason and social progress" (Steven Best and Douglas Kellner, *Postmodern Theory: Critical Interrogations* [New York: Guilford, 1991], 2).

The European encounter with religious others also contributed to the rise of modernity, as Clarke notes: "The list of thinkers from the Enlightenment and pre-Enlightenment period who professed more than a passing interest in Eastern philosophy is impressive and includes Montaigne, Malebranche, Bayle, Wolff, Leibniz, Voltaire, Montesquieu, Diderot, Helvetius, Quesnay, and Adam Smith. They were fascinated by its philosophy, by the conduct of the state, and by its education system, and in all kinds of ways sought to hold it up as a mirror in which to examine the philosophical and institutional inadequacies of Europe, as a model with which to instigate moral and political reform, and as a tool with which to strip Christianity of its pretensions to uniqueness" (Clarke, *Oriental Enlightenment*, 42). Clarke also notes the importance of the realization of the antiquity of non-Christian religious systems: "In particular, the discovery of the great civilizations in the East, and the acknowledgement of the great antiquity of China and India, meant that the historical priority given to the Israel of the Bible began to look highly questionable. . . . The antiquity of Indian religions was also beginning to be a subject of interest among scholars at that time, and Voltaire later came to the conclusion that India was the world's oldest culture and that it was here, rather than in Israel, that the roots of monotheism were to be found" (Clarke, *Oriental Enlightenment*, 45-46). The Asian religions in particular offered European proponents of modernity outside perspectives on Christianity and European culture. For example, to critique what they regarded as the superstition and corrupt institutions of Christianity, the French philosopher Voltaire, the German philosopher and mathematician Gottfried Leibniz, and the English Deist Matthew Tindal all claimed that the Chinese Confucian tradition had developed a religion based on reason rather than faith and revelation (Clarke, *Oriental Enlightenment*, 45, 46, 51).

31. The complex and problematic history of the category "world religions" exceeds the scope of the present discussion. For a detailed history and critique of this category, see Tomoko Masuzawa, *The Invention of World Religions: Or, How European Universalism Was Preserved in the Language of Pluralism* (Chicago: University of Chicago Press, 2005).

32 Clarke, *Oriental Enlightenment*, 84.

33. Quoted in Masuzawa, *The Invention of World Religions*, 312.

34. Ernst Troeltsch, *Christian Thought, Its History and Application*, trans. Mary E. Clarke (New York: Meridian Books, 1957), 41.

35. For my arguments in this regard, see Brockman, *No Longer the Same,* chap. 4.

36. See Rudolf Otto, *The Idea of the Holy*, trans. John W. Harvey (New York: Oxford University Press, 1958). Otto writes that the cross is the complete revelation "of the transcendent mysteriousness and 'beyondness' of God. . . . Here rational are enfolded with non-rational elements, the revealed commingled with the un-revealed, the most exalted love with the most awe-inspiring 'wrath' of the numen, and therefore, in applying to the Cross of Christ the category 'holy,' Christian religious feeling has given birth to a religious intuition profounder and more vital than any to be found in the whole history of religion" (Otto, *The Idea of the Holy*, 173). Thus John B. Cobb, Jr., writes of Otto: "Christian theology in the context of the history of religions reached its highest flowering in the early twentieth century in the work of Rudolf Otto. Otto penetrated deeply into the meaning and nature of religion and saw with imaginative appreciation the manifold ways in which it came to expression. More than any predecessor, and better than most successors, he developed his categories from the study of the history of religions in general instead of by generalization of Christian experience. He was able to employ these categories in his theological interpretation of Christianity as well. The task he undertook, however, was an enormous one, and theologically he was not himself ready for a complete pluralism. In order to show the unity of all religions, he exaggerated the centrality to each of that element of the numinous which he found common to all. Since it was still important for him to show the superiority or finality of Christianity, his interpretation of the numinous was skewed in favor of the form it took in Christianity" (John B. Cobb, Jr., *Christ in a Pluralistic Age* [Philadelphia, PA: Westminster, 1975], 48).

37. See Brockman, *No Longer the Same,* chap. 5.

38. Kenneth Cracknell, *Justice, Courtesy and Love: Theologians and Missionaries Encountering World Religions, 1846-1914* (London: Epworth, 1995), 37-38.

39. Ibid., 45.

40. Ibid., 53.

41. Troeltsch, "Christianity and the History of Religion," in *Christian Thought,* 78.

42. Cobb, *Christ in a Pluralistic Age,* 48-49.

43. Troeltsch, "Christianity and the History of Religion," 58.

44. For a brief account of this 1893 event, see Diana Eck, *Encountering God: A Spiritual Journey from Bozeman to Banaras* (Boston: Beacon, 1993), 23-30.

45. An example of this argument is Paul F. Knitter, *One Earth Many Religions: Multifaith Dialogue & Global Responsibility* (Maryknoll, NY: Orbis Books, 1995).

46. An English translation vetted by the Vatican is available online at http://www.vatican.va/archive/hist_councils/ii_vatican_council/documents/vat-ii_decl_19651028_nostra-aetate_en.html.

47. Ibid.

48. For a discussion of the "twists and turns" of WCC policy development in this area, see Kenneth Cracknell, *In Good and Generous Faith: Christian Responses to Religious Pluralism* (Cleveland, OH: Pilgrim Press, 2006), 180-227. A recent WCC document suggests just how far it has traveled from the medieval teaching *extra ecclesiam nulla salus*: "[Interreligious dialogue] must be a process of mutual empowerment, not a negotiation between parties who have conflicting interests and claims. . . . [P]artners in dialogue should be empowered to join in a common pursuit of justice, peace and constructive action for the good of all people. . . . Dialogue drives all communities to self-criticism and to re-thinking the ways in which they have interpreted their faith traditions. Dialogue brings about change in the experience of faith, helping people to deepen and grow in their faith in unexpected ways. . . . In dialogue we affirm hope. In the midst of the many divisions, conflicts and violence there is hope that it is possible to create a human community that lives in justice and peace. . . . In dialogue we nurture relations. Building bonds of relationship with those considered 'the other' is the goal of all dialogues" (Report from the interreligious consultation on "Conversion—Assessing the Reality," May 2006, "Ecumenical considerations for dialogue and relations with people of other religions"; online at http://www.oikoumene.org/en/resources/documents/wcc-programmes/interreligious-dialogue-and-cooperation/interreligious-trust-and-respect/04-ecumenical-considerations-for-dialogue-and-relations-with-people-of-other-religions.html; accessed June 2007).

49. The term "metanarrative" or "grand narrative" is from Jean-François Lyotard, *The Postmodern Condition: A Report on Knowledge,* trans. Geoff Bennington and Brian Massumi (Minneapolis: University of Minnesota Press, 1979), and refers to large-scale theories about the world, such as the Enlightenment notion that human reason would lead humanity to moral and technological progress, or the capitalist notion that free markets create the greatest good for the greatest number.

50. Steven Best connects the post-ist critique with a critique of Eurocentrism: "The proclivity of the white middle classes of European descent to proclaim themselves the representatives of all humanity and to project their own values and interests onto other cultures is aptly described . . . as the 'transcendental pretense.' Through appeal to universal principles, above all to the idea of human nature, many in the modern tradition sought to represent their ideas as the only valid ones, as grounded in nature itself. . . . On the occasions when modern theorists analyzed cultures outside of the temporal and spatial boundaries of central Europe, they typically came armed with a host of ready-made, a priori assumptions that sought universal conditions and characteristics of 'man in general.' They thereby found in the mirror of history only their own reflections. . . . Where Eurocentrism is the theory, imperialism is the practice" (Best, *The Politics of Historical Vision,* 10).

51. For example, an evangelical Web site called "Faith Facts" holds that "Objective evidence must be the basis for Christian truth claims . . . *[T]he evidence validates that Christianity is correct*, while the other religions are wrong" (emphasis in the original). The "evidence," however, includes the highly dubious claim that non-Christian religions teach salvation purely by human efforts, whereas Christianity alone teaches salvation through divine grace (http://faithfacts.gospelcom.net/quest_religions_same.html; accessed June 16, 2007).

52. David Tracy, *Dialogue with the Other: The Inter-Religious Dialogue* (Grand Rapids, MI: William B. Eerdmans, 1990), 2-3.

53. Knitter, *One Earth Many Religions*, 36. Aloysius Pieris similarly links interreligious encounter with a concern for the liberation of poor and suffering others. See his *An Asian Theology of Liberation* (Maryknoll, NY: Orbis Books, 1988).

54. Rita M. Gross, "Feminist Theology as Theology of Religions," *Feminist Theology* 26 (2001): 83-101.

55. A landmark example of interreligious theological conversation is John B. Cobb, Jr., and Christopher Ives, eds., *The Emptying God: A Buddhist-Jewish-Christian Conversation* (Maryknoll, NY: Orbis Books, 1990). In this work, the Japanese Buddhist Masao Abe presents a Zen interpretation of the self-emptying nature of God, and major Jewish and Christian theologians (Thomas J. J. Altizer, Eugene Borowitz, John B. Cobb, Jr., Catherine Keller, Schubert M. Ogden, Jürgen Moltmann, and David Tracy) respond.

56. Hick is more of a modernist, however, in his neo-Kantian assertion of a single, and apparently universal, noumenal Real.

57. George A. Lindbeck, *The Nature of Doctrine: Religion and Theology in a Postliberal Age* (Philadelphia, PA: Westminster, 1984), 40.

58. S. Mark Heim, *The Depth of the Riches: A Trinitarian Theology of Religious Ends* (Grand Rapids, MI: William B. Eerdmans, 2001), 19-20, 18. Heim gives three characteristics that define "religious end" in *The Depth of the Riches*, 21.

59. Knitter, *Introducing Theologies of Religions*, 193.

60. Representative works of comparative theology include Francis X. Clooney, *Hindu God, Christian God: How Reason Helps Break Down the Boundaries between Religions* (New York: Oxford University Press, 2001); James L. Fredericks, *Buddhists and Christians: Through Comparative Theology to Solidarity* (Maryknoll, NY: Orbis Books, 2004); Fredericks, *Faith among Faiths: Christian Theology and Non-Christian Religions* (Mahwah, NJ: Paulist, 1999); and John P. Keenan, *The Meaning of Christ: A Mahāyāna Theology* (Maryknoll, NY: Orbis Books, 1989). In the interests of full disclosure, I should note that much of my own public work to date has been in the area of Buddhist-Christian comparative theology. See David R. Brockman, "The Challenge of Yogācāra to David Tracy's Epistemology," *Koinonia* 15 (2003): 1-22; and Brockman, "An All-Pervading Self: The Challenge of the Tathāgatagarbha Tradition to Christian Theological Anthropology," unpublished presentation to the Philosophy of Religion section, Southwest regional meeting of the American Academy of Religion, March 2004.

61. Fredericks, *Faith among Faiths*, 167-68.

62. Fredericks, *Buddhists and Christians*, 26.

63. Although Knitter classifies comparative theology, along with postliberalism and Heim's "many religious ends" approach, under the "Acceptance" model (Knitter, *Introducing Theologies of Religions*, 173), Fredericks sees it as a move beyond the theology of religions paradigm (Fredericks, *Faith among Faiths*, 166-67). I make a similar argument in Brockman, "Turning to Religious Others."

64. Michael Amaladoss, "Interreligious Dialogue: A View from Asia," *International Bulletin of Missionary Research* 19, no. 1 (1995): 2-5, at 2. Accessed online via ATLA (article no. ATLA0000896639); accessed June 28, 2007.

65. Federation of Asian Bishops' Conferences, Final Statement of Fourth Plenary Assembly, September 16-25, 1986, Tokyo, Japan. Available at http://www.ucanews.com/html/fabc_plenary/fabc-86.htm. Accessed June 24, 2007.

66. Federation of Asian Bishops' Conferences, "Christian Discipleship in Asia Today: Service to Life," Final Statement of Sixth Plenary Assembly, January 10-19, 1995, Manila, Philippines; available at http://www.ucanews.com/html/fabc_plenary/fabc-95.htm; accessed June 24, 2007.

67. John Paul II, *Slavorum Apostoli* (2 June 1985); available at http://www.vatican.va/holy_father/john_paul_ii/encyclicals/documents/hf_jp-ii_enc_19850602_slavorum-apostoli_en.html; accessed June 30, 2008.

68. Heup Young Kim, *Christ and the Tao* (Hong Kong: Christian Conference of Asia, 2003); Jung Young Lee, *The Trinity in Asian Perspective* (Nashville, TN: Abingdon, 1996).

69. Kim, *Christ and the Tao*, 126. "Any Christian identity disconnected from our own people, community, and collective identity is not only inappropriate but also false" (126). As Kim puts it, the religions of Korea "are rooted in my spirituality to constitute an essential part of my spiritual identity (something like a religio-cultural DNA), yet the Western Christianity I was taught superficially hangs about. Spiritually and religiously, Confucianism and Taoism (Neo-Confucianism) still function as my native languages, while the Western Christianity remains as a foreign language like English" (125).

70. Representative works by these scholars include Wesley Ariarajah, *The Bible and People of Other Faiths* (Geneva: World Council of Churches, 1985); Lynn A. De Silva, *The Problem of the Self in Buddhism and Christianity* (New York: Barnes & Noble, 1979); Raimundo Panikkar, *The Cosmotheandric Experience: Emerging Religious Consciousness*, ed. Scott Eastham (Maryknoll, NY: Orbis Books, 1993); Aloysius Pieris, *An Asian Theology of Liberation* (Maryknoll, NY: Orbis Books, 1988); M. Thomas Thangaraj, *The Crucified Guru: An Experiment in Cross-cultural Christology* (Nashville, TN: Abingdon, 1994).

71. An alternative way to think about developments in recent Christian thought about religious others is in terms of the "centricity" of the theological formulations. This view is presented by Jacques Dupuis (borrowing from J. P. Schineller) to identify shifts in the paradigm governing theological reflection about religious others. See Dupuis, *Toward a Christian Theology of Religious Pluralism*, 182ff. The doctrine *extra ecclesiam nulla salus* can be characterized as *ecclesiocentric*: it presumes that theological reflection about religious others should center on their relation to the church. Dupuis argues that there has been a shift from ecclesiocentric paradigm to a Christocentric paradigm: "the abandonment of the untenable ecclesiological perspective according to which salvation was deemed available to people only through faith in Jesus Christ explicitly professed in the Christian community." This Christocentric approach is seen in Karl Barth, who wants to focus theology on Christ rather than the institutions and practices of his human followers. But for many other theologians, the Christocentric paradigm, Dupuis writes, "must be replaced by a theocentric worldview. The underlying implication is that it is no longer possible to refer universal salvation to Jesus Christ, whether or not faith in him be explicitly professed in the Church. Jesus Christ is no longer to be seen as the constitutive Savior for all humankind whose saving power is operative beyond the boundaries of the Christian Church. Rejected here is not only the notion of obligatory belonging to the

Church for salvation but the universal mediatorship of Jesus Christ in the order of salvation" (Dupuis, *Toward a Christian Theology of Religious Pluralism*, 183). John Hick's approach can be seen as theocentric (Hick calls it "Reality-centered"). More recently, other orientations have been proposed: *regnocentric* (focusing on signs of the presence of God's reign in other religions), *soteriocentric* (focusing on how the religions propose methods of salvation or liberation), *logocentric* (how the religions reflect or manifest what Christians call the pre-existent Logos of God), and *pneumatocentric* (how the religions reflect the presence of what Christians recognize as the Holy Spirit). These are discussed in Dupuis, *Toward a Christian Theology of Religious Pluralism*, 193-201. While the "centricity" thematization has much to recommend it, it is less widely recognized than the Race and Knitter categories.

72. Paul F. Knitter, *Introducing Theologies of Religions* (Maryknoll, NY: Orbis Books, 2002). Knitter's four-model scheme represents the latest in a succession of attempts to categorize the different approaches to the theology of religions. In 1985, Knitter proposed four categories: three confessional models (conservative Evangelical, mainline Protestant, Roman Catholic), and one cross-denominational "theocentric" model. See *No Other Name? A Critical Survey of Christian Attitudes toward the World Religions* (Maryknoll, NY: Orbis Books, 1985), 73. However, in *One Earth Many Religions,* Knitter returned to Race's threefold categorization. For his rationale, see *One Earth*, 25-26.

73. Race, *Christians and Religious Pluralism*, 11.

74. Fredericks, *Faith among Faiths*, 14-15.

75. Knitter, *Introducing Theologies of Religions*, 19. Knitter further divides this model into Total Replacement, exemplified by Barth, and Partial Replacement, exemplified by Paul Tillich, Wolfhart Pannenberg, Carl Braaten, and Clark Pinnock.

76. As Race puts it, inclusivism "aims to hold together two equally binding convictions: the operation of the grace of God in all the great religions of the world working for salvation, and the uniqueness of the manifestation of the grace of God in Christ, which makes a universal claim as the final way of salvation" (Race, *Christians and Religious Pluralism*, 38). Fredericks notes the key differences between inclusivism and exclusivism: "Inclusivist theologies, like exclusivist theologies, insist that all salvation is through Jesus Christ. But unlike exclusivism, inclusivism is willing to recognize that the saving grace of Christ is at work outside of the boundaries of the institutional church. Thus, although they do not acknowledge Christ to be the savior explicitly, [adherents of other religions] are not strangers to the Holy Spirit and must be counted, at least potentially, among the saved" (Fredericks, *Faith among Faiths*, 23).

77. Knitter, *Introducing Theologies of Religions*, 73. Rahner's discussion can be found in "Christianity and the Non-Christian Religions," in *Ministry and Theology in Global Perspective*, ed. Pittman et al., 87-93.

78. Knitter, *Introducing Theologies of Religions*, 90-93. Dupuis writes that Jesus Christ "is constitutive of salvation for all," yet "neither excludes nor includes other saving figures or traditions." Christ brings salvation history to its climax by way of "confirmation and accomplishment" rather than "substitution or supercession" (Dupuis, *Toward a Christian Theology of Religious Pluralism*, 388).

79. Quoted in Knitter, *Introducing Theologies of Religions*, 86.

80. Fredericks traces the development of Roman Catholic inclusivism in *Buddhists and Christians*, 1-8. Pope John Paul II, for example, speaks of the participation of other religions in the saving mystery of Christ (ibid., 5). With the publication of *Dominus Iesus* (2000), however, the Roman magisterium seems to be sliding back toward a less inclusive position. See Fredericks's discussion in "The Catholic Church and the Other Religious

Paths: Rejecting Nothing That Is True and Holy," *Theological Studies* 64, no. 2 (June 2003): 225-54.

81. Knitter, *One Earth Many Religions*, 23.

82. Fredericks, *Faith among Faiths*, 7.

83. Ibid. Race grounds pluralism in terms of the notion of religious experience: "The starting-point for the pluralist theory is the validity of the notion of religious experience, which is embodied in various ways in the religious traditions of the world. Valued as an authentic encounter with the divine, the experience is describable and is characterized differently within the traditions" (Race, *Christians and Religious Pluralism*, 139). Knitter notes that pluralists recognize what Langdon Gilkey calls a "rough parity" among religions: "Such rough parity means, not that all religions deep down are saying 'the same thing,' but that *because of* their differences from Christianity, other religions *may be* just as effective and successful in bringing their followers to truth, and peace, and well-being with God as Christianity has been for Christians; also, that these other religions, again because they are so different from Christianity, may have just as important a message and vision for all peoples as Christianity does" (Knitter, *One Earth Many Religions*, 30).

84. Knitter, *Introducing Theologies of Religions*, 110.

85. Ibid., 112. Knitter refers to these as three "bridges," enabling Christians to "cross the Rubicon" to the Mutuality Model.

86. Ibid.

87. Ibid., 125.

88. While I appreciate Knitter's reasons for grouping these approaches together, I am less sanguine about whether they actually belong together. As I argue in my dissertation, the structure of Lindbeck's and Heim's theological discourse is less open to religious diversity than is that of comparative theologians. See Brockman, "Turning to Religious Others," 96-99 (Heim), 292-324 (Lindbeck).

89. At least this has been the official position. The reality has often been quite different, as can be seen in the syncretistic blend of Christian and indigenous traditions in Latin American Catholicism.

90. See the essays collected in Catherine Cornille, ed., *Many Mansions? Multiple Religious Belonging and Christian Identity* (Maryknoll, NY: Orbis Books, 2002).

91. The following remarks summarize a much more complex argument presented in Brockman, "Turning to Religious Others," particularly chapters 4 and 9, and Brockman, *No Longer the Same*.

92. By *discourse* I mean its sense as generally found in cultural studies: "the forms of representation, conventions and habits of language use producing specific fields of culturally and historically located meanings" (Peter Brooker, *A Concise Glossary of Cultural Theory* [New York: Oxford University Press (Arnold), 1999], s.v. "Discourse," 66-67). I have removed the small capitals used to indicate that terms have their own entries elsewhere in this glossary.) This sense of discourse owes much to the work of Michel Foucault, particularly *The Archaeology of Knowledge*. Foucault's important insight is that discourse works to *construct* what its practitioners—for example, psychiatrists and psychologists in the discourse of psychopathology—accept as "real," "true," and/or "given." Foucault shows that the objects of a given discourse—e.g., madness—do not exist "outside" or "before" the discourse, which then describes or enumerates them. Rather, discourses "systematically form the objects of which they speak" (Michel Foucault, *The Archaeology of Knowledge and the Discourse on Language*, trans. A. M. Sheridan Smith [New York: Pantheon Books, 1972], 49). Foucault writes: "It would be quite wrong to see discourse as a place where previously established objects are laid one after another like words on a page" (42-43). Elsewhere he writes: "I would like to show that 'discourses,' in

the form in which they can be heard or read, are not, as one might expect, a mere inter-section of things and words: an obscure web of things, and a manifest, visible, coloured chain of words; I would like to show that discourse is not a slender surface of contact, or confrontation, between a reality and a language (*langue*), the intrication of a lexicon and an experience; I would like to show . . . that in analysing discourses themselves, one sees the loosening of the embrace, apparently so tight, of words and things, and the emergence of a group of rules proper to discursive practice. . . . [The task] consists of not—or no longer—treating discourses as groups of signs (signifying elements referring to contents or representations) but as practices that systematically form the objects of which they speak" (48-49).

93. David Tracy alludes to this problem when he writes: "Both the 'pagan' and the 'Jew' have too often served as the projected other of 'Christian' self-understanding" (Tracy, *Dialogue with the Other*, 4-5).

94. Fredericks, *Faith among Faiths*, 170-71.

95. As I have argued in Brockman, "Turning to Religious Others," 384-402, an important implication of this turn to the witness of religious others is a rethinking of the sources and norms used in Christian theological reflection: "The witness of religious others should not be relegated to a subordinate status. Rather, I envision something analogous to David Tracy's correlation of human experience and Christian witness, where both are brought into fully reciprocal, mutually critical conversation. In like fashion, the witness of religious others would be brought into fully reciprocal, mutually critical dialogue with Christian witness; in this way, *both* Christian witness *and* that of religious others would function as sources and norms for Christian theological reflection" (387).

Readings

New Testament Texts

NEW TESTAMENT TEXTS ARE NOT WORKS OF THEOLOGY, BUT RATHER are to be considered as sources and norms for theological reflection; that is, they provide authoritative material for theological interpretation and stand as norms by which the validity of theological reflection is evaluated.[1] Accordingly, it will be useful to examine some New Testament texts germane to a Christian theology of religions.

Christians sometimes reduce the New Testament witness regarding religious others to a set of "proof texts," scriptural passages cited without regard to their context. In particular, John 14:6 and Acts 4:12 (included in the selections below) are frequently cited to support two related claims: that divine revelation and salvation come solely through faith in the divinity of Jesus, and thus that non-Christians are outside the realm of divine revelation and salvation (or, put differently, that Christians alone stand inside that realm).

There are at least two significant problems with such an approach. First, when seen in the light of their overall context, these passages may be less definitively "exclusivist" than they might first appear.[2] Second, as James Fredericks points out, there are, in fact, two facets of the biblical witness regarding religious others.[3] On the one hand, there are those texts (including John 14:6 and Acts 4:12) that witness to the uniqueness and decisiveness of God's action in Jesus Christ. On the other hand, texts such as John 1:1-9 and Acts 17:22-31 affirm God's self-revelation to all humanity and God's will (or desire) to save all humanity. Paul Knitter refers to this latter aspect of the Good News as "God's revealing presence in others."[4] Both strands of the New Testament witness are represented in the selections included below.

A complication with the use of New Testament texts in theological reflection about religious others is the fact that, with the possible exception of Judaism, the Bible does not speak explicitly about the religious traditions active in our contemporary world.[5] For example, the Bible does not discuss Hinduism, Buddhism, the religions of the indigenous peoples of the Americas, or African Atlantic religions such as Santería. Islam did not even arise as a religious community until well after the biblical canon was established. Furthermore, the religions to which the New Testament explicitly refers (again, with the possible exception of Judaism) largely no longer exist today: the Roman imperial cult, the polytheism of Greece and

Rome, and mystery religions such as the cults of Isis/Osiris and Mithras. When New Testament writers talk about "idolatry" or otherwise criticize religious beliefs and practices, they are explicitly referring to the religions of their own time, not (necessarily) to the religions we encounter today.

Accordingly, applying the New Testament texts to the religions of our contemporary world requires an interpretive move. For example, the theologian might seek to apply Paul's condemnation of the Athenians' "idolatry" in Acts 17 to the beliefs and practices of Hindus or the indigenous American peoples. While this may well be a legitimate theological move, one should keep in mind that it reflects the theologian's hermeneutical decision, not (necessarily) the content of the biblical texts themselves, since those texts do not explicitly mention the religious life of Hindus or indigenous Americans.

With these cautions in mind, let us turn to some of the key New Testament texts of relevance to Christian theological reflection about religious others.

Jesus and Religious Outsiders (Matthew 8:5-12; 15:21-28)

These passages from the Gospel of Matthew are germane to a Christian theology of religions because they suggest glimmerings of wisdom and faith outside the Jewish community. In these texts, Jesus interacts with a Roman centurion and a Canaanite woman. It is likely that neither had access to that divine revelation to which the Jewish scriptures and tradition attest. Consequently, their example suggests the "prevenient" presence and work of God among those whom the Jewish community of Jesus' time considered religious outsiders. As Jacques Dupuis writes of these and other passages in which Jesus ministers to Gentiles: "Clearly . . . for Jesus, saving faith is not only remotely accessible to pagans and foreigners; it is actually operative among them. So too foreigners may already belong to the Kingdom of God, the call to which extends beyond the limits of Israel's chosen people."[6]

What significance do these passages have for a contemporary Christian theology of religions? On the one hand, one might see their importance as minimal. They may be taken to testify only to the charisma of Jesus himself, or to these "pagans" as exceptions to a general spiritual darkness among Gentiles. They might also be taken as foreshadowing the later Gentile character of the church. However, along with passages such as the Lucan parable of the Good Samaritan (see below), these passages may be taken to suggest the more general lesson that religious outsiders may not be utterly without faithfulness.

The Good Samaritan (Luke 10:29-37)

In this familiar text, Jesus challenges the exclusionism of the religious insiders of his time, and suggests that they may have much to learn from religious outsiders. Addressed to a religious insider—a *nomikos*, or expert in the Jewish law—this parable shows that the second great commandment, love of neighbor, may be exemplified not by religious insiders (represented in the parable by the priest and the Levite), but by a despised outsider, a Samaritan. This story takes on an added "edge" when one considers the enmity that prevailed between Jews and Samaritans at that time—not to mention the fact that only a few verses earlier, the evangelist tells us that Jesus and his disciples had recently been rejected by a Samaritan village (Luke 9:51-56).[7]

Having told the story, Jesus then asks the *nomikos* which of the three characters displayed neighbor-love, and the latter has no choice but to answer, "The one who showed him mercy," meaning the Samaritan. (It is perhaps symptomatic of the Jewish community's contempt for Samaritans that the *nomikos* cannot bring himself to say "the Samaritan.") Jesus replies, "Go and do likewise" (Luke 10:37); in other words, follow the example of the religious outsider, not the priest or the Levite.

In constructing the story in this way, Jesus indicates that the dominant religious, ethnic, and social conceptions of "inside" and "outside" have no part in the kingdom of God. Furthermore, the story of the compassionate Samaritan and similar passages suggest that Jesus believed that the outsider may have much to teach insiders. In other words, insider status conveys no assurance of righteousness or truth.[8] This should serve as a caution to those of us who are religious insiders within the Christian community today.

The Prologue to John's Gospel (John 1:1-9)

The scriptural foundations for the Logos theology exhibited by Justin Martyr and Clement of Alexandria (see next section) are laid in the following passage from the opening to the Fourth Gospel. In this passage, the author identifies Jesus Christ with the force responsible for the creation of the universe, the Logos, or Word, of God.

The author appeals to the idea of the Logos without comment, suggesting that the author intends it to be a term with which the intended readers are familiar. While John uses the concept in his own way, the absence of explication establishes common ground with non-Christian thought by evoking associations with ideas about the Logos in contemporaneous Greek and Jewish philosophy. Heraclitus, Plato, and the Stoics conceived of the Logos as the organizing principle which gives unity, order, and rationality to the cosmos, and which operates on the human plane as reason. This notion was deployed by the Jewish philosopher Philo (ca. 20 B.C.E.–ca. 50 C.E.) in his synthesis of Greek and Jewish thought. As C. H. Dodd writes, Philo understood the Logos as "the Platonic world of ideas, conceived not as self-existent, but as expressing the mind of the One God. It is this that mediates between God and our world."[9]

This passage can be seen as illustrating the two facets mentioned by Fredericks. On the one hand, it suggests the decisive role of Christ in salvation ("to all who received him, who believed in his name, he gave power to become children of God"), and thus echoes John 14:6 (see below). On the other hand, it also suggests what Knitter calls "God's revealing presence in others," in that Christ is depicted as the light that "enlightens everyone," a light that was not "overcome" by the "darkness." While the author asserts that "the world did not know him," this does not entail that divine revelation was utterly absent apart from the incarnate Christ.[10]

"I am the way . . ." (John 14:1-9)

Along with Acts 4:12, this Johannine passage is often used to support an exclusivist approach. There are two problems with this approach. First, as Kenneth Cracknell explains, the common exclusivist reading of John 14:6 may in fact be a *mis*reading. In the context of the Logos theology suggested by John's Gospel as a whole, Cracknell reads this passage as referring to Jesus' self-identification with "the Universal Word at work everywhere," including in the "ways of non-Christians."[11]

A second problem with the exclusivist interpretation involves the interpretation of "through me" in v. 6. Frequently, this has been taken to mean "through faith in the divinity and saving power of Christ."[12] While that is a possible interpretation, it should be noted that in v. 6 Jesus does not mention faith (or belief) explicitly (as he does, for instance, in v. 1). Consequently, "through me" could just as well signify that Christ is also active, as Cracknell notes, even among the "ways of non-Christians." In other words, the most one can say about John 14:6 is that it affirms that Christ is essential to salvation; but it leaves ambiguous the precise way in which that salvation is effected.

"No other name . . ." (Acts 4:1-12)

Along with John 14:6, this passage from Acts is often used to justify a narrowly exclusivist approach to religious others. However, while this passage certainly holds that Jesus Christ is necessary to salvation, it does not rule out the possibility that Christ may work behind the scenes through other religions. It does not explicitly state that baptism or belief in the divinity of Christ is necessary for salvation: only that Christ—or more precisely, the "name" of Christ, a more ambiguous concept—is necessary. Furthermore, it does not specify precisely *how* Christ (or his name) is necessary.

Reading Acts 4:12 in the context of the overall narrative in Acts 3 and 4, Cracknell finds that this verse is about healing (from sickness or demon possession) rather than some claim that Jesus is the only bearer of salvation: "rather than pointing to an exclusiveness, Acts 4:12 might help us to think of ways in which the grace and love of God operate in the world without being named at all."[13]

"God shows no partiality . . ." (Acts 10:34-35, 43-45)

The passage also suggests both aspects of the New Testament witness discussed above. First, it asserts that belief in Christ brings forgiveness of sins. Second, it also asserts that "in every nation" those who fear God and do "what is right" are "acceptable" to God—presumably without specific faith in, or even knowledge of, Jesus of Nazareth.

Paul's Sermon in Athens (Acts 17:22-31)

This text finds Paul visiting the Areopagus in Athens. It is of particular interest for Christian theological reflection about religious others for at least two reasons. First, it depicts Paul as giving a nuanced presentation of Greek religiosity, foreshadowing the apologetic work of Justin Martyr (see next section). Paul "is deeply distressed" by the proliferation of idols. Yet he also praises the Athenians for being "extremely religious" (Gk. *deisidaimonesterous*) (17:22). While the Greek adjective can signify "superstitious," both the Bauer-Danker Greek-English lexicon and many commentators regard its use here as laudatory, meaning "devout," as befits Paul's diplomatic approach in Athens.[14]

Second, Paul seems to suggest that ethnic, cultural, and perhaps religious differences are divinely intended, as ways for humans to seek, and perhaps find, God (vv. 26-28). This suggests the possibility that some humans—not only the Jewish people, to whom God has revealed Godself in the scriptures—do find God or have found God. As evidence of this divine inspiration, Paul cites testimony from the Greek tradition itself: "In him we live and move and have our being" comes from the philosophical tradition, perhaps Epimenides or Posidonius; and "For we too are his offspring" is from the Greek poet Aratus.[15] This amounts to an implicit affirmation of the Greek tradition.

While Paul goes on immediately to criticize idolatry and to declare that God now "commands all people everywhere to repent," he appeals to a kind of divine witness already present among the Greeks—thus the quotes from Greek thinkers. In other words, Paul does not reduce his message to the Athenians to a critique of their "idolatry." Instead, he appeals to them on the basis of their own experience, their own witness of the divine, but adds information—about Jesus of Nazareth—that would have been unknown to them.

Paul on Gentiles and the Law (Romans 2:14-15)

Paul's argument in this passage foreshadows Justin Martyr's later use of the concept of a universal *logos spermatikos*, or seed-Logos (see next section). Despite the fact that Gentiles are without the Law, the covenant binding God and the Jewish community, Paul holds that they nonetheless have an instinctive grasp of what God requires. The human conscience functions here as a kind of divine revelation outside the Jewish community. While the phrase "a law to themselves" in v. 14 today suggests lack of responsibility, v. 15 suggests quite the opposite: that, even in the absence of the Law, the Gentiles' conscience guides them in living faithfully.

Notes

1. On the categories source and norm, see Pamela Dickey Young, *Feminist Theology/Christian Theology: In Search of Method* (Minneapolis, MN: Augsburg Fortress, 1990), 19-20.

2. See the commentary on John 14:6 and Acts 4:12, below.

3. James L. Fredericks, *Faith among Faiths: Christian Theology and Non-Christian Religions* (Mahwah, NJ: Paulist Press, 1999), 13-14.

4. Knitter, *Introducing Theologies of Religions* (Maryknoll, NY: Orbis Books, 2002), 34. For a helpful exploration of other "non-exclusivist" passages in the Hebrew Bible and the New Testament, see Jacques Dupuis, *Toward a Christian Theology of Religious Pluralism* (Maryknoll, NY: Orbis Books, 1997), 41-83.

5. It could also be argued that contemporary Judaism is sufficiently different from the Judaism(s) of first-century Palestine that even the New Testament references to Jewish persons and practices no longer straightforwardly apply.

6. Dupuis, *Toward a Christian Theology of Religious Pluralism*, 47.

7. For a historical survey of the Jewish-Samaritan conflict, see Gerard S. Sloyan, "The Samaritans in the New Testament," *Horizons* 10 (Spring 1983): 7-21.

8. One might object that these stories have to do only with the specific religious insiders Jesus himself encountered in his own time (e.g., certain Pharisees). By that reading, Christ was not attacking religious insiders in general, and certainly not his own followers (i.e., Christians). After all, is it not true that Christians have "the mind of Christ," as Paul says (1 Cor 2:16)? Doesn't faith in Christ confer a kind of epistemological privilege on Christian insiders that is not available to those outside the Christian faith? First, I have little sympathy with Christian claims of epistemological privilege. Even if faith in Christ (or the action of the Holy Spirit, or some other putative mechanism) were to convey some such privilege, the biblical accounts insist that we remain limited and fallible beings. As such, our faith is always lived out in limited and fallible forms. Second, I do not see how we can separate "the mind of Christ" from the teachings and actions of Jesus remembered in the Gospel accounts. Thus, "the mind of Christ," insofar as it is *Christ's*, must be as critical of closed-mindedness toward religious others as Christ himself was.

9. C. H. Dodd, *The Interpretation of the Fourth Gospel* (New York: Cambridge University Press, 1980 [1953]), 68.

10. Regarding John 1:9-13, Dodd writes: "There were some who received the word of God, into whose souls Wisdom entered, making them not only friends of God and prophets, but children of God, generated by no physical process and by no merely human act of will, but by the creative will of God. Thus the Logos, or Wisdom, which was the original principle of creation, acts creatively once again in giving men a new birth as sons of God. It does not seem necessary to confine this divine generation to pre-Christian Israel. That there are children of God scattered abroad through the world is stated in [John 11:52], and it is unlikely that the evangelist was thinking only of Jews of the Dispersion. They are the 'other sheep not of this fold,' whom it is Christ's mission to gather into one. Thus it is quite consistent with his thought to interpret the [*tekna theou*] of [John 1:12] in the sense that already before the coming of Christ there were in the world those in whom the divine Logos was present, and who therefore had the 'right' to be children of God" (Dodd, *The Interpretation of the Fourth Gospel*, 281-82). For a conflicting view, see Raymond E. Brown, *The Gospel According to John: I-XII* (New York: Doubleday, 1966), 29-30.

11. Kenneth Cracknell, *In Good and Generous Faith: Christian Responses to Religious Pluralism* (Peterborough, UK: Epworth, 2005), 88.

12. For example, this is the approach taken by Hilary of Poitiers: "no one comes to the Father except through the Son, because we cannot know the Father, unless faith in the Son is active in us, since we cannot approach the Father in worship, unless we first adore the Son, while if we know the Son, the Father draws us to eternal life and receives us. But each result is the work of the Son, for by the preaching of the Father, Whom the Son preaches, the Father brings us to the Son, and the Son leads us to the Father" (Hilary of

Poitiers, *De Trinitate*, Book XI, NPNF 2-09, trans. E. W. Watson et al., 213; see *Hilary of Poitier, John of Damascus,* ed. Philip Schaff [Christian Classics Ethereal Library], http://www.ccel.org/ccel/schaff/npnf209.ii.v.ii.xi.html).

13. Cracknell, *In Good and Generous Faith,* 95.

14. Frederick W. Danker, ed., *A Greek-English Lexicon of the New Testament and Other Early Christian Literature,* 3d ed. (Chicago: University of Chicago Press, 2000), s.v. *deisidaimon,* 216.

15. C. K. Barrett, *A Critical and Exegetical Commentary on the Acts of the Apostles,* vol. 2 (Edinburgh: T&T Clark, 1998), 847-48.

Readings

Early Christian Voices

Justin Martyr

Born around 100 C.E., Justin Martyr is responsible for some of the earliest surviving Christian texts outside the New Testament canon itself. In response to early and intense persecution of Christians (to which he himself would fall victim in the 160s), Justin composed some of the first works of "apology" (defense) of the Christian faith and influenced several subsequent patristic thinkers, including Clement of Alexandria (see below) and Irenaeus of Lyon.

In the works excerpted here, Justin contends that Christianity is worthy of respect by non-Christians because it is consistent with the highest insights of the Greek philosophical tradition. A philosopher himself, Justin argues that Christ both affirms and completes the Greek philosophical tradition embodied in Socrates, Plato, and the Stoics. Like Paul at the Areopagus (see above), Justin is unsparing in his critique of idol worship, yet does not consign the entire non-Christian tradition to that category (as will be the case with Tertullian later in the second century).

To contemporary readers, Justin's argument might at first seem irrelevant to a discussion of Christian theologies of religions, since philosophy today is a largely secular enterprise. However, philosophers in Justin's day concerned themselves with many of the questions we would today associate with "religion": What is ultimately real? How did the cosmos come to be? What is the nature of the human soul? How does one live a virtuous life? How does one know good from evil? What happens to the human at death?[1] Each of the various philosophical schools—including Platonism, Neoplatonism, Stoicism, and Epicureanism—offered its own answers to these questions. Furthermore, some philosophical schools, such as Neoplatonism, had mystical dimensions that gave them what we today would consider a "religious" character.

As in much interreligious dialogue today, Justin begins by asserting common ground between Christians and those who persecute them. That common ground is none other than Christ himself, who is the full embodiment of the divine Logos which has informed the world from its beginnings. Even before the birth of Jesus of Nazareth, the Logos was already active in the world, "implanted in every race," sown like divine seed (the *logos spermatikos,* translated below as "spermatic word") in the minds and hearts of all people.

Walter Wagner describes Justin's argument as follows: "the Logos sowed the logoi of reason, justice, courage, and temperance throughout the cosmos. The Word imparted the seeds as receptors of God's will and generators of devout response in all humans."[2] Prior to the incarnation of Christ in Jesus of Nazareth, divine truth was evidenced not only among the house of Israel, but also in the works of Greek philosophers such as Socrates, Heraclitus, Plato, and the Stoics. Anticipating Karl Rahner's notion of "anonymous Christians," Justin claims that those who have lived *meta logou,* "reasonably" (literally, "with the Word"), have in fact been Christians without knowing it. Far from being in utter darkness and ignorance of God, "pagans" unknowingly partook in the selfsame divine wisdom proclaimed by Christians.

While Gentiles may have been without the words of God (the Hebrew scriptures), they have never been without the Word of God. This is evidenced in the wisdom and righteousness of "pagans." Christians celebrate what is good and true in the pagan tradition and claim it as scattered witness to the Word embodied in Jesus Christ. As Jacques Dupuis writes, "all persons who have known the Truth and lived righteously are Christians, for, and insofar as, all have partaken of, and lived according to, the Logos who is all Truth."[3]

Consequently, whatever truth is uttered by the philosophers is not solely the product of human reason, but represents a contemplation of the Logos, although the philosophers do not recognize it as such. However, Justin argues, the philosophers knew the Logos only in part, and the truth of their formulations is limited accordingly. Because Jesus Christ is the full embodiment of the divine Logos, Christianity represents the complete culmination of the wisdom to be found in the Jewish and Greek traditions. Thus, all that is true belongs to Christians as well, for all truth springs ultimately from the spermatic Logos.

The fact that Justin Martyr is one of the earliest surviving voices in the Christian tradition—writing not long after the latest New Testament texts—serves as a reminder that the narrow exclusivism of some later Christian thinkers was not a uniform characteristic of the early church.

Source: *The Apostolic Fathers with Justin Martyr and Irenaeus,* ed. Philip Schaff (Christian Classics Ethereal Library), http://www.ccel.org/ccel/schaff/anf01.html.

From "The First Apology of Justin"[4]

To the Emperor Titus Ælius Adrianus Antoninus Pius Augustus Cæsar, and to his son Verissimus the Philosopher . . . with the whole People of the Romans, I, Justin . . . present this address and petition in behalf of those of all nations who are unjustly hated and wantonly abused, myself being one of them.

Reason directs those who are truly pious and philosophical to honour and love only what is true, declining to follow traditional opinions, if these be worthless. For not only does sound reason direct us to refuse the guidance of those who did or taught anything wrong, but it is incumbent on the lover of truth, by all means, and if death be threatened, even before his own life, to choose to do and say what is right. Do you, then, since ye are called pious and philosophers, guardians of justice and lovers of learning, give good heed, and hearken to my address; and if ye are indeed such, it will be manifested. . . .

[S]ince of old these evil demons, effecting apparitions of themselves, both defiled women and corrupted boys, and showed such fearful sights to men, that those who did not use their reason in judging of the actions that were done, were struck with terror; and being carried away by fear, and not knowing that these were demons, they called them gods, and gave to each the name which each of the demons chose for himself. . . . [N]ot only among the Greeks did reason (Logos) prevail to condemn these things through Socrates, but also among the barbarians were they condemned by Reason (or the Word, the Logos) Himself, who took shape, and became man, and was called Jesus Christ; and in obedience to Him, we not only deny that they who did such things as these are gods, but assert that they are wicked and impious demons, whose actions will not bear comparison with those even of men desirous of virtue.

Hence are we called atheists. And we confess that we are atheists, so far as gods of this sort are concerned, but not with respect to the most true God, the Father of righteousness and temperance and the other virtues, who is free from all impurity. But both Him, and the Son (who came forth from Him and taught us these things, and the host of the other good angels who follow and are made like to Him), and the prophetic Spirit, we worship and adore, knowing them in reason and truth, and declaring without grudging to every one who wishes to learn, as we have been taught. . . .

And neither do we honour with many sacrifices and garlands of flowers such deities as men have formed and set in shrines and called gods; since we see that these are soulless and dead, and have not the form of God (for we do not consider that God has such a form as some say that they imitate to His honour), but have the names and forms of those wicked demons which have appeared. . . .

If . . . on some points we teach the same things as the poets and philosophers whom you honour, and on other points are fuller and more divine in our teaching, and if we alone afford proof of what we assert, why are we unjustly hated more than all others? For while we say that all things have been produced and arranged into a world by God, we shall seem to utter the doctrine of Plato; and while we say that there will be a burning up of all, we shall seem to utter the doctrine of the Stoics; and while we affirm that the souls of the wicked, being endowed with sensation even after death, are punished, and that those of the good being delivered from punishment spend a blessed existence, we shall seem to say the same things as the poets and philosophers; and while we maintain that men ought not to worship the works of their hands, we say the very things which have been said by the comic poet Menander, and other similar writers, for they have declared that the workman is greater than the work. . . .

We have been taught that Christ is the first-born of God, and we have declared above that He is the Word of whom every race of men were partakers; and those who lived reasonably are Christians, even though they have been thought atheists; as, among the Greeks, Socrates and Heraclitus, and men like them; and among the barbarians, Abraham, and Ananias, and Azarias, and Misael, and Elias, and many others whose actions and names we now decline to recount, because we know it would be tedious. So that even they who lived before Christ, and lived without reason, were wicked and hostile to Christ, and slew those who lived reasonably. But who, through the power of the Word, according to the will of God the Father and Lord of all, He was born of a virgin as a man, and was named Jesus, and was crucified, and died, and rose again, and ascended into heaven, an intelligent man will be able to comprehend from what has been already so largely said.

From "The Second Apology of Justin"[5]

[T]hose of the Stoic school—since, so far as their moral teaching went, they were admirable, as were also the poets in some particulars, on account of the seed of reason [the Logos] implanted in every race of men—were, we know, hated and put to death,—Heraclitus for instance, and, among those of our own time, Musonius and others. For, as we intimated, the devils have always effected, that all those who anyhow live a reasonable and earnest life, and shun vice, be hated. And it is nothing wonderful; if the devils are proved to cause those to be much worse hated who live not according to a part only of the word diffused [among men] but by the knowledge and contemplation of the whole Word, which is Christ. . . .

Our doctrines, then, appear to be greater than all human teaching; because Christ, who appeared for our sakes, became the whole rational being, both body, and reason, and soul. For whatever either lawgivers or philosophers uttered well, they elaborated by finding and contemplating some part of the Word. But since they did not know the whole of the Word, which is Christ, they often contradicted themselves. And those who by human birth were more ancient than Christ, when they attempted to consider and prove things by reason, were brought before the tribunals as impious persons and busybodies. And Socrates, who was more zealous in this direction than all of them, was accused of the very same crimes as ourselves. For they said that he was introducing new divinities, and did not consider those to be gods whom the state recognised. But he cast out from the state both Homer and the rest of the poets, and taught men to reject the wicked demons and those who did the things which the poets related; and he exhorted them to become acquainted with the God who was to them unknown, by means of the investigation of reason, saying, "That it is neither easy to find the Father and Maker of all, nor, having found Him, is it safe to declare Him to all."

But these things our Christ did through His own power. For no one trusted in Socrates so as to die for this doctrine, but in Christ, who was partially known even by Socrates (for He was and is the Word who is in every man, and who foretold the things that were to come to pass both through the prophets and in His own person when He was made of like passions, and taught these things), not only philosophers and scholars believed, but also artisans and people entirely uneducated, despising both glory, and fear, and death; since He is a power of the ineffable Father, not the mere instrument of human reason. . . .

. . . I both boast and with all my strength strive to be found a Christian; not because the teachings of Plato are different from those of Christ, but because they are not in all respects similar, as neither are those of the others, Stoics, and poets, and historians. For each man spoke well in proportion to the share he had of the spermatic word, seeing what was related to it. But they who contradict themselves on the more important points appear not to have possessed the heavenly wisdom, and the knowledge which cannot be spoken against. Whatever things were rightly said among all men, are the property of us Christians. For next to God, we worship and love the Word who is from the unbegotten and ineffable God, since also He became man for our sakes, that becoming a partaker of our sufferings, He might also bring us healing. For all the writers were able to see realities darkly through the sowing of the implanted word that was in them. For the seed and imitation impacted according to capacity is one thing, and quite another is the thing itself, of which there is the participation and imitation according to the grace which is from Him.

Clement of Alexandria

Clement was born around the middle of the second century c.e., and died early in the third. He was associated with the Egyptian port city of Alexandria, a center for scholarship which would later produce Athanasius and Cyril of Alexandria. Two of Clement's works are excerpted here: the *Exhortation to the Heathens* and the *Stromata* ("Miscellanies").

Clement employs the notion of Christ as divine Logos not only to establish common ground with the Greek philosophical tradition but also to attack Gnosticism. Against the Gnostic idea that the Logos was unconnected with the created universe, Clement argues (as Wagner writes) that no part of the cosmos

could ever be called God-forsaken, because the Logos had been everywhere. In the first coming as the agent of creation, the Logos not only planted the seeds of *gnōsis* in the world but made the world a place that God cherished and loved. . . . [H]umans were in the image of the Logos through the use of their soul's reason (*logos*), and they had the inner incentive as well as the ability to develop into the likeness of the Logos.[6]

In his *Exhortation to the Heathens*, Clement is able to recognize the traces of the divine Logos in the wisdom of the Greek philosophers and poets. Indeed, this "divine effluence" has been instilled into all people, especially those engaged in "intellectual pursuits." In the *Stromata*, Clement goes so far as to call Greek philosophy "the clear image of truth, a divine gift to the Greeks," for it serves as *praeparatio evangelica*, preparation for the gospel.

Source: *Fathers of the Second Century: Hermas, Tatian, Athenagoras, Theophilus, and Clement of Alexandria (Entire)*, ed. Philip Schaff (Christian Classics Ethereal Library), http://www.ccel.org/ccel/schaff/anf02.html.

From "Exhortation to the Heathens"[7]

It is the Lord of the spirits, the Lord of the fire, the Maker of the universe, Him who lighted up the sun, that I long for. I seek after God, not the works of God. Whom shall I take as a helper in my inquiry? We do not, if you have no objection, wholly disown Plato. How, then, is God to be searched out, O Plato? "For both to find the Father and Maker of this universe is a work of difficulty; and having found Him, to declare Him fully, is impossible."

Why so? by Himself, I beseech you! For He can by no means be expressed. Well done, Plato! Thou hast touched on the truth. But do not flag. Undertake with me the inquiry respecting the Good. For into all men whatever, especially those who are occupied with intellectual pursuits, a certain divine effluence has been instilled; wherefore, though reluctantly, they confess that God is one, indestructible, unbegotten, and that somewhere above in the tracts of heaven, in His own peculiar appropriate eminence, whence He surveys all things, He has an existence true and eternal.

"Tell me what I am to conceive God to be,
Who sees all things, and is Himself unseen,"

Euripides says. Accordingly, Menander seems to me to have fallen into error when he said:—

"O sun! for thou, first of gods, ought to be worshipped,
By whom it is that we are able to see the other gods."

For the sun never could show me the true God; but that healthful Word, that is the Sun of the soul, by whom alone, when He arises in the depths of the soul, the eye of the soul itself is irradiated. Whence accordingly, Democritus, not without reason, says, "that a few of the men of intellect, raising their hands upwards to what we Greeks now call the air (ἀήρ), called the whole expanse Zeus, or God: He, too, knows all things, gives and takes away, and He is King of all." . . .

We must not either keep the Pythagoreans in the background, who say: "God is one; and He is not, as some suppose, outside of this frame of things, but within it; but, in all the entireness of His being, is in the whole circle of existence, surveying all nature, and blending in harmonious union the whole,—the author of all His own forces and works, the giver of light in heaven, and Father of all,—the mind and vital power of the whole world,—the mover of all things." For the knowledge of God, these utterances, written by those we have mentioned through the inspiration of God, and selected by us, may suffice even for the man that has but small power to examine into truth.

From the Stromata[8]

[P]hilosophy does not ruin life by being the originator of false practices and base deeds, although some have calumniated it, though it be the clear image of truth, a divine gift to the Greeks; nor does it drag us away from the faith, as if we were bewitched by some delusive art, but rather, so to speak, by the use of an ampler circuit, obtains a common exercise demonstrative of the faith. Further, the juxtaposition of doctrines, by comparison, saves the truth, from which follows knowledge.

Philosophy came into existence, not on its own account, but for the advantages reaped by us from knowledge, we receiving a firm persuasion of true perception, through the knowledge of things comprehended by the mind. . . . "For the Hebrews seek signs," as the apostle says, "and the Greeks seek after wisdom." . . .

Accordingly, before the advent of the Lord, philosophy was necessary to the Greeks for righteousness. And now it becomes conducive to piety; being a kind of preparatory training to those who attain to faith through demonstration. . . . For God is the cause of all good things; but of some primarily, as of the Old and the New Testament; and of others by consequence, as philosophy. Perchance, too, philosophy was given to the Greeks directly and primarily, till the Lord should call the Greeks. For this was a schoolmaster to bring "the Hellenic mind," as the law, the Hebrews, "to Christ." Philosophy, therefore, was a preparation, paving the way for him who is perfected in Christ.

. . . The way of truth is therefore one. But into it, as into a perennial river, streams flow from all sides. . . . [W]hat was bestowed on each generation advantageously, and at seasonable times, is a preliminary training for the word of the Lord. . . . "But as the encyclical branches of study contribute to philosophy, which is their mistress; so also philosophy itself co-operates for the acquisition of wisdom. For philosophy is the study of wisdom, and wisdom is the knowledge of things divine and human; and their causes." Wisdom is therefore queen of philosophy, as philosophy is of preparatory culture. For if philosophy "professes control of the tongue, and the belly, and the parts below the belly, it is to be chosen on its own account. But it appears more worthy of respect and pre-eminence, if cultivated for the honour and knowledge of God." . . . We merely therefore assert here, that philosophy is characterized by investigation into truth and the nature of things (this is the truth of which the Lord Himself said, "I am the truth"); and that, again, the preparatory training for rest in Christ exercises the mind, rouses the intelligence, and begets an inquiring shrewdness, by means of the true philosophy, which the initiated possess, having found it, or rather received it, from the truth itself. . . .

[I]f the prophets and apostles knew not the arts by which the exercises of philosophy are exhibited, yet the mind of the prophetic and instructive spirit, uttered secretly, because all have not an intelligent ear, demands skilful modes of teaching in order to clear exposition. . . . Is not speaking our business, and does not action proceed from the Word? For if we act not for the Word, we shall act against reason. But a rational work is accomplished through God. "And nothing," it is said, "was made without Him"—the Word of God. . . .

Since, therefore, truth is one (for falsehood has ten thousand by-paths); just as the Bacchantes tore asunder the limbs of Pentheus, so the sects both of barbarian and Hellenic philosophy have done with truth, and each vaunts as the whole truth the portion which has fallen to its lot. But all, in my opinion, are illuminated by the dawn of Light. Let all, therefore, both Greeks and barbarians, who have aspired after the truth,—both those who possess not a little, and those who have any portion,—produce whatever they have of the word of truth.

. . . [T]he barbarian and Hellenic philosophy has torn off a fragment of eternal truth not from the mythology of Dionysus, but from the theology of the ever-living Word. And He who brings again together the separate fragments, and makes them one, will without peril, be assured, contemplate the perfect Word, the truth. . . .

[Clement cites Paul's speech to the Areopagites in Acts 17.]

. . . [I]t is evident that the apostle, by availing himself of poetical examples from the *Phenomena* of Aratus, approves of what had been well spoken by the Greeks; and intimates that, by the unknown God, God the Creator was in a roundabout way worshipped by the Greeks; but that it was necessary by positive knowledge to apprehend and learn Him by the Son. . . .

The divine apostle writes accordingly respecting us: "For now we see as through a glass"; knowing ourselves in it by reflection, and simultaneously contemplating, as we can, the efficient cause, from that, which, in us, is divine. . . . And by reflection and direct vision, those among the Greeks who have philosophized accurately, see God. For such, through our weakness, are our true views, as images are seen in the water, and as we see things through pellucid and transparent bodies. . . .

. . . Men must then be saved by learning the truth through Christ, even if they attain philosophy. For now that is clearly shown "which was not made known to other ages, which is now revealed to the sons of men." For there was always a natural manifestation of the one Almighty God, among all right-thinking men; and the most, who had not quite divested themselves of shame with respect to the truth, apprehended the eternal beneficence in divine providence.

Tertullian

Tertullian lived in Carthage (in present-day Tunisia) from about 155 to 230 C.E., and thus was a contemporary of Clement of Alexandria. A lawyer by training, Tertullian the theologian is known for the rigor of his arguments, his fiery rhetoric, and his uncompromising critique of what he considered the errors or heresies of the day. This was both a blessing and a curse, as Henry Chadwick notes in describing Tertullian as

> brilliant, exasperating, sarcastic, and intolerant, yet intensely vigorous and incisive in argument, delighting in logical tricks and with an advocate's love of a clever sophistry if it will make the adversary look foolish, but a powerful writer of splendid, torrential prose. . . . Every page [of his *Apology*] is written with the joy of inflicting discomfort on his adversaries for their error and unreasonableness, but in such a manner as to embarrass his own friends and supporters.[9]

In the following selections from *The Prescription against Heretics*, Tertullian is less concerned with non-Christians than heretics within the Christian community, those who have (to his way of thinking) turned away from orthodoxy. (Tertullian's principal *bêtes noires* here are the Gnostic Valentinus, the hyper-Hellenizer Marcion, and their followers.) However, his notions of the uniqueness of Christian teaching have clear implications for a theology of religions.

Tertullian arguably exhibits an early form of *fideism*, the notion that religious faith yields truths that cannot be arrived at by human reason and are not accessible to it. For Tertullian, an unbridgeable chasm separates reason and faith: they are essentially and utterly different. Consequently, he takes an uncompromising stand against any apologetic project (such as that epitomized by Justin Martyr), particularly the attempt to demonstrate continuity between Greek philosophy and Christian teaching. "What . . . has Athens to do with Jerusalem?" Tertullian famously writes. "What concord is there between the Academy and the Church? what between heretics and Christians? . . . Away with all attempts to produce a mottled Christianity of Stoic, Platonic, and dialectic composition!"[10] There can therefore be no "anonymous Christians" in Tertullian's view of the world. One is either wholly inside the community of the faithful, or wholly outside it.

Tertullian's stance has in its favor a certain straightforwardness, offering clear-cut boundaries between the Christian and the not-Christian. Yet this comes at the cost of coherence. For whereas the divine Logos theology of Justin and Clement both affirms the decisiveness of the incarnation and witnesses to the continuous prevenient presence of the Word in the world, Tertullian leaves us with the odd paradox of a world devoid of divine influence until the birth of Jesus, and the troubling possibility of wholesale damnation for those who have never heard the Gospel—calling into question the justice and love of God. It is ironic that so passionate a defender of orthodoxy should have ended his life a heretic. In the early third century, Tertullian became an adherent of the heretical Montanist sect. Tertullian's example serves as a reminder that even the most zealous and rigorous Christian thinker is not exempt from falling into the very errors he or she criticizes.

Source: *Latin Christianity: Its Founder, Tertullian*, ed. Philip Schaff (Christian Classics Ethereal Library), http://www.ccel.org/ccel/schaff/anf03.html.

From "The Prescription against Heretics"[11]

These are "the doctrines" of men and "of demons" produced for itching ears of the spirit of this world's wisdom: this the Lord called "foolishness," and "chose the foolish things of the world" to confound even philosophy itself. For (philosophy) it is which is the material of the world's wisdom, the rash interpreter of the nature and the dispensation of God. Indeed heresies are themselves instigated by philosophy. From this source came the Æons, and I know not what infinite forms, and the trinity of man in the system of Valentinus, who was of Plato's school. From the same source came Marcion's better god, with all his tranquility; he came of the Stoics. . . . [W]hen the apostle would restrain us, he expressly names *philosophy* as that which he would have us be on our guard against. Writing to the Colossians, he says, "See that no one beguile you through philosophy and vain deceit, after the tradition of men, and contrary to the wisdom of the Holy Ghost." He had been at Athens, and had in his interviews (with its philosophers) become acquainted with that human wisdom which pretends to know the truth, whilst it only corrupts it, and is itself divided into its own manifold heresies, by the variety of its mutually repugnant sects. What indeed has Athens to do with Jerusalem? What concord is there between the Academy and the Church? What between heretics and Christians? Our instruction comes from "the porch of Solomon," who had himself taught that "the Lord should be sought in simplicity of heart." Away with all attempts to produce a mottled Christianity of Stoic, Platonic, and dialectic composition! We want no curious disputation after possessing Christ Jesus, no inquisition after enjoying the gospel! With our faith, we desire no further belief. . . .

. . . No man gets instruction from that which tends to destruction. No man receives illumination from a quarter where all is darkness. Let our "seeking," therefore, be in that which is our own, and from those who are our own: and concerning that which is our own,—that, and only that, which can become an object of inquiry without impairing the rule of faith. . . .

From this, therefore, do we draw up our rule. Since the Lord Jesus Christ sent the apostles to preach, (our rule is) that no others ought to be received as preachers than those whom Christ appointed; for "no man knoweth the Father save the Son, and he to whomsoever the Son will reveal Him." Nor does the Son seem to have revealed Him to any other than the apostles, whom He sent forth to preach—that, of course, which He revealed to them.

Cyprian

A bishop of Carthage during the first half of the third century, Cyprian is often linked with the saying "There is no salvation outside the church" (*nulla salus extra ecclesiam*). While the notion can be traced to earlier thinkers, including Irenaeus and Origen, it does appear (in various forms) in Cyprian's own writings.[12]

The following selection is an excerpt from Cyprian's letter of reply to Jubaianus, who had asked for guidance regarding the efficacy of baptisms performed by heretic sects. As in the selection from Tertullian, Cyprian here is concerned specifically with heretics inside the Christian community. However, his response at least implies an exclusivist stance concerning those outside the (orthodox) Christian community: if "there is no salvation out of the Church," then not only heretics but non-Christians stand outside the realm of salvation.

Source: *Fathers of the Third Century: Hippolytus, Cyprian, Caius, Novatian, Appendix*, ed. Philip Schaff (Christian Classics Ethereal Library), http://www.ccel. org/ccel/schaff/anf05.html.

From "To *Jubaianus, Concerning the Baptism of Heretics*"[13]

Cyprian to Jubaianus his brother, greeting. You have written to me, dearest brother, wishing that the impression of my mind should be signified to you, as to what I think concerning the baptism of heretics; who, placed without, and established outside the Church, arrogate to themselves a matter neither within their right nor their power. This baptism we cannot consider as valid or legitimate, since it is manifestly unlawful among them. . . .

Can the power of baptism be greater or of more avail than confession, than suffering, when one confesses Christ before men and is baptized in his own blood? And yet even this baptism does not benefit a heretic, although he has confessed Christ, and been put to death outside the Church, unless the patrons and advocates of heretics declare that the heretics who are slain in a false confession of Christ are martyrs, and assign to them the glory and the crown of martyrdom contrary to the testimony of the apostle, who says that it will profit them nothing although they were burnt and slain. But if not even the baptism of a public confession and blood can profit a heretic to salvation, because there is no salvation out of the Church, how much less shall it be of advantage to him, if in a hiding-place and a cave of robbers, stained with the contagion of adulterous water, he has not only not put off his old sins, but rather heaped up still newer and greater ones! Wherefore baptism cannot be common to us and to heretics, to whom neither God the Father, nor Christ the Son, nor the Holy Ghost, nor the faith, nor the Church itself, is common. And therefore it behooves those to be baptized who come from heresy to the Church, that so they who are prepared, in the lawful, and true, and only baptism of the holy Church, by divine regeneration, for the kingdom of God, may be born of both sacraments, because it is written, "Except a man be born of water and of the Spirit, he cannot enter into the kingdom of God."

Augustine of Hippo

Augustine of Hippo (354-430) lived much of his life in Roman-controlled north Africa, becoming bishop of Hippo (in present-day Algeria). It is difficult to overestimate Augustine's impact on subsequent Christian theology, particularly on the thought of Martin Luther and John Calvin. He was a prolific author, who exhibited a strong confidence in his own rightness and a flair for rhetoric equaled only by Tertullian. Although an imaginative and rigorous theologian, Augustine sometimes allowed the force of his argument to lead him into positions that would be considered heterodox by later thinkers (for example, his theory of double predestination).

Determining Augustine's "real position" on any given subject is complicated by the fact that most of his writings are occasional in nature: they are responses to particular controversies that arose during his lifetime, most prominently the Donatist and Pelagian controversies. The exigencies of combating one opponent sometimes led him to take positions that he would later contradict or undermine in another context.

This may be the case with his view on the availability of salvation to those outside the church. Generally speaking, Augustine agreed with Cyprian, as Dupuis notes:

> On the one hand, as for the Jews and pagans after the Christ-event, Augustine was convinced that, unless they believed in Jesus Christ and were baptized, there was no salvation for them. Now that the Gospel had been preached and the Church established, they were held guilty for not having joined the Church in which salvation is found. . . . On the other hand, Augustine did know that there were tribes in Africa to which the Gospel had not been preached. These too he considered to be outside salvation.[14]

For Augustine, there is no injustice in this: due to Adam's sin, all humankind had become "a *massa damnata* that could be spared only through God's mercy by receiving the Christian faith and baptism. According to Augustine, God's salvific will, then, was not universal; it applied to those freely destined by God to be saved."[15]

Ironically, Augustine's notion of double predestination could also lead him to what seems to be the opposite opinion: that those whom God predestined to salvation were saved *despite* their living prior to the birth of Christ and the Church. In the following selection, from his "Letter to Deogratias," Augustine tackles one of the most vexing problems not only for a Christian theology of religions, but for Christian soteriology as well. This problem is commonly known as "the scandal of particularity": if Christ alone is the way of salvation, what becomes of good people who lived and died before the birth of Jesus? Were they deprived of salvation simply because of an accident of history, and if so, is this not unjust?

After opening with a *tu quoque* (arguing that the same charge of injustice can be made of the pagan traditions themselves), Augustine turns to the substance of these questions. In line with the prologue to John's Gospel, Augustine argues that although Christ took human form in a particular place and time, he has in all ages been "the same Son of God, co-eternal with the Father, and the unchangeable Wisdom by whom universal nature was called into existence, and by participation in whom every rational soul is made blessed." The divine Word has always been present, and has always spoken through the prophets, "at one time more obscurely, at another time more plainly, as seemed to divine wisdom best adapted to the time"

Accordingly, in all ages it has been possible for persons—even those outside Israel—to believe in Christ, to live according to his precepts, and thus to be saved. The "true religion" has existed throughout history, though "practised under other names and with other symbolical rites than it now has, and formerly more obscurely revealed and known to fewer persons than now." (Christianity, in other words, is not an innovation.)

Furthermore, there have always been believers in Christ, not only among the people of the "prophetic nation" of Israel, but also "among other nations." Augustine asks, rhetorically, "Why may we not believe that in other nations also, here and there, some more were found, although we do not read their names in these authoritative records [i.e., the biblical accounts]?"

Augustine's answer involves his doctrine of double predestination, by which God predestines some to salvation and some to damnation:

> Thus the salvation provided by this religion, by which alone, as alone true, true salvation is truly promised, was never wanting to any one who was worthy of it, and he to whom it was wanting was not worthy of it. . . . Accordingly, those to whom it has not been preached at all are those who were foreknown as persons who would not believe; those to whom, notwithstanding the certainty that they would not believe, the salvation has been proclaimed are set forth as an example of the class of unbelievers; and those to whom, as persons who would believe, the truth is proclaimed are being prepared for the kingdom of heaven.

Augustine here also seems to appeal to a notion of "anonymous Christians": "from the beginning of the human race, whosoever believed in Him, and in any way knew Him, and lived in a pious and just manner according to His precepts, was undoubtedly saved by Him, in whatever time and place he may have lived."

Source: *The Confessions and Letters of St. Augustin, with a Sketch of his Life and Work*, ed. Philip Schaff (Christian Classics Ethereal Library), http://www.ccel.org/ccel/schaff/npnf101.html.

From the "Letter to Deogratias"[16]

[Pagan critics of Christianity ask:] "If Christ . . . declares Himself to be the Way of salvation, the Grace and the Truth, and affirms that in Him alone, and only to souls believing in Him, is the way of return to God, what has become of men who lived in the many centuries before Christ came? . . . What, then, has become of such an innumerable multitude of souls, who were in no wise blameworthy, seeing that He in whom alone saving faith can be exercised had not yet favoured men with His advent? . . . Why, then . . . did He who is called the Saviour withhold Himself for so many centuries of the world? . . . What, then, became of the souls of men in Rome and Latium who lived before the time of the Cæsars, and were destitute of the grace of Christ, because He had not then come?"

To these statements we answer by requiring those who make them to tell us, in the first place, whether the sacred rites, which we know to have been introduced into the worship of their gods at times which can be ascertained, were or were not profitable to men. If they say that these were of no service for the salvation of men, they unite with us in putting them down. . . . If, on the other hand, they defend these rites, and maintain that they were wise and profitable institutions, what, I ask, has become of those who died before these were instituted? . . .

Wherefore, since we affirm that Christ is the Word of God, by whom all things were made and is the Son, because He is the Word, not a word uttered and belonging to the past but abides unchangeably with the unchangeable Father, Himself unchangeable, under whose rule the whole universe, spiritual and material, is ordered in the way best adapted to different times and places, and that He has perfect wisdom and knowledge as to what should be done, and when and where everything should be done in the controlling and ordering of the universe,—most certainly, both before He gave being to the Hebrew nation, by which He was pleased, through sacraments suited to the time, to prefigure the manifestation of Himself in His advent, and during the time of the Jewish commonwealth, and, after that, when He manifested Himself in the likeness of mortals to mortal men in the body which He received from the Virgin, and thenceforward even to our day, in which He is fulfilling all which He predicted of old by the prophets, and from this present time on to the end of the world, when He shall separate the holy from the wicked, and give to every man his due recompense,—in all these successive ages He is the same Son of God, co-eternal with the Father, and the unchangeable Wisdom by whom universal nature was called into existence, and by participation in whom every rational soul is made blessed. . . .

Therefore, from the beginning of the human race, whosoever believed in Him, and in any way knew Him, and lived in a pious and just manner according to His precepts, was undoubtedly saved by Him, in whatever time and place he may have lived. For as we believe in Him both as dwelling with the Father and as having come in the flesh, so the men of the former ages believed in Him both as dwelling with the Father and as destined to come in the flesh. And the nature of faith is not changed, nor is the salvation made different, in our age, by the fact that, in consequence of the difference between the two epochs, that which was then foretold as future is now proclaimed as past. . . . Wherefore the true religion, although formerly set forth and practised under other names and with other symbolical rites than it now has, and formerly more obscurely revealed and known to fewer persons than now in the time of clearer light and wider diffusion, is one and the same in both periods. . . .

. . . [F]rom the beginning of the human race, He never ceased to speak by His prophets, at one time more obscurely, at another time more plainly, as seemed to divine wisdom best adapted to the time; nor were there ever wanting men who believed in Him, from Adam to Moses, and among the people of Israel itself, which was by a special mysterious appointment a prophetic nation, and among other nations before He came in the flesh. For seeing that in the sacred Hebrew books some are mentioned, even from Abraham's time, not belonging to his natural posterity nor to the people of Israel, and not proselytes added to that people, who were nevertheless partakers of this holy mystery, why may we not believe that in other nations also, here and there, some more were found, although we do not read their names in these authoritative records? Thus the salvation provided by this religion, by which alone, as alone true, true salvation is truly promised, was never wanting to any one who was worthy of it, and he to whom it was wanting was not worthy of it. And from the beginning of the human family, even to the end of time, it is preached, to some for their advantage, to some for their condemnation. Accordingly, those to whom it has not been preached at all are those who were foreknown as persons who would not believe; those to whom, notwithstanding the certainty that they would not believe, the salvation has been proclaimed are set forth as an example of the class of unbelievers; and those to whom, as persons who would believe, the truth is proclaimed are being prepared for the kingdom of heaven and for the society of the holy angels.

Notes

1. Of course, some of these questions have continued to occupy philosophers up to the present day—a fact that should serve as a caution against drawing sharp distinctions between philosophy and religion.

2. Walter H. Wagner, *After the Apostles: Christianity in the Second Century* (Minneapolis, MN: Fortress, 1994), 160-61.

3. Dupuis, *Toward a Christian Theology of Religious Pluralism*, 59. "Justin argues that the light that all men [sic] have is implanted by the divine Reason, the Logos of God who was incarnate in Jesus and who is universally active and present in the highest goodness and intelligence wherever they may be found. Justin strikingly interprets in this sense the parable of the Sower. The divine Sower sowed his good seed throughout his creation. Justin does not make rigid and exclusive claims for divine revelation to the Hebrews so as to invalidate the value of other sources of wisdom. Abraham and Socrates are alike 'Christians before Christ.' But just as the aspirations of the Old Testament prophets

found their fulfillment in Christ, so the correct insights achieved by the Greek philosophers reached their completion in the gospel of Christ who embodies the highest moral ideal. Christ is for Justin the principle of unity and the criterion by which we may judge the truth, scattered like divided seeds among the different schools of philosophy in so far as they have dealt with religion and morals" (Henry Chadwick, *The Early Church* [New York: Penguin Books, 1982 (1967)], 76-77).

4. Selections from chapters I, II, V, VI, IX, XX, XLVI.

5. Selections from chapters VIII, X, XIII.

6. Wagner, *After the Apostles*, 174-75.

7. Selections from chapter VI.

8. Selections from sections 1.2, 1.5, 1.9, 1.13, 1.19, 5.13.

9. Chadwick, *The Early Church*, 91.

10. Despite Tertullian's critique of philosophy, he was more dependent on the philosophical tradition than such remarks might suggest, as Jaroslav Pelikan notes: "Biblical doctrine and philosophical speculation were . . . intermingled in the theology of Tertullian. . . . His question, 'What has Athens to do with Jerusalem?' and the resoundingly negative answer he repeatedly provided to that question have sometimes obscured the philosophical elements in his thought. . . . In theory Tertullian owed loyalty only to the Bible . . . 'what we are ourselves, that also the Scriptures are (and have been) from the beginning.' But it was by no means obvious what the Scriptures and the tradition of the church . . . taught about the origin and nature of the human soul. Therefore, he felt obliged to 'call on the Stoics also to help me. . . . ' By the time Tertullian had finished vindicating the biblical doctrine of the soul against the philosophers, he had invoked not only the Stoics, but Aristotle . . . and other philosophical sources ranging from the pre-Socratics Heraclitus and Democritus to the philosophical scholar of the Augustan age, Arius Didymus. . . . Tertullian can be said to illustrate the continuing and unavoidable, if not always acknowledged or even conscious, influence of philosophical ideas on Christian doctrine" (Jaroslav Pelikan, *The Christian Tradition: A History of the Development of Doctrine,* vol. 1 [Chicago: University of Chicago Press, 1971], 49-50). Pelikan's remarks should serve as a warning for those attempting *sola Scriptura* approaches today.

11. Selections from chapters VII, XII, XXI.

12. For a discussion of antecedents, see Dupuis, *Toward a Christian Theology of Religious Pluralism*, 86-87.

13. Selections from sections 1 and 21.

14. Dupuis, *Toward a Christian Theology of Religious Pluralism*, 90-91.

15. Ibid., 91.

16. Selections from sections 8, 9, 11, 12, 15.

Readings

The Christendom Synthesis

Thomas Aquinas

Widely considered one of the greatest theologians in the Christian tradition, Thomas Aquinas (ca. 1225-1274) is of particular importance to the Christian theology of religions for his theory of "baptism of desire" (*votum baptismi*).

Living more than two centuries before Europeans became aware of the peoples of the Americas, he shared the notion, common in his time, that the Christian message had already been made available to all nations. Consequently, "while allowing for the sufficiency of implicit faith in Christ before the Gospel had been promulgated, Thomas firmly upheld the necessity of explicit faith thereafter."[1] Nevertheless, systematic thinker that he was, he anticipated cases where one might die before receiving the sacrament of baptism, or where one might have not been exposed to the message of the gospel. To cover these cases, Thomas advanced the notion of baptism of desire, which reconciles the person to God. As Jacques Dupuis writes, "It is this doctrine of implicit *votum baptismi* that, in the new circumstances created by the discovery of the New World, later theologians would develop on a broad scale. . . . [I]t would also be followed by the Council of Trent, and through it would become received doctrine" of the Roman Catholic Church.[2]

> Source: *Summa Theologica*, trans. by the Fathers of the English Dominican Province (Benziger Brothers edition, 1947; Christian Classics Ethereal Library), http://www. ccel.org/ccel/aquinas/summa.html.

[Is explicit belief in Christ universally necessary to salvation?[3]]

. . . [T]he mystery of Christ's Incarnation and Passion is the way by which men obtain beatitude; for it is written (Acts 4:12): "There is no other name under heaven given to men, whereby we must be saved." Therefore belief of some kind in the mystery of Christ's Incarnation was necessary at all times and for all persons, but this belief differed according to differences of times and persons. The reason of this is that before the state of sin, man believed, explicitly in Christ's Incarnation, in so far as it was intended for the consummation of glory, but not as it was intended to deliver man from sin by the Passion and Resurrection, since man had no foreknowledge of his future sin. . . .

But after sin, man believed explicitly in Christ, not only as to the Incarnation, but also as to the Passion and Resurrection, whereby the human race is delivered from sin and death: for they would not, else, have foreshadowed Christ's Passion by certain sacrifices both before and after the Law, the meaning of which sacrifices was known by the learned explicitly, while the simple folk, under the veil of those sacrifices, believed them to be ordained by God in reference to Christ's coming. . . .

After grace had been revealed, both learned and simple folk are bound to explicit faith in the mysteries of Christ, chiefly as regards those which are observed throughout the Church, and publicly proclaimed, such as the articles which refer to the Incarnation. . . .

. . . Many of the gentiles received revelations of Christ, as is clear from their predictions. Thus we read (Job 19:25): "I know that my Redeemer liveth." The Sibyl too foretold certain things about Christ, as Augustine states (*Contra Faust.* xiii, 15). . . . If, however, some were saved without receiving any revelation, they were not saved without faith in a Mediator, for, though they did not believe in Him explicitly, they did, nevertheless, have implicit faith through believing in Divine providence. . . .

[Is every act of an unbeliever a sin?[4]]

It is said of Cornelius, while yet an unbeliever (Acts 10:4, 31), that his alms were acceptable to God. Therefore not every action of an unbeliever is a sin, but some of his actions are good.

I answer that, As stated above . . . mortal sin takes away sanctifying grace, but does not wholly corrupt the good of nature. . . .

. . . Unbelief does not so wholly destroy natural reason in unbelievers, but . . . some knowledge of the truth remains in them, whereby they are able to do deeds that are generically good. With regard, however, to Cornelius, it is to be observed that he was not an unbeliever, else his works would not have been acceptable to God, whom none can please without faith. Now he had implicit faith, as the truth of the Gospel was not yet made manifest: hence Peter was sent to him to give him fuller instruction in the faith.

[Are grace and virtues bestowed on man by Baptism?[5]]

. . . [M]an receives the forgiveness of sins before Baptism in so far as he has Baptism of desire, explicitly or implicitly; and yet when he actually receives Baptism, he receives a fuller remission, as to the remission of the entire punishment. So also before Baptism Cornelius and others like him receive grace and virtues through their faith in Christ and their desire for Baptism, implicit or explicit: but afterwards when baptized, they receive a yet greater fulness of grace and virtues. Hence in Ps. 22:2, "He hath brought me up on the water of refreshment," a gloss says: "He has brought us up by an increase of virtue and good deeds in Baptism."

Nicholas of Cusa

Born Nikolas Krebs in 1401 in the German town of Kues (latinized as Cusa), Nicholas of Cusa was a true polymath. Besides serving as a cardinal and bishop, he was a philosopher, a mathematician, an astronomer, and a sometime mystic. He worked to reunify the Eastern and Western churches, traveling in 1437 as papal representative to Constantinople. He died in 1464.

The work excerpted below, *De Pace Fidei* (The Peace of Faith), seems to have been written in response to the events surrounding the fall of Constantinople (modern-day Istanbul) to the Muslim Ottoman armies in 1453. In this work, a man who is troubled by the religious violence of his time is granted a vision of a heavenly conference concerning the possibility of harmony between the different religions. In the course of this conference, the personified Word of God converses with representatives of the various "religions" (including Eastern Orthodoxy, Roman Catholicism, Islam, and Hinduism). The Word holds that behind the different religious beliefs and practices, all people actually belong to the one religion, since all seek after Wisdom, and Wisdom is one. Even polytheists, the Word asserts, presuppose the one true deity. Therefore, if all believers would look deep into their own beliefs, they would see that religious differences are epiphenomenal, not essential. By insisting on the underlying unity of all religions, Nicholas anticipates the later work of theologians such as Karl Rahner and Kenneth Cracknell.

Source: Nicholas of Cusa, *De Pace Fidei and Cribratio Alkorani*, 2nd ed., trans. by Jasper Hopkins (Minneapolis, MN: Arthur J. Banning Press, 1994); http://cla.umn. edu/sites/jhopkins/CAI-12-2000.pdf. Accessed July 23, 2007.

. . . [An archangel addresses God:] "O Lord, King of the universe, what does any creature have that You did not give to it? It was fitting that the human body, formed from the clay of the earth, was inbreathed by You with a rational spirit, so that from within this body an image of Your ineffable power would shine forth. From one [man] there was multiplied the great number of people who inhabit the surface of dry land. . . .

"But You know, O Lord, that there cannot be a great multitude without much diversity. . . . You set over Your people different kings and different seers, called prophets—very many of whom, in their role as Your legates, instituted (in Your name) worship and laws and instructed an uneducated people. [Men] accepted these laws just as if You Yourself, the King of kings, had spoken to them face to face; they believed that they heard not kings and prophets but You Yourself in and through kings and prophets. Now, to various nations You sent various prophets and teachers—some at one time, others at another. But the earthly human condition has this characteristic: viz., that longstanding custom, which is regarded as having passed over into nature, is defended as the truth. In this way there arise great quarrels when each community prefers its own faith to another [faith]."

"Aid [us], then, O You who alone are able to. For this strife occurs for the sake of You, whom alone all [men] worship in everything they are seen to adore. For no one, in whatever he is seen to desire, desires [anything] except the good, which You are. And in all intellectual inference no one seeks anything other than the truth, which You are. . . . You, then, who are the giver of life and of existence, are the one who is seen to be sought in different ways in different rites, and You are named in different names; for as You are [in Yourself] You remain unknown and ineffable to all. . . . [D]o not hide Yourself any longer, O Lord. Be propitious, and manifest Your face; and all peoples will be saved, who no longer will be able to desert the Source of life and its sweetness, once having foretasted even a little thereof. For no one departs from You except because He is ignorant of You.

"If You will deign to do the foregoing, the sword will cease, as will also the malice of hatred and all evils; and all [men] will know that there is only one religion in a variety of rites. But perchance this difference of rites cannot be eliminated; or perhaps it is not expedient [that it be eliminated], in order that the diversity may make for an increase of devotion, since each region will devote more careful attention to making its ceremonies more 'favorable,' as it were, to You, the King. If so, then at least let there be one religion—just as You are one—and one true worship of You as Sovereign. Therefore, be placable, O Lord, because Your wrath is Your graciousness and Your justice is Your mercy. . . ."

[T]he Word that was made flesh and that held the preeminent position among all the heavenly inhabitants, answered on behalf of all: "Father of Mercies, Your works are most perfect, and there remains nothing to be added for their completion. Nevertheless, because You decreed from the beginning that man remain in possession of free choice, and since in the sensible world nothing remains stable, and since fluxible opinions and conjectures are changed from time to time, as are also tongues and interpretations, human nature needs frequent visitation in order that the false inferences which occur very often concerning Your Word may be eradicated and thereby truth may continually shine forth. Since truth is one and since it cannot fail to be grasped by every free intellect, all the diverse religions will be led unto one orthodox faith."

. . . To [the representatives of the various religious traditions] the Word of God spoke as follows: "The Lord, King of heaven and of earth, has heard the moaning of those who have been killed, those who have been imprisoned, and those who have been reduced unto servitude—[the moaning of those] who suffer on account of the diversity of the religions. All who either inflict or suffer this persecution are motivated only from their belief that such [action or passion] is expedient for salvation and is pleasing to their Creator. Therefore, the Lord has had mercy upon His people and is agreeable that henceforth all the diverse religions be harmoniously reduced, by the common consent of all men, unto one inviolable [religion]. . . ."

[Unless otherwise indicated, the following excerpts are statements by the Word:]

". . . You will [all] find to be everywhere presupposed not a faith that is *other* but a faith that is one and the same. For among the countrymen of your own language-groups, you who are now present are called wise—or, at least, [are called] philosophers, or lovers of wisdom."

". . . There can be only one Wisdom. For if it were possible for there to be more than one Wisdom, these wisdoms would have to derive from a single [Wisdom]; for oneness is prior to all plurality."

". . . You all agree . . . that there is one most simple Wisdom, whose power is ineffable. And in the unfolding of Wisdom's power, each [of you] experiences this ineffable and infinite power. . . ."

". . . Now, it is not possible that there be more than one eternity, because prior to all plurality there is oneness."

". . . Therefore, Wisdom is the one, simple, eternal God, the Beginning of all things."

". . . See how you philosophers of various sects agree on the religion of one God—whom you all presuppose, in that you profess to be lovers of Wisdom."

". . . Therefore, all men declare together with you that there is one Absolute Wisdom, which they presuppose and which is the one God."

". . . Therefore, for all those who are of sound understanding there is one religion and worship, which is presupposed in all the diversity of the rites."

". . . All who have ever worshiped a plurality of gods have presupposed there to be deity. For in all the gods, they adore the deity as [one and] the same in [all] its participants. For just as there are no white things if whiteness does not exist, so if the deity does not exist, there are no gods. Therefore, the worshiping of [a plurality of] gods bespeaks the deity; and he who says that there is more than one god says [implicitly] that there is, antecedently, one Beginning of them all—just as he who maintains that there is more than one holy [man] admits that there is one Most Holy, by participation in whom all [these] others are holy. For no race was ever so obtuse that it believed there to be a plurality of gods each of whom was the universe's First Cause, Beginning, or Creator. . . ."

". . . Therefore, if all those who worship a plurality of gods look unto that which they presuppose, viz., unto the deity, which is the cause of all [the gods], and if, as reason dictates, they accept this deity into their overt religious practices (even as, implicitly, they worship it in all whom they call gods), then the dispute is dissolved."

". . . If the people were informed about salvation—[informed] in a manner comparable to the aforesaid one—then they would rather seek salvation in Him who has given being and who is Saviour and Infinite Salvation than [seek it] in those who of themselves have nothing unless it is conceded [to them] by the Saviour. . . ."

. . . At this point a man from India[6] [asked]: "What about statues and effigies?"

Word: "Images that lead to a knowledge of the things which are admissible in the true worship of the one God are not condemned. But when they lead away from the true worshipping of the one God as Sovereign (as if in stones there were some portion of deity and as if [the deity] were bound to a statue), then, rightly, the images ought to be broken, because they deceive [men] and turn [them] away from the truth. . . ."

Bartolomé de Las Casas

A voice crying in a wilderness of greed, prejudice, and intolerance, the Dominican friar Bartolomé de Las Casas (1474-1566) was one of the few Europeans in the colonial period to speak out in defense of the indigenous peoples of the Americas and in opposition to their maltreatment at the hands of his fellow European Christians. His sympathy for the indigenous peoples, rooted in first-hand knowledge of their culture and religious beliefs and practices, led him to develop an inclusivist theology of religions that foreshadowed later work by Karl Rahner, Kenneth Cracknell, and others.

Las Casas emigrated to Hispaniola from Spain to the New World only ten years after Columbus's fateful voyage. At first, he participated in the brutal *encomienda* system, in which the indigenous peoples were forced to work as slaves in the fields and mines. After becoming a priest, he renounced his *encomienda* and in 1514 preached his first sermon against the system. As a Dominican friar and later as bishop of Chiapas, Las Casas wrote and preached against Spanish abuse of the indigenous peoples.

The liberation theologian Gustavo Gutiérrez notes that Las Casas, seeing how the Indians were treated by the "Christian" Spaniards, realized that "Gold is the real god of those who mistreat the Indians," and "was particularly scandalized by the fact that this real idolatry is disguised as though it were a service of the true God." For this reason, Las Casas held that "the worst idolatry is that of Christians and not that of the [non-Christian] Indians."[7] Clearly, Las Casas understood "Christian" to entail considerably more than mere profession of faith in Christ and membership in the church.

Las Casas also raised the possibility that non-Christians may be saved, as we see in the following excerpts. Appealing to the doctrine of predestination and to the inscrutability of God's designs, Las Casas argues that God denies salvific assistance to no one, "not even to those outside the church. The grace of God is offered to all, although God alone knows who will freely accept it. And these latter Las Casas calls predestined."[8] Indeed, Las Casas envisions a Day of Judgment in which Christians, because of their own oppression of the Indians and because of the latter's own good works, will be outnumbered by unbelievers at the right hand of God.[9]

While he regards Christianity as "the universal way to salvation," this does not mean that those outside the church are utterly without God—or indeed, outside the realm of the saved. Quite the contrary: "It must not be thought," he writes in his *History of the Indies*, "that, because a nation is discovered later than another, its Maker denied it His support, for He ordained things as He pleased." Furthermore, since the Elect will come from all nations, Las Casas argues, "divine Providence must have naturally disposed these people for indoctrination and divine grace, reserving the time of their calling and conversion, as it did and we believe will always do toward all other nations outside the holy Church, as long as it endures." Indeed, given the shameful record of Christians in the New World, Las Casas even speculates that there may be Indians in heaven: "However divine justice may punish and torture them in this life, however it may seem to have forsaken them by delivering them into our insatiable greed, no Christian will doubt that God's chosen few will indeed include those Indians whom He has predestined to enjoy divine vision in the eternal life." In his *The Only Way,* Las Casas comments that due to the work of Christ, God's chosen are called "from every race, every tribe, every language, every corner of the world. Thus, no race, no nation on this entire globe would be left totally untouched by the free gift of divine grace. Some among them, be they few or many, are to be taken into eternal life. We must hold this to be true also of our Indian nations." Gutiérrez comments:

> To none is God's salvific assistance denied: not even to those outside the church. The grace of God is offered to all, although God alone knows who will freely accept it. And these latter Las Casas calls predestined. . . . All are called. God alone knows who will respond adequately. We cannot close gates that the Lord wants permanently open. No theology can exclude anyone from salvation (especially with the certitude and arrogance with which, as we shall see, Oviedo so excludes them). Las Casas maintains the possibility of the salvation of the Indians despite their condition as heathen.[10]

Thus we find in Las Casas the paradox that those who profess faith in Christ may deny him with their works, while those who are outside the church may be his true followers. In other words, those who seem to be Christian insiders may be in fact outsiders, and the outsiders, insiders. It is still Christ who saves, even in and through the religions of the Indians; however, one's explicit knowledge of that fact, or one's lack thereof, is less important than one's lived relationship to others, and thereby, to God.

From History of the Indies[11]

> [T]here is not and there never has been in the history of mankind a nation from which, especially after the Incarnation and Passion of the Saviour, there cannot be selected and composed that innumerable multitude of St. John's vision—Chapter 7 of the Apocalypse—that body of the Elect which St. Paul called the mystical Body of Christ and Church. Consequently, divine Providence must have naturally disposed these people for indoctrination and divine grace, reserving the time of their calling and conversion, as it did and we believe will always do toward all other nations outside the holy Church, as long as it endures. . . . Since we believe that God predestined a

few select ones from all parts of the world, appointing a time for their calling and glorification, and since we do not know who these might be, we must esteem and judge all men, trying to help them inasmuch as we desire their salvation. As for ourselves, we must see that our works be instrumental to their predestination as if we were all sure of being Elect ourselves. . . . [T]he Creator of the universe, who created all things for well-being of man, inspires man to discover the wonders of the world which but confirm His perfection. . . .

The Christian religion is granted to different peoples as the universal way to salvation so that they may leave behind their various sects, which necessarily leads [sic] their worshippers to eternal exile and infinite misery, and, consequently, so that they may be guided to that unparalleled kingdom where everyone is King.

. . . [The historian] Oviedo[12] says that God must have a reason to permit them [the Indian peoples] to be destroyed, intending to wipe them out for their sins, and that Indians do not respond to punishment, reward or admonition. . . . But Oviedo . . . was not aware that God could destroy them justly only for original sin. They may be in a state of sin but we are not free to despise them for it, nor to rob and kill them. Woe unto us indeed if as robbers and killers and dispensers of bad examples (instead of the good examples we are to show them to attract them to Christ), we should corrupt them and prevent their salvation. However divine justice may punish and torture them in this life, however it may seem to have forsaken them by delivering them into our insatiable greed, no Christian will doubt that God's chosen few will indeed include those Indians whom He has predestined to enjoy divine vision in the eternal life. Just by chance (or even without chance), it may be that once God has exterminated these people through our cruel hands, He will spill His anger over us all for our violence and our tyranny, inspiring other nations to do unto us what we have done unto them, destroying us as we destroyed them, and it may be that more of those whom we held in such contempt will sit at the right hand of God than there will be of us, and this consideration ought to keep us in fear night and day.

From The Only Way[13]

It was due to the will and work of Christ, the head of the Church, that God's chosen should be called, should be culled from every race, every tribe, every language, every corner of the world. Thus, no race, no nation on this entire globe would be left totally untouched by the free gift of divine grace. Some among them, be they few or many, are to be taken into eternal life. We must hold this to be true also of our Indian nations. . . .

The reason is, they are all human beings. Their minds are very quick, alive, capable, clear. This mind comes to them primarily from the will of God who wished to make them so. Then, secondarily, it comes from . . . the kind conditions of the places God gave them to live in, the fair and clement weather. . . .

[On "True Evangelization":] One way, one way only, of teaching a living faith, to everyone, everywhere, always, was set by Divine Providence: the way that wins the mind with reasons, that wins the will with gentleness, with invitation. It has to fit all people on earth, no distinction made for sect, for error, even for evil. . . .

Divine Wisdom cares for all its creatures, not just by leading them to fulfill their natural purposes, but also by endowing them with inner powers, with potentialities which are at the source of performance, so they would be able to act on their own initiative as well. Thus actions invited by God are actions native to creatures, consonant with them; they flow easily. Creatures possess the sources of response within themselves. . . .

So each creature moves toward what Divine Wisdom wants for it by means of a nature divinity gives it, according to the leaning built into nature. It is the goodness in God from which all natures flow . . . so every creature has in it a power to want goodness due to the imprint of its Creator upon it. . . .

Those who wage wars for conversion, those who are in any way the cause of such wars being waged on unconverted peoples—those who declare war, counsel it, push it or supply it—all of them commit mortal sin of the worst kind. . . .

Notes

1. Jacques Dupuis, *Toward a Christian Theology of Religious Pluralism* (Maryknoll, NY: Orbis Books, 1997), 114.

2. Ibid., 116.

3. *Summa Theologica* 2-2, Q. 2, Art. 7.

4. *Summa Theologica* 2-2, Q. 10, Art. 4.

5. *Summa Theologica* III, Q. 69, Art. 4.

6. [Ed.] Representing the Hindu and possibly the Buddhist traditions.

7. Gustavo Gutiérrez, *The God of Life*, trans. Matthew J. O'Connell (Maryknoll, NY: Orbis Books, 1991), 61.

8. Gustavo Gutiérrez, *Las Casas: In Search of the Poor of Jesus Christ*, trans. Robert R. Barr (Maryknoll, NY: Orbis Books, 1993), 253.

9. Gutiérrez writes: "Heathen—those who make no explicit profession of faith in Christ (partly through the fault of Christians)—will perhaps, according to Fray Bartolomé, enter the Reign of God in greater numbers than will the faithful. They will be called to that Reign by the Son of Man, and only because—within their religious world and in their cultural categories—they will have given 'to eat and to drink' to their sibling in need, and in him or her to Christ himself. Works in behalf of one's neighbor are an exigency of salvific grace" (*Las Casas*, 261).

10. Ibid., 253.

11. Bartolomé de Las Casas, *History of the Indies*, trans. Andrée Collard (New York: Harper & Row, 1971), 5-6, 14, 281-82.

12. [Ed:] Fernández Gonzalo de Oviedo y Valdés in 1545 was appointed royal historian of the West Indies. His *Natural History* (1526) was a target of Las Casas's criticism.

13. Bartolomé de Las Casas, *The Only Way*, ed. Helen Rand Parish; trans. Francis Patrick Sullivan (Mahwah, NJ: Paulist, 1992), 63, 68-69, 164.

Readings

Modern and Postmodern Voices

Friedrich Schleiermacher

THE GERMAN REFORMED THEOLOGIAN FRIEDRICH SCHLEIERMACHER (1768-1834) is widely acknowledged to be the father of modern liberal Protestant theology. As Keith Clements notes, "Schleiermacher's ascription of religion to the realm of *feeling* marked the start of modern Protestantism's habitual emphasis on the knowledge of God as inward and experiential."[1] Rejecting both the Enlightenment elevation of human reason and premodern views of Christian doctrine, Schleiermacher makes two key theological moves. First, he grounds Christian theological reflection in immediate interior experience, specifically, in what he comes to call the "feeling of absolute dependence." Second, he claims that this experience is a universal feature of human consciousness, and is the essence of all "religion," a category of which Christianity is the most developed instance.

Schleiermacher is also one of the first major Western Christian theologians to recognize the significance of religions other than Christianity—indeed, to speak, in the modern sense, of Christianity *as* religion, as one religion among many. Although Schleiermacher cannot be said to have developed a full-blown theology of religions—his discussion of religions in *The Christian Faith* (excerpted below) is far too cursory, and functions purely in support of a systematic account of Christian teaching—his work sparked a tradition of thought about religion that emphasizes its experiential dimension. He did so in response to the Enlightenment critique of religion and of the Christian tradition, and to the growing European awareness of great religious diversity worldwide. His goal was to isolate Christianity's "peculiar essence," by distinguishing Christianity "from religions co-ordinate with it."[2] To do so, he laid out a set of criteria by which to define "religion" and then shows how Christianity alone satisfies them.

In his willingness to confront the fact of religious diversity, Schleiermacher sets the stage for contemporary conversation with religious others. In other ways, however, he represents the old Christendom paradigm. He takes it for granted that the Christian theologian's task is to establish the superiority of Christianity over all other religions. Yet the only religion of which Schleiermacher demonstrates substantial knowledge is Christianity itself.[3] That is, his comments about religious others are based on a priori beliefs, not on any genuine familiarity with them. In some cases, his remarks about religious others are distressingly inaccurate.[4]

Source: Friedrich Schleiermacher, *The Christian Faith*, ed. H. R. Macintosh and J. S. Stewart (Edinburgh: T&T Clark, 1999).[5]

The common element in all howsoever diverse expressions of piety, by which these are conjointly distinguished from all other feelings, or, in other words, the self-identical essence of piety, is this: the consciousness of being absolutely dependent, or, which is the same thing, of being in relation with God.
    . . . God is given to us in feeling in an original way; and if we speak of an original revelation of God to man or in man, the meaning will always be just this, that, along with the absolute dependence which characterizes not only man but all temporal existence, there is given to man also the immediate self-consciousness of it, which becomes a consciousness of God. . . .

If the feeling of absolute dependence, expressing itself as consciousness of God, is the highest grade of immediate self-consciousness, it is also an essential element of human nature. . . .

The various religious communions which have appeared in history with clearly defined limits are related to each other in two ways: as different stages of development, and as different kinds.
    . . . Our proposition does not assert, but it does tacitly presuppose the possibility, that there are other forms of piety which are related to Christianity as different forms on the same level of development, and thus so far similar. But this does not contradict the conviction, which we assume every Christian to possess, of the exclusive superiority of Christianity. . . . Our proposition excludes only the idea, which indeed is often met with, that the Christian religion (piety) should adopt towards at least most other forms of piety the attitude of the true towards the false. For if the religions belonging to the same stage as Christianity were entirely false, how could they have so much similarity to Christianity as to make that classification requisite? And if the religions which belong to the lower stages contained nothing but error, how would it be possible for a man to pass from them to Christianity? Only the true, and not the false, can be a basis of receptivity for the higher truth of Christianity. The whole delineation which we are here introducing is based rather on the maxim that error never exists in and for itself, but always along with some truth, and that we have never fully understood it until we have discovered its connexion with truth, and the true thing to which it is attached. With this agrees what the apostle [Paul] says when he represents even Polytheism as a perversion of the original consciousness of God which underlies it, and when, in this evidence of the longing which all these fancies have failed to satisfy, he finds an obscure presentiment of the true God.

. . . Those forms of piety in which all religious affections express the dependence of everything finite upon one Supreme and Infinite Being, i.e. the monotheistic forms, occupy the highest level; and all others are related to them as subordinate forms, from which men are destined to pass to those higher ones.

. . . As such subordinate stages we set down, generally speaking, Idol-worship proper (also called Fetichism) and Polytheism; of which, again, the first stands far lower than the second. . . . [T]here cannot fail to be here and there at least a presentiment of One Supreme Being behind the plurality of higher Beings; and then Polytheism is already beginning to disappear, and the way to Monotheism is open.

· · · [W]hen the higher self-consciousness, in distinction from the sensible, has been fully developed, then . . . in so far as we are constituent parts of the world, and therefore in so far as we take up the world into our self-consciousness and expand the latter into a general consciousness of finitude, we are conscious of ourselves as absolutely dependent. Now this self-consciousness can only be described in terms of Monotheism. . . .

. . . On this highest plane, of Monotheism, history exhibits only three great communions—the Jewish, the Christian, and the Mohammedan; the first being almost in process of extinction, the other two still contending for the mastery of the human race. Judaism, by its limitation of the love of Jehovah to the race of Abraham, betrays a lingering affinity with Fetichism; and the numerous vacillations towards idol-worship prove that during the political heyday of the nation the monotheistic faith had not yet taken fast root, and was not fully and purely developed until after the Babylonian Exile. Islam, on the other hand, with its passionate character, and the strongly sensuous content of its ideas, betrays, in spite of its strict Monotheism, a large measure of that influence of the sensible upon the character of the religious emotions which elsewhere keeps men on the level of Polytheism. Thus Christianity, because it remains free from both these weaknesses, stands higher than either of those other two forms, and takes its place as the purest form of Monotheism which has appeared in history. . . . And so this comparison of Christianity with other similar religions is in itself a sufficient warrant for saying that Christianity is, in fact, the most perfect of the most highly developed forms of religion.

. . . The above account is at variance with the view which sees no real piety at all, but only superstition, in the religions of the lower levels, mainly because they are supposed to have had their source simply in fear. But the honour of Christianity does not at all demand such an assertion. For since Christianity itself affirms that only perfect love casts out all fear, it must admit that imperfect love is never entirely free from fear. And likewise it is always the case, even in idol-worship, if the idol is worshipped as a protector at all, and not as an evil being, that the fear is by no means quite without any impulses of love, but is rather an adaptation, corresponding to the imperfect love, of the feeling of absolute dependence. . . . The truth is, rather, that we must never deny the homogeneity of all these products of the human spirit, but must acknowledge the same root even for the lower powers.

Ernst Troeltsch

No one more fully embodies the modern crisis of Christian thought in a religiously plural world than Ernst Troeltsch (1865-1923). A historian by training and a Christian by faith, Troeltsch struggled throughout his career to do justice to both commitments.

On the one hand, Troeltsch was a religious person; he sought "a vital and effective religious position, which could alone furnish . . . life with a center of reference . . . and could alone give meaning and purpose to reflection upon the things of this world."[6] For Troeltsch, Christianity offered this "center of reference." At the same time, as a historian, he recognized "the relativity and transitoriness of all things, even of the loftiest values of civilization." History, he writes, "presents a spectacle of bewildering diversity, and of historical institutions as all in a perpetual state of movement from within."[7] Viewed historically, Christianity itself was not an unchanging and eternal entity (as sometimes claimed); like other religious traditions, it had changed over time.

In the following selections from a posthumously published lecture, Troeltsch sets out the major challenges facing Christian thought in the modern period and offers a refreshingly candid appraisal of his own efforts to address them. Troeltsch focuses on what he describes as "the one fundamental conflict between the spirit of critical scepticism generated by the ceaseless flux and manifold contradictions within the sphere of history and the demand of the religious consciousness for certainty, for unity, and for peace."[8] Rather than suppressing the conflict by suppressing one of its terms (e.g., rejecting faith altogether, or adopting a fundamentalist rejection of the insights of historical research), Troeltsch actively engages it, allowing it to shape his theoretical perspective.

In the opening sections of this talk (prior to the excerpts below), Troeltsch looks back at an earlier work, *The Absolute Validity of Christianity*. There, he had argued that Christianity's "absolute validity" cannot be grounded on its claims of miracles (for other religions also claim miracles, and all miracles are subject to "the negative results of historical criticism"). Nor can it be grounded on the claim of a natural evolutionary trend toward Christianity, for neither such a trend nor Christianity as an unchanging entity can be demonstrated historically. The only basis for a claim of Christianity's absolute validity is that it "is the loftiest and most spiritual revelation we know."[9]

However, further study of Christianity and other religions—and in particular the close link between religion and culture—led Troeltsch to believe that Christianity can only be absolutely valid *for Christians*. In the following excerpts, Troeltsch argues that since Christianity is thoroughly bound up with Western civilization, shaping it and being shaped by it, it strikes Westerners as uniquely right and true. Yet other religions are as well suited to their cultural contexts as Christianity is suited to the Western context.[10] Furthermore, other religions "may experience their contact with the Divine Life in quite a different way. . . . And they may quite sincerely regard this as absolutely valid for them." In the end, Troeltsch concludes, only God can determine the relative validity and value of the different religions.

The relativity of religious truth has significant implications for Christian relations with religious others. While Troeltsch acknowledges a continuing Christian missionary duty to what he calls "the crude heathenism of smaller tribes," he argues that Christians must rethink their relation with "the great philosophical world religions." Rather than working to convert adherents of these religions to Christianity, Christians should instead focus on dialogue aimed at "a measure of agreement and of mutual understanding."

Ironically, Troeltsch's assertion of the relativity of perspectives is underscored by the fact that he himself is very much a creature of his own culture, and of the "orientalist" biases of European scholars of his time. We have already seen his dismissive reference to "the crude heathenism of smaller tribes"; his comments about Confucianism and Buddhism are equally questionable. His attempt to set aside these traditions by calling them "philosophies" rather than "religions" raises more questions than it answers.[11] More problematic is his claim that "Confucianism is essentially a national movement and Buddhism is . . . bound to the conditions of life in tropical countries." This does not account for Confucianism's strong influence outside its "national" context in China, dramatically affecting cultural and religious life in Korea, Japan, and Southeast Asia. Nor does it account for Buddhism's success in such manifestly non-tropical countries as Tibet or Japan.

Nonetheless, Troeltsch remains important to contemporary students of the theology of religions, not only for confronting questions which remain important today, but also for exemplifying the scholar of rigor and integrity, courageous enough to confront the theological problems of his context and to change his mind when his sense of the truth demanded.

Source: Ernst Troeltsch, *Christian Thought, Its History and Application*, trans. Mary E. Clarke (New York: Meridian Books, 1957).

"The Place of Christianity among the World Religions"[12]

. . . [I]t is historical facts that have welded Christianity into the closest connection with the civilizations of Greece, Rome and Northern Europe. All our thoughts and feelings are impregnated with Christian motives and Christian presuppositions; and, conversely, our whole Christianity is indissolubly bound up with elements of the ancient and modern civilizations of Europe. From being a Jewish sect Christianity has become the religion of all Europe. It stands or falls with European civilization; whilst, on its own part, it has entirely lost its Oriental character and has become hellenized and westernized. Our European conceptions of personality and its eternal, divine right, and of progress towards a kingdom of the spirit and of God, our enormous capacity for expansion and for the interconnection of spiritual and temporal, our whole social order, our science, our art—all these rest, whether we know it or not, whether we like it or not, upon the basis of this deorientalised Christianity. Its primary claim to validity is thus the fact that only through it have we become what we are, and that only in it can we preserve the religious forces that we need. . . . Christianity has grown up with us and has become a part of our very being. . . . Christianity could not be the religion of such a highly developed racial group if it did not possess a mighty spiritual power and truth; in short, if it were not, in some degree, a manifestation of the Divine Life itself. The evidence we have for this remains essentially the same, whatever may be our theory concerning absolute validity—it is the evidence of a profound inner experience. This experience is undoubtedly the criterion of its validity, but, be it noted, only of its validity *for us*. It is God's countenance as revealed to us; it is the way in which, being what we are, we receive, and react to, the revelation of God. It is binding upon us, and it brings us deliverance. It is final and unconditional for us, because we have nothing else, and because in what we have we can recognize the accents of the divine voice. But this does not preclude the possibility that other racial groups, living under entirely different cultural conditions, may experience their contact with the Divine Life in quite a different way, and may themselves also possess a religion which has grown up with them, and from which they cannot sever themselves so long as they remain what they are. And they may quite sincerely regard this as absolutely valid for them, and give expression to this absolute validity according to the demands of their own religious feeling. . . . If we wish to determine their relative value, it is not the religions alone that we must compare, but always only the civilizations of which the religion in each case constitutes a part incapable of severance from the rest. But who will presume to make a really final pronouncement here? Only God Himself, who has determined these differences, can do that. . . . The practical bearing of this new manner of thinking . . . has a considerable influence upon the question of foreign missions. Missionary enterprise has always been in part simply a concomitant of the political, military, and commercial expansion of a state or nation, but in part also an outcome of the religious enthusiast's zeal for conversion. . . . The latter aspect . . . is intimately connected with the claim to absolute validity. But here we have to maintain, in accordance with all our conclusions hitherto, that directly religious missionary enterprise must stand in quite a different relation to the great philosophical world religions from that in which it stands to the crude heathenism of smaller tribes. There can be always only a spiritual wrestling of missionary Christianity with the other world religions, possibly a certain contact with them. . . . [I]n relation to the great world religions we need to recognize that they are expressions of the religious consciousness corresponding to certain definite types of culture, and that it is their duty to increase in depth and purity by means of their own interior impulses, a task in which the contact with Christianity may prove helpful, to them as to us, in such processes of development from within. The great religions might indeed be described as crystallizations of the thought of great races, as these races are themselves crystallizations of the various biological and anthropological forms. There can be no conversion or transformation of one into the other, but only a measure of agreement and of mutual understanding. . . .

. . . [A]s all religion has thus a common goal in the Unknown, the Future, perchance in the Beyond, so too it has a common ground in the Divine Spirit ever pressing the finite mind onward towards further light and fuller consciousness, a Spirit Which indwells the finite spirit, and Whose ultimate union with it is the purpose of the whole many-sided process. Between these two poles, however,—the divine Source and the divine Goal—lie all the individual differentiations of race and civilization, and, with them also, the individual differences of the great, comprehensive religions. There may be mutual understanding between them, if they are willing to renounce those sorry things, self-will and the spirit of violent domination. . . . But, so far as human eye can penetrate into the future, it would seem probable that the great revelations to the various civilizations will remain distinct. . . .

. . . I hope you feel that I am not speaking in any spirit of scepticism or uncertainty. A truth which, in the first instance, is *a truth for us* does not cease, because of this, to be very Truth and Life. What we learn daily through our love for our fellow-men, viz. that they are independent beings with standards of their own, we ought also to be able to learn through our love for mankind as a whole—that here too there exist autonomous civilizations with standards of their own. This does not exclude rivalry, but it must be a rivalry for the attainment of interior purity and clearness of vision. If each racial group strives to develop its own highest potentialities, we may hope to come nearer to one another. This applies to the great world religions, but it also applies to the various religious denominations, and to individuals in their intercourse with one another. In our earthly experience the Divine Life is not One, but Many. But to apprehend the One in the Many constitutes the special character of love.

Karl Barth

Perhaps the preeminent Protestant theologian of the twentieth century, Karl Barth (1886-1968) devoted his long theological career to counteracting the turn to the human in modern theology and to restoring God—or at least his conception of God—to the place of prominence. His theological reflection about religion and religious others was very much in the service of this broader theological project. In the following selection from Barth's magnum opus, *Church Dogmatics*, Barth—like Schleiermacher (and the Troeltsch of *The Absolute Validity of Christianity*)—asserts the superiority and supremacy of the Christian religion. However, his argument in support of this claim differs markedly from the approaches taken by his predecessors.

As we saw in the selections from Troeltsch, the new historical consciousness and the emphasis on human experience in theology could easily lead to relativism. Barth would have none of that. He sought to restore absolute certainty to Christian theology by grounding theological reflection not in human experience (à la Schleiermacher and Otto) or in a comparison of Christianity with other religions (à la Troeltsch), but in "revelation," in other words, in God's self-revelation in Jesus Christ, which for Barth is absolute and unchanging.[13] According to Barth, what this "revelation" reveals is the absolute opposition between the human and God as "Wholly Other."[14]

This sharp dualism between divine and human translates into an equally absolute opposition between two other categories: "revelation" and "religion." Whereas Schleiermacher looks favorably upon the (allegedly) universal human religious impulse and builds his theology upon it, Barth sees it as fundamentally negative, a mark of the fallenness of humanity. Religion is for Barth a thoroughly human construct; it is the utterly sinful human's efforts to know God. Religion, Barth contends, is unbelief.[15] Accordingly, he speaks of revelation as the "abolition of religion."

It is important to note that Barth's "religion" is an a priori category: Barth does not derive the concept a posteriori, after gathering evidence from empirical study of the various religions.[16] Equally important, Barth's critique of "religion" was not so much a critique of non-Christian religions as a critique of corruption in Christianity itself. As an instance of religion, Barth contends, Christianity is "idolatry and self-righteousness, unbelief, and therefore sin."[17]

Nonetheless, Barth contends that the Christian religion can be spoken of as the one true religion. Insofar as it is faithful to divine revelation, Christianity— and Christianity alone—recognizes the true character of religion as unbelief. Christianity is thus that aspect of the world of human religion that calls religion itself into question. Given his assertion of the superiority of Christianity over other religions—qualified though that assertion may be—Barth is often cited as an example of the exclusivist (or replacement) orientation toward religious others.[18]

Barth's approach raises numerous troubling questions. First, does the revelation recognized by Christians actually say what Barth claims it does? Does Barth's rather crude opposition between revelation and religion, and his negative portrayal of the latter, in fact reflect the New Testament witness?[19] Has Barth overemphasized the particularistic strand of New Testament witness to the exclusion of the universalistic strand? Second, can an a priori construal of religion—one which does not build on actual encounter with religious others—really be useful theologically? Does it not run the risk of bearing false witness about the actual beliefs and practices of religious others? Finally, as I have argued elsewhere, does Barth not undermine his stress on the otherness of God by restricting revelation to that recognized by Christians? Put differently: if God is Wholly Other, why should God behave only in ways that Christians have come to expect?[20]

While these are serious difficulties, Barth's theological contributions are rich and complex, and merit continued study.

Source: Karl Barth, *Church Dogmatics,* I/2, 2nd ed., trans. G. W. Bromiley; ed. G. W. Bromiley and T. F. Torrance (New York: T&T Clark International, 2004).[21]

The revelation of God in the outpouring of the Holy Spirit is the judging but also reconciling presence of God in the world of human religion, that is, in the realm of man's attempts to justify and to sanctify himself before a capricious and arbitrary picture of God. The Church is the locus of true religion, so far as through grace it lives by grace.

[The Problem of Religion in Theology]

. . . We could not . . . regard the event of revelation as an interplay between God and man, between grace and nature.[22] On the contrary, as we tried to be faithful to Holy Scripture as the only valid testimony to revelation, we saw that we were committed to the statement that as an event which encounters man, this event represents a self-enclosed circle. Not only the objective but also the subjective element in revelation, not only its actuality but also its potentiality, is the being and action of the self-revealing God alone.

But this revelation is in fact an event which encounters man. It is an event which has at least the form of human competence, experience and activity. And it is at this point that we come up against the problem of man's religion. . . .

. . . It is always the sign of definite misunderstanding when an attempt is made systematically to co-ordinate revelation and religion, i.e., to treat them as comparable spheres, to mark them off from each other, to fix their mutual relationship. . . . For where we think that revelation can be compared or equated with religion, we have not understood it as revelation. Within the problem which now engrosses us it can be understood only where *a priori* and with no possible alternative we accept its superiority over human religion, a superiority which does not allow us even to consider religion except in the light of revelation. . . . Revelation is understood only where we expect from it, and from it alone, the first and the last word about religion. The inquiry into the problem of religion in theology involves an either-or, in which the slightest deviation, the slightest concession to religionism, at once makes the right answer absolutely impossible. . . .

To sum up: we do not need to delete or retract anything from the admission that in His revelation God is present in the world of human religion. But what we have to discern is that this means that *God* is present. Our basic task is so to order the concepts revelation and religion that the connexion between the two can again be seen as identical with that event between God and man in which God is God, i.e., the Lord and Master of man, who Himself judges and alone justifies and sanctifies, and man is the man of God, i.e., man as he is adopted and received by God in His severity and goodness. It is because we remember and apply the christological doctrine of the *assumptio carnis* that we speak of revelation as the abolition of religion.

[Religion as Unbelief]

. . . Revelation singles out the Church as the *locus* of true religion. But this does not mean that the Christian religion as such is the fulfilled nature of human religion. It does not mean that the Christian religion is the true religion, fundamentally superior to all other religions. . . . We have to give particular emphasis to the fact that through grace the Church lives by grace, and to that extent it is the *locus* of true religion. . . .

We begin by stating that religion is unbelief. It is a concern, indeed, we must say that it is the one great concern, of godless man. . . .

. . . [T]his proposition . . . does not affect only other men with their religion. Above all it affects ourselves also as adherents of the Christian religion. It formulates the judgment of divine revelation upon all religion. . . .

To realise that religion is really unbelief, we have to consider it from the standpoint of the revelation attested in Holy Scripture. . . .

. . . In revelation God tells man that He is God, and that as such He is his Lord. In telling him this, revelation tells him something utterly new, something which apart from revelation he does not know and cannot tell either himself or others. . . . This "coming to us" of the truth is revelation. . . . [I]t reaches us as religious men; i.e., it reaches us in the attempt to know God from our standpoint. . . . From the standpoint of revelation religion is clearly seen to be a human attempt to anticipate what God in His revelation wills to do and does do. It is the attempted replacement of the divine work by a human manufacture. The divine reality offered and manifested to us in revelation is replaced by a concept of God arbitrarily and wilfully evolved by man. . . .

. . . [R]eligion is the contradiction of revelation, the concentrated expression of human unbelief, i.e., an attitude and activity which is directly opposed to faith. . . . We cannot, therefore, interpret the attempt as a harmonious co-operating of man with the revelation of God, as though religion were a kind of outstretched hand which is filled by God in His revelation. . . . On the contrary, we have here an exclusive contradiction. In religion man bolts and bars himself against revelation by providing a substitute, by taking away in advance the very thing which has to be given by God. . . .

Revelation does not link up with a human religion which is already present and practised. It contradicts it, just as religion previously contradicted revelation. It displaces it, just as religion previously displaced revelation; just as faith cannot link up with a mistaken faith, but must contradict and displace it as unbelief, as an act of contradiction. . . .

. . . [I]t is only by the revelation of God in Jesus Christ that we can characterise religion as idolatry and self-righteousness, and in this way show it to be unbelief. . . .

[True Religion]

The preceding expositions have established the fact that we can speak of "true" religion only in the sense in which we speak of a "justified sinner."

Religion is never true in itself and as such. The revelation of God denies that any religion is true, i.e., that it is in truth the knowledge and worship of God and the reconciliation of man with God. . . . [R]evelation is the truth beside which there is no other truth, over against which there is only lying and wrong. . . . No religion is true. It can only become true, i.e., according to that which it purports to be and for which it is upheld. And it can become true only in the way in which man is justified, from without; i.e., not of its own nature and being, but only in virtue of a reckoning and adopting and separating which are foreign to its own nature and being. . . . Like justified man, religion is a creature of grace. But grace is the revelation of God. No religion can stand before it as true religion. No man is righteous in its presence. . . . The abolishing of religion by revelation need not mean only its negation: the judgment that religion is unbelief. Religion can just as well be exalted in revelation, even though the judgment still stands. . . . It can be justified by it, and—we must at once add—sanctified. Revelation can adopt religion and mark it off as true religion. . . . There is a true religion: just as there are justified sinners. If we abide strictly by that analogy—and we are dealing not merely with an analogy, but in a comprehensive sense with the thing itself—we need have no hesitation in saying that the Christian religion is the true religion.

. . . We must insist, therefore, that at the beginning of a knowledge of the truth of the Christian religion, there stands the recognition that this religion, too, stands under the judgment that religion is unbelief, and that it is not acquitted by any inward worthiness, but only by the grace of God, proclaimed and effectual in His revelation. . . .

. . . That there is a true religion is an event in the act of the grace of God in Jesus Christ. To be more precise, it is an event in the outpouring of the Holy Spirit. To be even more precise, it is an event in the existence of the Church and the children of God. The existence of the Church of God and the children of God means that true religion exists even in the world of human religion. In other words, there is a knowledge and worship of God and a corresponding human activity. We can only say of them that they are corrupt. . . . And yet we have also to say of them that (in their corruption) they do reach their goal. In spite of the lying and wrong committed, in spite of the futility of the means applied, God is really known and worshipped, there is a genuine activity of man as reconciled to God. The Church and the children of God and therefore the bearers of true religion live by the grace of God. . . . It is of grace that the Church and the children of God live by His grace. It is of grace that they attain the status of the bearers of true religion.

Karl Rahner

Karl Rahner (1904-1984) was one of the most influential Roman Catholic theologians of the twentieth century. His theology laid the groundwork for many of the developments of the Second Vatican Council (1962-1965), where he served as theological adviser. A pioneer of the inclusivist (or fulfillment) orientation toward religious others, Rahner stands in the long tradition of Roman Catholic thought about the relationship between Christians and non-Christians. Like his predecessors, Rahner worked to reconcile belief in the centrality and necessity of God's self-revelation in Christ and of the church, with the belief that a just and loving God would not condemn those who had not encountered the gospel (or, put positively, that God's grace touches all persons).

Like his contemporary Karl Barth, Rahner holds that knowledge of God is impossible apart from God's self-communication (revelation) to humans. Rahner, however, has a broader understanding of revelation than Barth: he sees the cosmos as pervaded by divine grace, by God's self-revelation. The Incarnation reveals that God saves humans not *from* history, but *in* history. Since humans are intrinsically and necessarily historical and social beings, God acts in history through their social institutions—including religions other than Christianity. Although all salvation is through Christ, Christ's salvific action includes non-Christians, whether they are aware of it or not. Thus, Rahner speaks of "anonymous Christians": those who have experienced divine grace even before Christian teaching reaches them. Therefore, Rahner writes, "the proclamation of the gospel does not simply turn someone absolutely abandoned by God and Christ into a Christian, but turns an anonymous Christian into someone who now also knows about his Christian belief in the depths of his grace-endowed being by objective reflection and in the profession of faith which is given a social form in the Church."[23]

The following selection from Rahner's *Theological Investigations* lays out his basic argument. Here, he speaks of an "Open Catholicism," by which he means a Catholicism in active encounter with the world, understanding historical forces, acknowledging their significance for the church, and realizing itself as the "higher unity" of those forces. One of these historical forces is religious diversity ("pluralism"), which is a problem for Christianity—indeed, its "greatest scandal" and "greatest vexation"—because Christianity claims itself as *the* religion.

Rahner addresses the problem of religious diversity by proposing four "theses." The first, which he regards as self-evident, is that Christianity understands itself as the absolute religion, beside which no other religion has equal standing. Yet Christianity also has a historical existence: it began at a point in time, and must come in a historical/cultural way to all persons. Christianity, like every religion, only exists in a social-historical form.

Second, until the gospel enters a person's historical situation, God acts graciously in and through the various religions, which express humans' natural religious inclinations. Thus, any given non-Christian religion contains not only natural knowledge of God admixed with human depravity, but also elements of divine grace. The assertion of grace in other religions is an a priori based on the belief (which Rahner regards as necessary for Christians) in "the universal and serious salvific purpose of God towards all men." Because persons can only be religious socially, God's grace must operate in and through other religions: "by the fact that in practice man as he really is can live his proffered relationship to God only in society, man must have had the right and indeed the duty to live his relationship to God within the religious and social realities offered to him in his particular historical situation." Rahner holds that Christians can be agnostic about the salvific status of any individual person outside Christianity, but optimistic about the power of God's salvific will for all people.

This is the basis for Rahner's third thesis, that non-Christians may be "anonymous Christians" (discussed above). His fourth thesis follows logically from the third. The church is not the exclusive community of the saved, but should instead be understood as "the historically tangible vanguard and the historically and socially constituted explicit expression of what the Christian hopes is present as a hidden reality even outside the visible Church."

The notion of anonymous Christianity offers Rahner a way to balance the particularity of the Christ-event (and of the church which proclaims and mediates its benefits) with the universality of God's love and grace. It gives Christians a way to be faithful to the gospel witness without dismissing the witness of religious others, and indeed could set the stage for interreligious dialogue in which Christians seek signs of God's presence in other religious traditions.

However, as with any theological formulation, Rahner's approach is not without problems. If Christians already know in advance that their own religious tradition offers complete and final saving truth, can they really learn anything of importance from religious others? Isn't interreligious conversation on such terms—to borrow one critic's picturesque metaphor—"dialogue between the elephant and the mouse"?[24] Perhaps even more important, if God truly does work in and through other religious traditions, how can Christians be sure a priori that only Christianity offers fullness of saving truth? Is not such certainty only available after dialogue with religious others?

Source: Karl Rahner, *Theological Investigations, Vol. 5: Later Writings*, trans. Karl-H. Kruger (Baltimore, MD: Helicon, 1966).[25]

From "Christianity and the Non-Christian Religions"

. . . *1st Thesis:*. . . . Christianity understands itself as the absolute religion, intended for all men, which cannot recognize any other religion beside itself as of equal right. This proposition is self-evident and basic for Christianity's understanding of itself. . . . Valid and lawful religion for Christianity is . . . God's action on men, God's free self-revelation by communicating himself to man. It is God's relationship to men, freely instituted by God himself and revealed by God in this institution. This relationship of God to man is basically the same for all men, because it rests on the Incarnation, death and resurrection of the one Word of God become flesh. Christianity is God's own interpretation in his Word of this relationship of God to man founded in Christ by God himself. And so Christianity can recognize itself as the true and lawful religion for all men only where and when it enters with existential power and demanding force into the realm of another religion and—judging it by itself—puts it in question.[26] . . . [T]he Christian religion as such has a beginning in history; it did not always exist but began at some point in time. It has not always and everywhere been *the* way of salvation for men—at least not in its historically tangible ecclesio-sociological constitution and in the reflex fruition of God's saving activity in, and in view of, Christ. As a historical quantity Christianity has, therefore, a temporal and spatial starting point in Jesus of Nazareth and in the saving event of the unique Cross and the empty tomb in Jerusalem. It follows from this, however, that this absolute religion—even when it begins to be this for practically all men—must come in a historical way to men, facing them as the only legitimate and demanding religion for them. . . . We leave it, however, an open question (at least in principle) at what exact point in time the absolute obligation of the Christian religion has in fact come into effect for every man and culture. . . . [I]n concrete human existence as such, the nature of religion itself must include a social constitution—which means that religion can exist only in a social form. This means, therefore, that man, who is commanded to have a religion, is also commanded to seek and accept a *social* form of religion.

. . . *2nd Thesis:* Until the moment when the gospel really enters into the historical situation of an individual, a non-Christian religion (even outside the Mosaic religion) does not merely contain elements of a natural knowledge of God, elements, moreover, mixed up with human depravity which is the result of original sin and later aberrations. It contains also supernatural elements arising out of the grace which is given to men as a gratuitous gift on account of Christ. For this reason a non-Christian religion can be recognized as a *lawful* religion (although only in different degrees) without thereby denying the error and depravity contained in it.

. . . [This] means first of all that it is a priori quite possible to suppose that there are supernatural, grace-filled elements in non-Christian religions. . . . It does not mean, of course, that all the elements of a polytheistic conception of the divine . . . are to be or may be treated as harmless either in theory or in practice. . . . The decisive reason . . . is basically a theological consideration. This consideration . . . rests ultimately on the fact that, if we wish to be Christians, we must profess belief in the universal and serious salvific purpose of God towards all men which is true even within the post-paradisean phase of salvation dominated by original sin. We know, to be sure, that this proposition of faith does not say anything certain about the *individual* salvation of man understood as something which has in fact been reached. But God desires the salvation of everyone. And this salvation willed by God is the salvation won by Christ, the salvation of supernatural grace which divinizes man, the salvation of the beatific vision. It is a salvation really intended for all those millions upon millions of men who lived perhaps a million years before Christ—and also for those who have lived after Christ—in nations, cultures and epochs of a very wide range which were still completely shut off from the viewpoint of those living in the light of the New Testament. . . . It is senseless to suppose cruelly—and without any hope of acceptance by the man of today, in view of the enormous extent of the extra-Christian history of salvation and damnation—that nearly all men living outside the official and public Christianity are so evil and stubborn that the offer of supernatural grace ought not even to be made in fact in most cases. . . .

. . . We must . . . rid ourselves of the prejudice that we can face a non-Christian religion with the dilemma that it must either come from God in everything it contains and thus correspond to God's will and positive providence, or be simply a purely human construction. . . .

. . . If, however, man can always have a positive, saving relationship to God, and if he always had to have it, then he has always had it within *that* religion which in practice was at his disposal by being a factor in his sphere of existence. . . . [B]y the fact that in practice man as he really is can live his proffered relationship to God only in society, man must have had the right and indeed the duty to live his relationship to God within the religious and social realities offered to him in his particular historical situation.

3rd Thesis: If the second thesis is correct, then Christianity does not simply confront the member of an extra-Christian religion as a mere non-Christian but as someone who can and must already be regarded in this or that respect as an anonymous Christian. It would be wrong to regard the pagan as someone who has not yet been touched in any way by God's grace and truth. If, however, he has experienced the grace of God . . . then he has already been given revelation in a true sense even before he has been affected by missionary preaching from without. . . . [I]f it is true that a person who becomes the object of the Church's missionary efforts is or may be already someone on the way towards his salvation, and someone who in certain circumstances finds it, without being reached by the proclamation of the Church's message—and if it is at the same time true that this salvation which reaches him in this way is Christ's salvation, since there is no other salvation—then it must be possible to be not only an anonymous theist but also an anonymous Christian. And then it is quite true that in the last analysis, the proclamation of the gospel does not simply turn someone absolutely abandoned by God and Christ into a Christian, but turns an anonymous Christian into someone who now also knows about his Christian belief in the depths of his grace-endowed being by objective reflection and in the profession of faith which is given a social form in the Church. . . . The reflex self-realization of a previously anonymous Christianity is demanded (1) by the incarnational and social structure of grace and of Christianity, and (2) because the individual who grasps Christianity in a clearer, purer and more reflective way has, other things being equal, a still greater chance of salvation than someone who is merely an anonymous Christian. . . .

4th Thesis: It is possibly too much to hope, on the one hand, that the religious pluralism which exists in the concrete situation of Christians will disappear in the foreseeable future. On the other hand, it is nevertheless absolutely permissible for the Christian himself to interpret this non-Christianity as Christianity of an anonymous kind which he does always still go out to meet as a missionary, seeing it as a world which is to be brought to the explicit consciousness of what already belongs to it as a divine offer or already pertains to it also over and above this as a divine gift of grace accepted unreflectedly and implicitly. If both these statements are true, then the Church will not so much regard herself today as the exclusive community of those who have a claim to salvation but rather as the historically tangible vanguard and the historically and socially constituted explicit expression of what the Christian hopes is present as a hidden reality even outside the visible Church. . . . [T]he Church is not the communion of those who possess God's grace as opposed to those who lack it, but is the communion of those who can explicitly confess what they *and* the others hope to be. Non-Christians . . . may think it presumption for the Christian to regard the non-Christian as a Christian who has not yet come to himself reflectively. But the Christian cannot renounce this "presumption" which is really the source of the greatest humility both for himself and for the Church. For it is a profound admission of the fact that God is greater than man and the Church. . . . On such a basis one can be tolerant, humble and yet firm towards all non-Christian religions.

John Hick

Often cited as the leading exponent of the pluralist orientation toward religious others, the British philosopher and theologian John Hick (b. 1922) ironically began his career as an evangelical Christian convinced, as he later wrote, "that Christianity is uniquely superior to all [other religions] and the world in process of being converted to Christian faith," a belief rooted largely in unfamiliarity: "like most of my generation, I had never met anyone of another faith and knew virtually nothing about the other world religions—and the little that I thought I knew has turned out to be largely caricature."[27] He found his early exclusivism less and less tenable as he learned about other religions and began to note similarities between their teachings and those of Christianity. Prominent among these similarities, as he notes in the essay excerpted below, is a common belief among the "post-axial religions"[28] that the Ultimately Real is "ineffable and unobservable." This common stress on divine ineffability serves as the lynchpin for his theology of religions.

In *An Interpretation of Religion* (1989), Hick formulates his "pluralist hypothesis":

> the great world faiths embody different perceptions and conceptions of, and correspondingly different responses to, the Real from within the major variant ways of being human; and that within each of them the transformation of human existence from self-centredness to Reality-centredness is taking place. These traditions are accordingly to be regarded as alternative soteriological "spaces" within which, or "ways" along which, men and women can find salvation/liberation/ultimate fulfilment.[29]

For Hick, there is one Real—one ultimate divine Reality—which serves as the common focus of all the "the great post-axial faiths." The various religions, Hick writes, "constitute different ways of experiencing, conceiving, and living in relation to an ultimate divine Reality which transcends all our varied versions of it."[30] Although they call this Real by different names (God, Brahman, the Dao, the Dharmakaya, and so on), the major religions all attest to the ineffability of the Real. Hick's approach turns on a distinction he borrows from the Enlightenment philosopher Immanuel Kant: that between the *noumenal* and the *phenomenal*. Hick asserts that the Real is noumenal: it is "beyond our human concepts," and thus "cannot be directly experienced by us as it is in itself."[31] On the other hand, the various conceptions of deities or absolutes are *phenomenal*, the "joint products of the universal presence of the Real and of the varying sets of concepts and images that have crystallized within the religious traditions." Attributes such as singular/plural, personal/impersonal, good/evil, or purposive/ non-purposive belong to this phenomenal realm, not to the noumenal Real. In this way Hick seeks to account for both religious diversity and the intriguing similarities between religions. Religious differences occur at the phenomenal level, as products of different cultural and historical circumstances; yet at the noumenal level, there is real common ground between religions.

Insofar as they mediate experience of the Real, the various religions function as "ways of salvation," transforming human existence from self-centeredness to Reality-centeredness (centeredness in the noumenal Real).[32] Religions are salvific insofar as they promote this transformation.

It is important to note that Hick does not claim that all religions are equally true or equally salvific. It is self-evident, he argues, "that not all religious persons, practices, and beliefs are of equal value."[33] Hick in effect argues that the value of a given religious tradition may be judged by its "fruits," its ability to produce saintliness and unselfish behavior among its adherents. Theoretically, then, Hick avoids relativism. In practice, however, he is less successful. In the selection below, he suggests that "the great religious traditions" produce saintliness and unselfish behavior more or less equally, and takes this as evidence that they are all in touch, to more or less the same extent, with the one ultimate Reality. Thus, he concludes, "so far as we can tell, no one of the great world religions is salvifically superior to the rest." Whether this amounts to relativism is an open question.[34]

A second problem lies in Hick's claim that the post-axial faiths are different paths to the same transcendent and ineffable Reality. Although he offers supporting examples from many religious traditions,[35] Hick implicitly claims special insight which the adherents of the different religions lack: that is, where adherents may see different Ultimates—say, a personal Allah versus an impersonal Dao versus the Christian Trinity—Hick somehow knows that they are all talking about the "same thing," the same Ultimate Reality. Yet since the noumenal Real is by definition beyond description, how can Hick be sure that the Real is in fact what the various religions are talking about? And for the same reason, how can Hick be sure that there is *one* Real, rather than many Reals, or that attributes such as personal/impersonal and one/many are not essential to it? While such questions do not take away from the importance of Hick's theoretical contribution to the theology of religions, they do indicate areas deserving further investigation.

Source: John Hick, "Religious Pluralism and Salvation," in *The Philosophical Challenge of Religious Diversity,* ed. Philip L. Quinn and Kevin Meeker (New York: Oxford University Press, 2000), 54-63.

Let us approach the problems of religious pluralism through the claims of the different traditions to offer salvation—generically, the transformation of human existence from self-centeredness to Reality-centeredness. This approach leads to a recognition of the great world faiths as spheres of salvation; and so far as we can tell, more or less equally so. Their different truth-claims express (a) their differing perceptions, through different religio-cultural "lenses," of the one ultimate divine Reality; (b) their different answers to the boundary questions of origin and destiny, true answers to which are however not necessary for salvation; and (c) their different historical memories. . . .

The fact that there is a plurality of religious traditions . . . creates an obvious problem for those of us who see them, not simply as human phenomena, but as responses to the Divine. . . . [W]hilst there are various overlaps between their teachings there are also radical differences: is the divine reality (let us refer to it as the Real) personal or non-personal; if personal, is it unitary or triune; is the universe created, or emanated, or itself eternal; do we live only once on this earth or are we repeatedly reborn? and so on and so on. When the problem of understanding religious plurality is approached through these rival truth-claims it appears particularly intractable.

I want to suggest, however, that it may more profitably be approached from a different direction, in terms of the claims of the various traditions to provide, or to be effective contexts of, salvation. "Salvation" is primarily a Christian term, though I shall use it here to include its functional analogues in the other major world traditions. In this broader sense we can say that both Christianity and these other faiths are paths of salvation. For whereas pre-axial religion was (and is) centrally concerned to keep life going on an even keel, the post-axial traditions, originating or rooted in the "axial age" of the first millennium B.C.E.—principally Hinduism, Judaism, Buddhism, Christianity, Islam—are centrally concerned with a radical transformation of the human situation.

. . . [I]f we stand back from these different conceptions to compare them, we can, I think, very naturally and properly see them as different forms of the more fundamental conception of a radical change from a profoundly unsatisfactory state to one that is limitlessly better because rightly related to the Real. . . . I suggest that [the religions' different] conceptions of salvation are specifications of what, in a generic formula, is the transformation of human existence from self-centeredness to a new orientation, centered in the divine Reality. . . . Each tradition sets forth the way to attain this great good: faithfulness to the Torah, discipleship to Jesus, obedient living out of the Qur'anic way of life, the Eightfold Path of the Buddhist dharma, or the three great Hindu *margas* of mystical insight, activity in the world, and self-giving devotion to God. . . .

The great world religions, then, are ways of salvation. Each claims to constitute an effective context within which the transformation of human existence can and does take place from self-centeredness to Reality-centeredness. How are we to judge such claims? We cannot directly observe the inner spiritual quality of a human relationship to the Real; but we can observe how that relationship, as one's deepest and most pervasive orientation, affects the moral and spiritual quality of a human personality and of a man's or woman's relationship to others. It would seem, then, that we can only assess these salvation-projects insofar as we are able to observe their fruits in human life. The inquiry has to be, in a broad sense, empirical. For the issue is one of fact, even though hard to define and difficult to measure fact, rather than being settleable by *a priori* stipulation. . . .

The ethical aspect of this salvific transformation consists in observable modes of behavior. But how do we identify the kind of behavior which, to the degree that it characterizes a life, reflects a corresponding degree of reorientation to the divine Reality? Should we use Christian ethical criteria, or Buddhist, or Muslim . . . ? The answer, I suggest, is that at the level of their most basic moral insights the great traditions use a common criterion. For they agree in giving a central and normative role to the unselfish regard for others that we call love or compassion. This is commonly expressed in the principle of valuing others as we value ourselves, and treating them accordingly. . . . Clearly, if everyone acted on this basic principle, taught by all the major faiths, there would be no injustice, no avoidable suffering, and the human family would everywhere live in peace.

When we turn from this general principle of love/compassion to the actual behavior of people within the different traditions, wondering to what extent they live in this way, we realize how little research has been done on so important a question. We do not have much more to go on than general impressions, supplemented by travellers' tales and anecdotal reports. . . .

All this constitutes a haphazard and impressionistic body of data. . . . I suggest that all that we can presently arrive at is the cautious and negative conclusion that we have no good reason to believe that any one of the great religious traditions has proved itself to be more productive of love/compassion than another.

. . . [A]n objective ethical comparison of such vast and complex totalities is at present an unattainable ideal. And the result is that we are not in a position to claim an over-all moral superiority for any one of the great living religious traditions.

. . . [T]he picture that I am suggesting can be outlined as follows: our human religious experience, variously shaped as it is by our sets of religious concepts, is a cognitive response to the universal presence of the ultimate divine Reality that, in itself, exceeds human conceptuality. This Reality is however manifested to us in ways formed by a variety of human concepts, as the range of divine personae and metaphysical impersonae witnessed to in the history of religions. Each major tradition, built around its own distinctive way of thinking-and-experiencing the Real, has developed its own answers to the perennial questions of our origin and destiny, constituting more or less comprehensive and coherent cosmologies and eschatologies. These are human creations which have, by their association with living streams of religious experience, become invested with a sacred authority. However they cannot all be wholly true; quite possibly none is wholly true; perhaps all are partly true. But since the salvific process has been going on through the centuries despite this unknown distribution of truth and falsity in our cosmologies and eschatologies, it follows that it is not necessary for salvation to adopt any one of them. We would therefore do well to learn to tolerate unresolved, and at present unresolvable, differences concerning these ultimate mysteries. . . .

There may indeed well be a variety of ways in which Christian thought can develop in response to our acute late twentieth century awareness of the other world religions, as there were of responding to the nineteenth century awareness of the evolution of the forms of life and the historical character of the holy scriptures. And likewise there will no doubt be a variety of ways in which each of the other great traditions can rethink its inherited assumption of its own unique superiority. But it is not for us to tell people of other traditions how to do their own business. Rather, we should attend to our own.

Rosemary Radford Ruether

The Catholic feminist theologian Rosemary Radford Ruether is Emerita Professor at the Pacific School of Religion. Her many published works—including the landmark *Sexism and God-Talk: Toward a Feminist Theology* (1983)—have addressed a number of critical contemporary issues, including feminism, social justice, and environmentalism. As the following reading indicates, Radford Ruether has also given serious consideration to Christian relations with other religions (particularly Judaism), informed by her feminist commitments.

In this essay she considers two "relationships": the feminist critique of all patriarchal religions, and the ongoing dialogue between Christians and religious others (especially Jews). She argues that both relationships challenge the traditional Christian notion of "a single universal biblical faith," that is, that "In Christianity all the nations . . . are to be gathered . . . in order to worship the true God of biblical faith."

The feminist critique challenges Christian claims of "a single universal biblical faith" by revealing how women's voices and experience have been excluded from a role in shaping the biblical texts and doctrine. An androcentric bias pervades both Judaism and Christianity: "the revelations of the biblical tradition were *male* revelations, not female revelations. This does not mean that the divinity to which they point is male, but rather that men received these revelations in the context of male experience and shaped their telling from a male perspective." In other words, Jewish and Christian women have been treated as religious others by their own traditions. Accordingly, Radford Ruether calls for "a new midrash on scripture or a 'Third Testament' that can tell stories of God's presence in experiences where God's presence was never allowed or imagined before in a religious culture controlled by men and defined by male experience."

Interreligious dialogue also challenges claims that Christianity constitutes the one universal faith. Interreligious dialogue reveals the many ways "in which experience of the divine has been localized in human experience." Rejecting the claim that Christianity has "a monopoly on religious truth," she contends instead that the ground of all beings is the God/ess, the divine Primal Matrix. The God/ess—not any single religion—"is truly universal, and is the father and mother of all peoples without discrimination"; thus, all religions offer "true revelation and true relationship to the divine." "True universality," she writes, "lies in accepting one's own finiteness, one's own particularity and, in so doing, not making that particularity the only true faith, but allowing other particularities to stand side by side with yours as having equal integrity. Each [religion] is limited and particular, and yet each is, in its own way, an adequate way of experiencing the whole for a particular people at a particular time." In this respect, Radford Ruether adopts a position similar to that of John Hick's notion of multiple culturally mediated phenomenal experiences of the one noumenal Real.

Like Michael Amaladoss, Radford Ruether reminds us that the theology of religions cannot be separated from the lives and experience of the people engaged in it.

Source: "Feminism and Jewish-Christian Dialogue: Particularism and Universalism in the Search for Religious Truth," 137-42, in *The Myth of Christian Uniqueness*, ed. John Hick and Paul F. Knitter (Maryknoll, NY: Orbis Books, 1987).

Christianity has traditionally regarded Judaism as a religion of obsolete particularism, tied to the idea of God's election of a particular people and land, which has been superseded by the superior revelation of God's redemption of all peoples throughout the earth by the one universal faith. But this view misconstrues the potential of Judaism for its own distinct understanding of universalism, as well as the hidden particularism behind Christian claims to universalism.

Christian claims to universalism were shaped culturally within the Greco-Roman Empire, which believed itself to be a universal empire containing the one true humanistic culture. All persons of other cultures became "human" by assimilating into Greco-Roman culture and accepting its political sway. Those who remained outside this imperial orbit or rejected its culture were seen as "barbarians"—that is, persons of uncivilized status, less than fully human. In the fourth century, Christianity saw its universalism as an expression of the messianic promises to the Jews that, in the last days, all nations would be gathered to Zion and worship the one God (e.g., Isaiah 26:6-8). This promise, it was claimed, was being fulfilled in Christianity. In Christianity all the nations of the gentiles are to be gathered into Zion in order to worship the true God of biblical faith. Israel itself, unfortunately, failed to recognize and accept its own universal fulfillment.

Christianity synthesized these two kinds of universalism—messianic universalism and Greco-Roman imperialist universalism. . . . Nowhere has Christianity become the predominant form of religion among peoples who are not heirs of Greco-Roman culture. Thus Christian universalism, in practice, has remained mostly limited to areas shaped culturally by Greco-Roman and European civilization. . . .

. . . Is the Christian claim to be the one universal faith by which all persons relate authentically to God still credible? . . . Christianity has not succeeded in breaking the power of the great historical religions, such as Buddhism, Judaism, and Islam. These have not been conquered by the great missionary and imperialist expansion of the West in modern times. . . .

. . . Theologically, Christianity has never accepted an equal status with other major religions and has shown various ways of relating to other religious traditions. The most negative approach was to view other religions as mere idolatry and demon worship, which must be destroyed, root and branch, in order to be replaced by the one true faith. This view has tended to identify Christianity totally with its cultural expressions and to regard any retention of indigenous culture as a failure of full conversion.

A more benign view has been to see other religions as partial or incomplete expressions of truth, which have glimpses of the true God available through a general or natural revelation but lack the complete or final expression of God's revelation in Christ. . . .

Toward Judaism, Christianity has reserved its most intense ambivalence. On the one hand, it acknowledges it as its parental faith and accepted its Bible as its Old Testament in Christian scriptures. But Christianity has regarded its parental religion not only as incomplete, having failed to accept the fulfillment of its own revelation of God in Christ, but also it has seen Judaism and Jews as perverse, deliberately rejecting Christ and seeking to kill him. . . .

Modern efforts to prescind from the Christian mission to the Jews, without rejecting the finality of Christianity, have varied. Some have suggested that Judaism already contains a sufficient and redeeming relationship to God through its historical revelation in the Torah. . . . Paul Van Buren has recently sought to reverse the pattern by declaring that it is Christianity that is apostate for having departed from Judaism, as the one true chosen people. . . . But this leaves in doubt whether Jews must also recognize Christianity as their mission to the Gentiles in the process.

I believe that we must rethink these views much more radically. The idea that Christianity, or even the biblical faiths, have a monopoly on religious truth is an outrageous and absurd religious chauvinism. It is astonishing that even Christian liberals and radicals fail to seriously question this assumption. My own assumption is that the Divine Being that generates, upholds, and renews the world is truly universal, and is the father and mother of all peoples without discrimination. This means that true revelation and true relationship to the divine is to be found in all religions. God/ess is the ground of all beings, and not just of human beings. . . .

Although there is true relationship to the divine, authentic spirituality, and viable morality in all religious systems, this does not mean that they are all just different words for the same thing. Each religion, like each culture, is a unique configuration of symbolic expressions that has been shaped by the total experience of peoples, their particular histories, and ecological settings. Although there is much overlap among religions, they also represent a broad spectrum of possible ways of experiencing the divine. Some may focus on the historical struggle for justice, some on the renewal of natural processes, and some on mystical ecstasy. Each has incarnated its way of symbolizing life and its relationship to the higher powers in unique ways that make it impossible simply to translate one religion to the other, or to create some abstraction of them all into a universal, ethical faith, as was often imagined among eighteenth-century European rationalists. . . .

We should see ourselves in need of becoming multi-cultural in religious understanding, entering deeply into perhaps two or three cultural configurations of religion and being able to experience our own life renewed through them in different ways. This means that a universal code for all religions eludes us. One can, at most, enter deeply into only two or three such communities of faith, not all of them. But this cultivation of the ability to enter in depth into several symbolic cultures gives us a basic sympathy for the possibilities of truth in all religions.

> True universality lies not in trying to make one cultural synthesis that can embrace all possibilities. . . . True universality lies in accepting one's own finiteness, one's own particularity and, in so doing, not making that particularity the only true faith, but allowing other particularities to stand side by side with yours as having equal integrity. Each is limited and particular, and yet each is, in its own way, an adequate way of experiencing the whole for a particular people at a particular time. . . .

Feminism is a new challenge to Christian claims of universalism that poses different problems from those of interreligious relationships. Interreligious relationships speak of many different ways in which experience of the divine has been localized in human experience and the mutual recognition of these historico-cultural configurations by each other. Feminism speaks of new contexts where the divine needs to be localized. By and large, not only Judaism and Christianity, Islam, and Buddhism, but even ancient tribal religions have not allowed the divine to be experienced in a way defined by women. Feminism looks back at the history of all religions as expressions of male-dominated cultures that have marginalized women to some extent, although women have been more radically and totally marginalized in some religious systems than in others.

Marjorie Hewitt Suchocki

The pluralist orientation toward religious others has been criticized for tending toward relativism, and thus for offering no effective means of critiquing forms of religion. Marjorie Hewitt Suchocki brings a feminist/liberation perspective to bear on this problem. While she affirms a pluralistic perspective—indeed, insists on it—she resists relativism by arguing that a norm or criterion from feminist/liberation theology, justice, is equally pertinent for judging various forms of religion. Her approach has much in common with the comparativism advocated by James Fredericks, in that the norm is derived through interreligious dialogue, rather than a priori from a single religion's perspective.

Suchocki grounds her appropriation of justice as norm for reflection about religious others by drawing parallels between the dynamics of sexism and those associated with absolutizing one religious tradition (elevating it as normative for all others). She describes "the invidious effects when one mode of humanity"—whether male experience or the witness of a particular religion—"is made normative for others." First, it results in the erasure or exploitation of those who fall outside the norm: "Measurement against an absolute norm, whether sex or religion, renders invisible or secondary all those in whom the norm is not found." Second, it distorts the perspective of those who fall within that norm: "The presumption of superiority dulls one's self-critical stance."

The solution, however, does not lie in what she calls an "unrelieved relativism." Instead, justice can serve as "the fundamental criterion of value and the focus of dialogue and action among religions."[36] For Suchocki, justice involves physical, social, and personal well-being. Yet to avoid replacing one a priori absolute with another, she argues that the definition of justice must be worked out dialogically, from "[c]oncrete forms of well-being in community." Dialogue is crucial because understandings of what constitutes well-being will vary from one community to the next. Indeed, the calculation of well-being invites appreciation of diversity, the "recognition of multiple modes of being human, with this multiplicity valued positively." Furthermore, agreement regarding what constitutes well-being should not be sought within religious interpretations of society, but rather in each religion's projection of the ideal. Since religious ideals are inherently diverse, it is imperative that we listen to and learn from others who are different.

Source: Marjorie Hewitt Suchocki, "In Search of Justice: Religious Pluralism from a Feminist Perspective," 149-60, in *The Myth of Christian Uniqueness*, ed. John Hick and Paul F. Knitter (Maryknoll, NY: Orbis Books, 1987).

"In Search of Justice: Religious Pluralism from a Feminist Perspective"

Liberation theology has pointed to the invidious effects that follow when one mode of humanity is made normative for others. Such normativeness, combined with power, allows and invites exploitation of all those falling outside the norm. Furthermore, it distorts the perspective of those counted as falling within the norm, leading to problems in adequately knowing either self or others. As liberation theologians—whether feminist, black, or Third World—have dealt with this theme, they have focused on universalized norms in the realm of social, political, and personal structures of existence. The thesis of this essay is that the principle holds for religion as well: universalizing one religion such that it is taken as the norm whereby all other religions are judged and valued leads to oppression, and hence falls short of the norm that liberationists consider ultimate—the normative justice that creates well-being in the world community.

A feminist perspective, therefore, suggests that one must radically affirm religious pluralism, but not without bringing a critical consciousness of well-being in human community to interreligious and intrareligious discussion. Justice is thus to be the fundamental criterion of value and the focus of dialogue and action among religions. . . .

My feminist rejection of absolutizing one religion as the norm for all others accepts the uniqueness and self-naming quality of each religion. I reject, however, the possibility of entering into dialogue with no judgments whatsoever. We are not creatures suspended from some skyhook, impartially surveying the human scene; we are part and parcel of its buzzing confusion, and enter into dialogue value-laden and value-projecting. What is called for is not a nonjudgmental dialogue with other religions in light of the relativism of belief systems, but a shift of judgment from ideological ground to ethical ground, along with an open recognition of the conditioned nature of the norm of justice we bring, and a commitment to critical exploration of the norm in the very dialogue wherein it is brought to bear. . . .

Absolutizing one religion, such that it becomes normative for all others, is a dynamic with clear parallels to sexism, whereby one gender is established as the norm for human existence. Therefore the critique of sexism can be extended as a critique of religious imperialism. . . .

. . . Just as the universalization of male experience functions either to absorb women within the masculine norm or to ascribe to women those character- istics that men are not willing to name clearly as belonging to themselves, even so the universalization of one religion leads to similar distortions. . . .

[Suchocki discusses the depiction of other religions in Hans Küng's *On Being a Christian*. In Küng's approach,] Christianity is the norm whereby other religions can continue to improve what is best within themselves. Christians, in turn, can affirm what is positive in other religions, accepting what is of value and discarding the worthless. The criterion of judgment is the essence of Christianity, which is Christ himself—the "ultimately deci- sive, definitive, archetypal" man.

Parallels with sexism can be drawn in that the norm of Christ is applied to other religions regardless of norms that may be generated from within those religions. Just as the norm of masculinity is applied to women regard- less of women's protestations that their own experience of humanity is suf- ficient to generate their own norms, even so Christian norms are projected uncritically upon non-Christian religions. Such inclusivist stances toward other religions violate their integrity. Also, just as women are measured and judged by masculine experience, even so Küng measures and judges other religions by Christian experience. Further, the form of sexism that separates reprehensible qualities from men and projects them upon women is also operative in Küng's treatment. The qualities which he specifically names as negative in other religions have parallels within Christianity. These parallels are not acknowledged. Rather, they are rendered invisible in Christianity by projecting them as somehow appropriately descriptive of other religions. Here the exclusivist attitude toward women finds its echo in an exclusivist attitude toward other religions. . . .

. . . That the utilization of religious absolutism leads to a failure in self- knowledge is also evident in Küng's account. Just as men, projecting quali- ties devalued in themselves onto women, fail to have a full understanding of themselves, even so a Christian theologian fails to understand the reality of Christianity when its negative characteristics are projected onto other religions. . . .

The same dynamics that promote sexism with repercussions against men as well as women apply with regard to the absolutizing of one religion vis-à-vis all others. Distortions in knowledge and exploitation in relation- ships follow.

If no religion can set itself up as a norm for all others, do we find ourselves in a situation of unrelieved relativism? Is there no transcendence of
our particularity that allows us to determine what is a valid stance toward
self and others in the world? I suggest that the norm championed by femi-
nists and other liberation theologians is also a norm for reflection on the
world religions. That norm is justice. . . .

The justice applied normatively by liberation theologians centers upon
inclusiveness of well-being. . . . When justice is defined from the perspective of the oppressed, certain consequences follow. First, justice is named
as a concrete reality manifested in concrete communities. Laws are to be
abstracted from situations that exhibit well-being. Concrete forms of well-
being in community provide the norm by which the laws are themselves
judged. Consequently, situations reflecting the absence of well-being in
community are sufficient reason to call into question the adequacy of the
formulated laws governing community life.

Valuation in a concrete mode of justice would begin with fundamental,
physical well-being. Food, water, shelter, work, and community are primary,
constituting as they do needs fundamental to all human existence. Building
upon these values is a second level of justice in terms of human dignity and
recognition in the human community. This level involves a self-naming, an
appreciation of self and others. A third level of justice is openness to self-
development and self-determination within the context of community. The
levels are successive, each building upon the other, and each moving toward
a multiplicity of forms. . . .

The ultimate test of justice is precisely the degree to which it knows no
boundaries to well-being. A justice that establishes well-being within the
context of its own community and ignores the well-being of those outside
that community is to that degree unjust. Likewise, a community that establishes its own well-being through exploitation of the well-being of those
outside the community is to that degree unjust. A supposition underlying
this statement is that the world is a network of interrelationship and interdependence. Thus a value of concrete forms of justice implicitly and explicitly pushes toward an affirmation of pluralism. It provides, however, not
only an affirmation of pluralism, but a criterion for judging the forms of
pluralism that it engenders. . . .

[M]odes of Christianity that systematically engage in destructive
action with regard to other groups of persons may in fact be Christian, but
they are poor forms of religion in general and of Christianity in particular. Modes that are destructive of justice for their own members are likewise poor forms of religion, regardless of their conformity to intrareligious
norms. . . .

With regard to the relativity of justice, the concrete interpretation of what
constitutes well-being is conditioned by one's personal and societal con-

text. The notion of justice can be as culture-bound and imperialistic as any other notion. My attempt to locate justice in specific modes of well-being—physical, societal, and personal—runs into the difficulty that what constitutes these modes of well-being can be differently defined in different societies. The problem for interreligious dialogue is that there are variations of interpretation about what constitutes physical well-being, as well as variations in interpreting societal and personal well-being. Diversity with regard to personal and societal well-being is in fact called for by the norm of justice outlined above, for the norm supports and even expects cultural diversity. Internal rather than external critiques would be most appropriate in these realms. There is a certain intransigence to the norm, however, when it comes to fundamental aspects of human existence, such as peaceful access to food, water, health, shelter, work, and community. To use justice normatively in interreligious dialogue implies, first, a fundamental importance accorded to these values for all peoples, and secondly, a commitment to work cooperatively with any religious group toward the creation of such well-being for the various communities of the world. . . .

. . . Religions will therefore have different valuations of what constitutes the justice of physical well-being in society, and these valuations may well have their source in the historical development of the religion within its society. . . .

I suggest, however, that there is another base of contact among the religions that allows a nonimperialistic criterion of justice. . . . By looking at each religion's vision of the ultimately perfect mode of existence for its saints or holy ones, whether that vision be otherworldly or not, we might find some echo of unanimity on the value of freedom from suffering.

My point is that justice is not given a universally acceptable content, not even with regard to physical well-being. . . . On the contrary, we must look to the heart of justice in each religion as that which renders life meaningful in light of a vision of what existence should be. Using justice as a norm means that the primary visions within each religion of what societal life should be in a "perfect" world is a source of judgment that can be used internally within each religion to judge its present societal forms of justice. Dialogue among the religions can likewise proceed from the development of mutual concerns for justice that can lead to concerted actions for justice in the world. Justice is a dynamic and transformative notion, capable of being used even to judge itself. . . .

Interreligious dialogue at the societal/personal levels of justice will discover that what constitutes dignity will be defined differently in various cultures. There may be no single standard. The situation may be even more culturally specific at the third level—that is, openness to self-development and self-determination within the context of community. . . . Divergences of communities on these issues are not antithetical to justice, but in fact become the test of justice.

Affirming religious pluralism within the context of justice shifts the focus of dialogue to the concreteness of human well-being. The very exploration of human well-being, however, inevitably directs our attention to questions concerning how we determine what constitutes well-being, or into the heart of the ideological nature of the religions. Interreligious dialogue focused on justice promotes intrareligious dialogue concerning ultimate and penultimate values. The pluralism among religions then finds itself calling attention to the pluralism within each religion; dialogue engenders dialogues. Affirming one another's diversity may grant us the privilege of "listening in" to the internal dialogues, in the hope of understanding and mutual transformations. One vision of justice can temper, criticize, and deepen another, and through dialogue each vision might grow richer in understanding and implementation.

In any case, a norm of justice used in the valuation of religions allows the affirmation of religious pluralism without plunging us into religious relativism, wherein we have no rational ground for distinguishing between a "Jonestown" religion and an Amish village. The norm, however, must be used self-consciously and dialogically in recognition of the fact that the norm is hardly culture-free. In the process of dialogue, justice is not only affirmed, but also created.

Aloysius Pieris

Aloysius Pieris, S.J., is the founder and director of the Tulana Research Center in Kelaniya, Sri Lanka. A scholar of Theravada Buddhism as well as a Christian theologian, Pieris has been at the forefront of Buddhist-Christian dialogue, in works such as *Love Meets Wisdom: A Christian Experience of Buddhism* (1988) and *Fire and Water: Basic Issues in Asian Buddhism and Christianity* (1996).

In *An Asian Theology of Liberation*, from which the following excerpt is drawn, Pieris seeks to connect two projects previously thought to be at cross-purposes: liberation theology and inculturation. Pieris makes three fundamental points of interest to students of Christian theologies of religions. First, the "irruption of the Third World" proclaimed by liberation theologians, Pieris argues, is also "the irruption of the non-Christian world." A theology of liberation, therefore, must speak to and through the non-Christian peoples of the Third World. Second, Pieris understands "the religious instinct . . . as a revolutionary urge, a psycho-social impulse, to generate a new humanity." Liberation or soteriology, and not God-talk, is therefore the proper basis for "interreligious collaboration with the Third World." Third, Pieris argues that every religion—including Christianity—is both liberative and enslaving, both "a sign and countersign of the kingdom of God." The question of inculturation, then, becomes: "Into which stream of non-Christian religiousness does Christianity hope to enter—the reactionary or the revolutionary?" Finally, Pieris draws on both Christian and non-Christian sources to rethink three categories key to liberation theology: *basileia*, *metanoia*, and *martyrion*.

Source: Aloysius Pieris, *An Asian Theology of Liberation* (Maryknoll, NY: Orbis Books, 1988).[37]

Because . . . there is no people unless summoned by God, and no God worth talking about except the God who speaks through a people, all theology is about a people's God—that is, about God's people. The major focus of all "God-talk" or theology, then, must be the Third World's irruption as a new peoplehood announcing the liberating presence of a God who claims to humanize this cruel world.

But the irruption of the Third World is also the irruption of the non-Christian world. The vast majority of God's poor perceive their ultimate concern and symbolize their struggle for liberation in the idiom of non-Christian religions and cultures. Therefore, a theology that does not speak to or speak through this non-Christian peoplehood is an esoteric luxury of a Christian minority. Hence, we need a theology of religions that will expand the existing boundaries of orthodoxy as we enter into the liberative streams of other religions and cultures. . . .

. . . [The analysis presented here] presumes that every religion, Christianity included, is at once a sign and countersign of the kingdom of God; that the revolutionary impetus launching a religion into existence is both fettered and fostered by the need for an ideological formulation; that its institution-alization both constrains and conserves its liberative force; that religion, therefore, is a potential means of either emancipation or enslavement. . . .

. . . Religiousness—especially in Asia—is for a greater part of humanity metatheistic, or at least nontheistic, if not, at times, explicitly atheistic. The common thrust, however, remains *soteriological*, the concern of most religions being *liberation* (*vimukti*, *moksa*, nirvana) rather than specula-tion about a hypothetical liberator. Many metacosmic religions[38] point to a future that is attainable as the present moment of total human emancipa-tion, putting the accent on a metapersonal Beyond, if not on an "imper-sonal" but transphenomenal It: Tao, dharma, *tathata*, *Brahman*, nirvana. The cosmic religions, on the other hand, look up to many gods and spiritual forces, which constitute the spectrum of a complex unity of being envelop-ing the whole of human cosmic existence. Even where the two forms of reli-gions—the cosmic and metacosmic—merge, the net result is not a simple equivalent of biblical monotheism.

Hence, theology as God-talk or God's talk is not necessarily the uni-versally valid starting point, or the direct object, or the only basis, of inter-religious collaboration with the Third World. But liberation is. Soteriology is the foundation of theology. Regrettably, the contemporary theologies of religions (with Christ pitted *against* religions or niched *within* them) are devoid of any Third World perspective: they take off from textual accounts of non-Christian religiousness and ignore the historical fact that a religion's

micro-ethical concern for self-purification of individuals . . . is often projected onto the macro-ethical level of socio-political catharsis. . . .

I submit that the religious instinct should be defined as a revolutionary
urge, a psycho-social impulse, to generate a new humanity. It is none other
than the piercing thrust of evolution in its self-conscious state, the human
version of nature's thirst for higher forms of life. The religious quest, in
other words, is an irresistible drive to *humanize* what has merely been *homi-
nized*. As in the biosphere, where it can end up in blind alleys, so also in
the *noosphere*, this evolutionary upsurge can be sidetracked to regressive
states of inertia. Revolution could turn reactionary religion irreligious. But
the foundation of a Third World theology of religions remains unshaken—
namely, that it is this revolutionary impulse that constitutes, and therefore
defines, the essence of *homo religiosus*. . . .

. . . Inculturation . . . has fortunately come to mean, in present usage, the
Christian search for meaning within the *religious* ethos of non-Christian
cultures. . . . Into which stream of non-Christian religiousness does Christianity hope to enter—the reactionary or the revolutionary? To allay the liberationists' misgivings about inculturation, one more crucial question has
to be raised: Which brand of Christianity seeks to be inculturated, the one
framed within a cosmology that is repudiated in the Third World, or the
one derived from a Third World hermeneusis of the gospel?

A Third World hermeneusis vivifies the Christian kerygma by recharg-
ing the three key words around which it revolves, words now worn out by
ideological misuse: *basileia* (the kingdom, or new order), *metanoia* (interior
conversion to that order), and *martyrion* (overt commitment to it).

True to our non-Christian religious traditions, we can neither describe
nor define the new order but can only boldly strive toward it by the *via nega-
tiva*—namely, by negating the present order not only in theory and analysis,
but also in the commitment to overthrow it! The future that calls in question
the present ever remains the "unnamable" or at least the "unmentioned presupposition" of every true revolution. For the intimate encounter with Ultimate Reality—the core of mysticism—almost overlaps with a profoundly
transforming experience of present unreality. The salvific truth dawns as
the unmasking of delusion. Being shines in the darkest depths of nonbeing.
Brahma/atman is reached by piercing through *maya*. Nirvana culminates
the pilgrimage of *samsara*. Life is the passage through death. Grace over-
whelms where sin abounds. Revolution is born of bondage. Yahweh abides
in the *anawin* (the poor). God's saving power erupts from the earth's slav-
ing poor.

Can we touch the one without being touched by the other? Only the
victim of the present order is qualified to be its judge and authorized to
"proclaim the imminent future"—which is what the kerygma means. *Metanoia*, then, is the disturbance of heart and change of life that such mysticism
evokes. It is a religiously motivated desire and decision to move toward the
new humanity—a "cultural revolution" in the vocabulary of those who are

allergic to the term "religious conversion." *Martyrion* is the concomitant growth of a collective testimony in the communities of converts, a personalized anticipation and a visible guarantee of the new order. Like the supreme martyr, Jesus, they too are the victim-judge of the existing system and the paradigm of the future they announce. This incipient "structural revolution" is known as the church—which is good news to the poor, because the poor by birth and the poor by option constitute it.

Engelbert Mveng

The Jesuit theologian, historian, and artist Fr. Engelbert Mveng (1930-1995) taught at the University of Yaoundé in his native Cameroon.[39] In the following excerpt, Mveng discusses the five sources upon which African Christian theology draws. Of particular interest to students of Christian theology of religions is the inclusion of African traditional religions as a theological source. While Mveng recognizes African traditional religions as religions of salvation, he notes that they do not understand salvation in precisely the same sense as does Christianity. Nonetheless, he contends that these religions provide African Christian theologians "with the basic structures of African religious experience." Consequently, Mveng argues, the gospel of Jesus Christ "as a strictly religious message, can only reach the African soul by using the language that the people can understand." From a theology of religions standpoint, Mveng's approach to inculturating the Christian gospel in an African context implies that Christians can learn from religious others without sacrificing their identity as Christians.

Source: Engelbert Mveng, "African Liberation Theology," in *Theologies of the Third World: Convergences and Differences*, ed. Leonardo Boff and Virgil Elizondo (Concilium 199; Edinburgh: T&TClark, 1988), 17-34.[40]

The Sources of African Theology

The Accra Declaration[41] mentions five sources of African theology. It is an indicative rather than an exhaustive list. These five sources are: the Bible, traditional religion, African anthropology, the Independent Churches, and the African cultural heritage.

The Bible: African theologians know that the Bible is the word of God revealed to all men. They approach the Bible as believers. Their basic problem is that of an African reading of the Bible. An African reading looks for what God, through the Bible, has to say to the African people today about their life and destiny, in their context and situation of weakness, poverty and oppression. Such a reading discovers the word of God to be a message of salvation and freedom addressed to every man and every race. The God of the Bible is the God of the weak and the oppressed. . . . It is important to emphasise that the African reader neither adds to nor subtracts anything from the Bible. He simply adheres to the essential truth of the word of God. The liberating God of the Bible, he has not put him there, he has found him there. It is the very essence of the word of God. That is why the African reading of the Bible is also a fight for the freedom of the word of God, held captive and disfigured by the reading of the oppressors. . . .

The African Religions constitute, with the Bible, one of the major sources of African theology. The questions which are at the centre of traditional African religions are certainly not those of a discourse on God. The God of African monotheism is a God who is worshipped only in silence. Human chatter is dumb before the ineffable mystery of God. On the other hand, African religious reasoning concerns the fate of man, the struggle in each of us between life and death, and the final victory of life over death. The African religions, then, are religions of salvation. The initiation rites are the search for a universal way of salvation, leading to the victory of life over death. The whole universe is a vast battlefield where the battle of life and death is fought, and the initiation teaches man to read the names of life's allies in the great book of the cosmos, and to mobilise them against the adversary: death. Humanity is torn between the camp of life and the camp of death, and the basis of moral action lies in the choice between the two camps.

It is easy to understand why the religious praxis in traditional Africa is completely centred on the life of man and his *raisons d'être*: health, disease, birth, death, survival, the other world, fortune, misfortune, fertility, offspring, family, the community, success, failure, and finally harmony between members of the community, and harmony between man and the cosmos.

Consequently one can understand the importance of the ritual which is the cosmic celebration of man's religious experience.

The traditional religions provide the African theologians with the basic structures of African religious experience; the categories and concepts which take account of the intelligibility of this experience and which weave the thread of all strictly religious reasoning. The good news of Jesus Christ as a message of freedom and salvation, and therefore as a strictly religious message, can only reach the African soul by using the language that the people can understand.

However, it is important to draw attention to certain fundamental aspects of the traditional African religions. Although it is true that they are religions of salvation, the ways of salvation are not always the same. The convention known as *ancestor worship* is a celebration of consanguinity and family life. The way to salvation here is a *via communis* leading to the fulfilment and the culmination of life shared in the family between the living and the dead. When we speak of inculturation, we must never forget that, at this level, the transition from the natural biological family to the family of grace and of union with God, does not occur without problems. The question is not that of the natural and the supernatural. Far from it! The question is an unavoidable one, which African tradition had very well observed: the question of same and other, of own and other people's, of kinsman and stranger. The transition from the order of kinship to the order of affiliation and adoption is common to mystery cults and all initiation systems. In ancestor worship the way of salvation leads to fidelity and identification with the ancestor. In mystery calls [sic] and initiation systems fidelity and identification are aimed at the other being, the stranger, the benevolent and liberating model who must come from elsewhere. The initiate must destroy the old man to reach the status of new man. He must pass through death to enter into the real life; he must change his name, speak another language, become a new man. At this level, the problems of Christian conversion and inculturation appear particularly relevant. Christology, soteriology, African spirituality can then espouse an authentically African reasoning, without betraying the mystery of man's meeting with the other being in whom he fulfills and completes himself.

(Chung) Hyun Kyung

The Korean feminist theologian (Chung) Hyun Kyung is an associate professor of Ecumenical Theology at Union Theological Seminary. The author of the groundbreaking *Struggle to Be the Sun Again: Introducing Asian Women's Theology*, she has been at the forefront of emerging efforts to inculturate Christian thought in an Asian—specifically, Korean women's—frame of reference. As the following excerpt shows, Chung's Christian theological work draws freely (though not uncritically) from non-Christian sources, including Korean shamanism. Consequently, some have leveled charges of syncretism against her, to which she responded in a 2003 interview:

> If they ask me, "Are you a syncretist?" I say, "You are right, I am a syncretist, but so are you." My response is that I know I am a syncretist, but you don't know you are a syncretist because you have hegemonic power . . . non-Christian cultures, when they try to interpret the gospel out of their life experience, they are syncretists! But they are just being true to their identity, history and culture.[42]

The following excerpt illustrates Chung's theological method and her implicit theology of religions. Korean Christian women, she argues, define their Christian identity in terms of their "lived inherited experience" reaching back prior to the arrival of Christianity in Korea not to mention the birth of Christianity itself; this religious inheritance includes the experience of shamanism, Buddhism, and Confucianism. Turning to the specific problem of the liberation of Korean women from oppression and suffering, she interprets the liberative power of the Christian gospel in terms of two key concepts drawn from Korean shamanism: *han*, which refers to the root experience of oppression, injustice, and suffering; and *han-pu-ri*, which can be translated as "liberation," but also carries the sense of collective healing. By treating non-Christian resources as both source and norm for Christian theology, Chung implies (as does Mveng)

that Christian encounter with religious others serves to enrich Christian theological reflection.

Source: Chung Hyun Kyung, "'*Han-pu-ri*': Doing Theology from Korean Women's
Perspective," in *Frontiers in Asian Christian Theology: Emerging Trends*, ed. R. S.
Sugirtharajah (Maryknoll, NY: Orbis Books, 1994), 52-62.[43]

How can we . . . solve and untangle the accumulated *han* of Korean women?
In Korea we call the release of *han* "*han-pu-ri*." I think *han-pu-ri* must be
the purpose of doing women's theology in Korea.

Originally the term *han-pu-ri* came from Korean shamanistic tradition.
Korean shamans have played the role of the priest or priestess of *han-pu-ri*
in his or her communities. Shamanistic *kut* (ritual) gave the opportunity
for voiceless ghosts to speak out their stories of *han*. The community must
then solve the *han* of the ghost collectively either by eliminating the source
of the oppression for the ghosts or by comforting and negotiating with the
ghosts. Therefore *han-pu-ri* has been an opportunity for collective repentance, group therapy, and collective healing for the ghosts and their communities in Korean society.

The most fascinating things about Korean *han-pu-ri* for me are the following three factors:

1.   The majority (65-70 percent) of shamans who play the role of the priest
     or priestess of *han-pu-ri* in Korean society are women.

2.   The majority of people who participate in the *han-pu-ri kut* in Korean
     society are women.

3.   The majority of characters in ghost stories are women. . . .

. . . [W]hy are women the majority in the above situation? When I look
at the three factors with the "epistemological privilege" of third-world
women, the answer is clear. Korean women have been the embodiment of
the worst *han* in our history. They usually did not have the public channels
to express their *han*. This developed a sense of impassibility among Korean
women. Many of them died without releasing the sense of impassibility in
their lives. That is why there are so many women ghosts in our traditional
stories. Women who endured the helpless impassibility could understand
one another through their shared life experience as women. *Han-pu-ri*
became one of the few spaces where poor Korean women played their spiritual role without being dominated by male-centered religious authority.
Han-ridden women got together and tried to release their accumulated *han*
through *han-pu-ri kut*.

There are three important steps in *han-pu-ri*. The first step is *speaking and hearing*. The shaman gives the *han*-ridden persons or ghosts the
chance to break their silence. The shaman enables the persons or ghosts to
let their *han* out publicly. The shaman makes the community hear the *han*-
ridden stories. The second step is *naming*. The shaman enables the *han*-

ridden persons or ghosts (or their communities) to name the source of their oppression. The third step is *changing* the unjust situation by action so that *han*-ridden persons or ghosts can have peace. . . .

I can find four main theological sources in the Korean women's emerging theologies. The most important source . . . is the Korean women's lived experience. However, this experience is not the universal, abstract, and standardized human experience as alluded to by some traditional European male theologians. The specific historical experience of Korean women is manifested in their experience as victims and agents of liberation, and through the experience of *han* and *han-pu-ri*. Korean women's experience is the starting point and ending point of Korean women's hermeneutical circle. The second source is critical consciousness. Critical consciousness is different from a neutral, detached, objective reason. Critical consciousness is an engaged subjective reason that takes sides. Critical consciousness is the thinking power that can uncover the ideology of domination. The third source is tradition. Korean women use all of the traditions we have in order to fully articulate Korean women's theology.

We use our own religious traditions, such as Shamanism, Buddhism, Confucianism, and Christianity, and political ideologies. However we do not use all the traditions uncritically. We distinguish from a specifically women's perspective the liberative traditions from the oppressive traditions. We women learn from our experiences that male-defined liberation did not always include women's liberation. We use liberative traditions to empower women and our critical analysis of the oppressive traditions to name the source of oppression. The fourth source is Scripture. We use the Old and New Testaments along with other scriptures from our traditional religions. We selectively choose liberating messages from the texts. Scriptural texts are our references from women. We learn by the texts, but we go beyond the texts to meet the community behind the text.

When we Korean women do theology with the above methodology and resources, we come up with the question of the norm for our theology. What makes our theology good theology? I will say the norm of Korean women's theology is the power of liberation (*han-pu-ri*) and life-giving. If a theology untangles the Korean women's *han* and liberates us from bondage, it is a good theology. If a theology keeps us accumulating our *han* and staying in our *han*-ridden women's places, it is a bad theology no matter how important church unity, the authority of the Bible, and church traditions are. If a theology has a life-giving power to Korean women and empowers us to grow in our full humanhood, that is a good theology. If a theology makes us die inside and wither away in our everyday bodily and spiritual life, it is a bad theology.

Can this Korean women's theology be a Christian theology with these two norms: liberation (*han-pu-ri*) and life-giving power? Surely it can because we Korean women believe in good news (gospel), not bad news. For us, the gospel of Jesus means liberation (*han-pu-ri*) and life-giving power.

In that sense, we are Christians. Where there is genuine experience of liberation (*han-pu-ri*) and life-giving power, we meet our God, Christ, and the
power of the Spirit. That is good news. We Korean Christian women define
our Christian identity according to our lived inherited experience, which
stretches five thousand years back, even beyond the birth of Jesus.

S. Mark Heim

How can Christian theology respect the witness of other religions in their diversity, and at the same time affirm the ultimacy of the Christian way to salvation?
This is the problem theologian S. Mark Heim sets for himself in two recent
works: *Salvations: Truth and Difference in Religion*, which is excerpted below;
and *The Depth of the Riches: A Trinitarian Theology of Religious Ends*.[44] His
solution is to propose that there are "many salvations," rooted in the plural
nature of the triunity of the Christian God.

Heim contends that the pluralism of theologians such as John Hick is not
as pluralistic as it claims, because it, like exclusivism and inclusivism, assumes
that "there is and could be only one religious fulfillment or 'salvation.'"[45] This
has the effect of papering over the real differences between religions. If we wish
to take those differences seriously, Heim argues, we must accept the fact that different religions offer different "religious ends": "religious paths in fact lead persons to the distinctively varied states they advertise and on which they set such
transcendent value."[46] By this logic, Buddhist nirvana and Christian salvation
(for example) are not different experiences of the same noumenal Real (as Hick
would have it), but are truly different religious ends, each real and each achiev-
able by means of the practices and beliefs prescribed by the respective tradition.
As Knitter describes Heim's stance, "Buddhists arrive at Nirvana, Christians
arrive at union with God. And both are happy."[47]

Heim grounds the existence of many religious ends in the Christian doctrine of the Trinity. Manyness characterizes human religious life because it
characterizes the nature of God as Trinity. Thus, religious diversity arises from
the diversity within the life of the triune God.[48] Even though the religious ends
proclaimed by the religions differ markedly from one another, Christians can
recognize them as real and valid because they offer real relation with the triune
God. Indeed, Heim goes so far as to say that Christians do not in fact believe in
the Trinity if they do not also believe that God intends the differences among
the religions.[49]

Heim contends that the life of the triune God is manifested in three dimensions: the impersonal, the personal (the unitary agency of one divine person),
and communion. Human relations with this triune God "can be tuned or concentrated in one of these channels, with distinctive religious results." If one
such "channel of relation" with God "is maintained in isolation from others,"
a distinct religious end results.[50] While other religions realize some aspects of
relation with God, Heim contends that Christianity alone recognizes the third
and crucial dimension to the life of the triune God: communion.[51] Indeed, Heim

construes the religious end of Christianity, salvation, as "communion of relation-in-difference with God and with others."[52] It is this third dimension of the triune God that other religions miss in their focus on the impersonal or the personal.

Thus, Heim is able to affirm that there is truth in Buddhism, Islam, and other religions—indeed, to affirm that these religions offer a kind of relationship with the God whom Christians confess—while simultaneously maintaining the distinctiveness of Christian teaching.[53] He is also able to affirm the need for Christians to listen to and learn from religious others. Heim argues that each religion claims the superiority of its own path, and that, from within its own cultural-religious context, such claims are valid. Yet the religions also recognize that their truth is only partially grasped. Thus, there is a need for each religion to learn from others who see the world differently.

Does the validity of various religious ends other than (Christian) salvation mean that non-Christians do not suffer what Christians have called loss or damnation? Not at all, answers Heim: "A relation with God is not the same thing as salvation. Insofar as alternative religious ends lack or rule out real dimensions of communion with the triune God, they embody some measure of what the Christian tradition regards as loss or damnation."[54] Christians have real reason to regret the failure of religious others to realize salvation-as-communion, and consequently have a real impetus to witness to the Christian *kerygma*.[55]

How viable is Heim's alternative? On the plus side, the concept of "religious ends" is a helpful category for thinking about the differences between the aims or goals proclaimed by the different religions. If we wish to affirm the real differences between religions, rather than domesticating them, we need to be prepared to extend these differences to the religious ends claimed by those religions. We need to acknowledge the possibility that different religions are in fact talking about different things. To do so is to recognize that religious others know what they are taking about, rather than simply being mistaken about the true nature of what they believe. Furthermore, Heim's approach reminds us that truth and validity of those religious ends does not mean that they all amount to the same thing. Truth does not equate to identity. Reality, especially (to use a Christian term) *eschatological* reality, may be plural. Ironically, many pluralists seem not to have recognized this possibility.

Yet important questions remain. Since Heim makes it clear that only Christianity offers the fullness of salvation (because Christianity alone recognizes all three dimensions of the divine life), does his theory of many "religious ends" really respect the truth in and of other religions? By deciding a priori that Christian salvation is essentially different from, and superior to, other religious ends, does his approach have the unintended effect of insulating Christians from any radical challenges to Christian teaching from religious others? By regarding the experience/witness of religious others as incomplete in comparison to that of Christians, does he not forestall the possibility that Christianity may be radically challenged by what religious others have to say, and thus that we may learn anything of importance from religious others?

Source: S. Mark Heim, *Salvations: Truth and Difference in Religion* (Maryknoll, NY: Orbis Books, 1995).[56]

A More Pluralistic Hypothesis

In expositions of pluralistic theologies of religion by their primary advocates one word never appears in the plural: salvation. This is the more dramatic since diversity is otherwise their constant theme. One writer, for instance, suggests it is wisest to affirm that God has different histories and different natures, that in fact there may be many gods. . . . But in all the speculation and professed radicalism "salvation" remains a comfortable and unitary reference point. The prominent figures I have reviewed make salvation the universal, cross-cultural constant in interpreting religious traditions. John Hick adopts what he calls "the soteriological criterion" to test the validity of such traditions. . . . Paul Knitter revises his theocentric approach to the theology of religions in favor of "soteriocentrism," with its absolute presupposition of a single "soteria." . . . At first sight, the use of a traditional Christian term to designate the standard to judge all religions seems odd in those who explicitly warn us against such particularism. But they regard "'salvation" as shorthand for one process taking place within all major religious traditions, though not normatively understood or described in any of them. . . . The largely undefended assumption that there is and can be only one religious end is a crucial constitutive element of "pluralistic" theologies. Despite their appropriation of the title, these theologies are not religiously pluralistic at all. Difference in religious aims and ends is what they bend their impressive efforts to deny. I would suggest that more adequate perspectives are possible which diverge sharply at this point. . . . What would a truly pluralistic hypothesis look like, one that was interested in affirming—as religiously significant—a much more substantial portion of the various faith traditions? This alternative would explore the conditions under which the various believers' accounts of their faith could be most extensively and simultaneously valid. It would open the possibility of affirming religious traditions as truthful in a much more concrete sense than pluralistic theologies provide. It would mean that the traditions themselves would not be superseded by the philosophical framework placed on them. The key to such a hypothesis is the willingness to consider more than one realizable religious aim. . . .

A Real Pluralism of Religious Ends

. . . The question, then, is what theories or theologies of religion will allow for the maximum truth value in the specifics of the traditions and will most significantly ground the importance of concrete knowledge of them? . . .

. . . [Various faiths testify that] there are states of religious fulfillment which have already become actual for at least some human beings in connection with the ineffable referents (righteousness, nirvana, the *tao,* God). While even under these circumstances of fulfillment the referents may remain ineffable—unable to be fully described—they would be actual for those human beings who participate in them. *What* is actual for them, whether it is one and the same thing, as Hick suggests, and whether or not even those persons are in a position to be able to determine such questions, we simply do not know. Certainly if we are to credit the various religious accounts of their aims, the presumption is that they are different. . . .

. . . [T]he hypothesis of multiple religious ends "relativizes" each faith path. . . . It affirms that more than one may be truthful in their account of themselves, and that these truths are distinct. That is, it relativizes the religions precisely by actual relation to each other. This contrasts with the relativizing of traditions on Hick's hypothesis by referring them to his postulated absolute, which as such figures in no one's lived religious life. . . .

In order to participate in the distinctive dimensions of Buddhist religious fulfillment in this life, there is no path but the Buddhist path. And the same is true of each tradition. Indeed, this can be seen as a complementary truth to the fact that at another level any serious attempt simply to understand the character of a faith tradition requires immersion in its "one and only" history, practices, texts, and beliefs. Here again, the hypothesis of multiple religious ends coheres with an emphasis on the importance of a religion's concrete texture. . . .

"Plenitude and Trinity: A Christian Perspective on Religious Diversity"

. . . I have argued that inclusivist religious approaches which recognize diverse religious ends constitute the most adequate set of responses to religious diversity. Similarly, I will argue that the Christian theological perspective I outline is one of the most adequate Christian approaches to religious diversity. In both cases the orientation from which I work is a Christian one, an orientation constantly subject to . . . enlargement and transformation.

. . . In line with the orientational pluralism I have described, it is appropriate to argue in this manner for the universal validity of my position in the first instance, and the preferability of my view among Christian alternatives in the second. . . .

Neither Heaven nor Hell

. . . The fundamental challenge of my proposal for Christians is to reflect on the possibility of the providential provision of a diversity of religious ends for human beings.

As Joseph DiNoia puts it, Christian theology can affirm "the distinctiveness of the aims fostered by other religions without prejudice to an affirmation of the unique valuation of the Christian community or of its doctrines about salvation." . . . Such distinctiveness raises the question of a providential role for the religions in the divine plan other than or in addition to serving as channels for salvation as Christians understand it. These are roles "that are now only dimly perceived and that will be fully disclosed in the consummation of history for which Christians long." . . . On the other hand, the alternativeness of these ends to Christian aims allows and even requires a judgment from the Christian perspective that subordinates them to the consummation of the Christian life. To realize something other than communion with the triune God and with others in the continuing relationship of created being is to achieve a lesser good. It is not the abundant life that Christians know and hope for in Christ. There is no reason to avoid this judgment, as long as we grasp that others make reciprocal judgments. The new factor we have added to the picture is the expectation, to be tested by encounter, that these reciprocal judgments may in fact be grounded in their own distinct religious fulfillments.

The discussion of religious difference shifts then from a sole focus on flat issues of truth and falsehood, or degrees of these, to include consideration of alternatives: not "Which religion alone is true?" but "What end is most ultimate, even if many are real?" The cessation of self, the realization of an absolute actual self which is "non-dual," communion with the triune God, living on only in our effects on historical posterity: let us presume for the moment that these and other aims are actual possibilities. These are real experiential human states, significantly constituted by the practice and aspiration of the person who attains them. They are not identical. . . .

A religious end or aim is defined by a set of practices, images, stories, and conceptions which collectively has three characteristics. First, the set provides material for a pervasive pattern of life. The "ultimacy" often spoken of in definitions of religion is here given a quite concrete interpretation; it is not some single dimension of life that is addressed but all its features, sublime and mundane. Second, at least some of these elements are understood to be *constitutive* of a final human fulfillment and/or to be the sole means of achieving that fulfillment. For instance, for Christians, there is a texture of such elements making reference to Jesus Christ, and Christ is believed to be integral to the fulfillment itself. Most Buddhists may maintain that all the instruments used to follow the dharma way are ultimately themselves dispensable, even the eight-fold path itself. But it can only be discarded *after* being used, and nothing else is fit to serve the same purpose. Third, for any individual or community the pattern is in practice exclusive of some alternative options. The set of stories and practices in its nature involves choices. "The ascetic life leads to peace" and "the sensual life leads to joy" may both be true reports. But one can practice the observance of one more comprehensively only at the expense of the other. For our purposes it makes no difference that some may make the tantric claim that some combined practice of asceticism/sensuality will lead to peace *and* joy. This is itself a claim, a pattern, and a practice which, if followed, rules out either of the other two paths.

The relations among religious ends are as diverse as the ends themselves. Some fulfillments may be similar enough that the paths associated with them reinforce each other to some degree, as typing and piano playing may both train the fingers. Other ends may simply pose no obstacle, one to the other, save the intrinsic division of finite time and effort: say marathon running and single parenthood. Yet others diverge so sharply that a decisive step in one direction moves away from the other: strict nonviolence and participation in armed revolution. . . .

"Salvation" or religious fulfillment for any religious community is integrally related to a comprehensive pattern of life. Any particular religious tradition would regard someone as "saved" whose life had been most fully shaped by the distinctive pattern it fosters. Even if the person in question had his or her life formed entirely outside explicit relation to this particular religious tradition, the person would be perceived and evaluated on the basis of the pattern provided by this faith tradition. Religious ends are not extrinsic awards granted for unrelated performances, like trips to Hawaii won in lotteries. No one is unhappy "in" nirvana or arrives at it unready, because the state of cessation is an achievement the path makes possible. It is not "enjoyed" until one has become what the path makes you. The way and the end are one. . . .

. . . From a Christian perspective this requires the somewhat unfamiliar admission that other religious fulfillments may be both distinct and quite real. At the same time Christians may rightly continue to view the achievement of these alternative religious ends as something to be avoided, even in cases carrying some measure of the meaning of "damnation." That is, they are not positive evils (though such evils may also be live possibilities), but they are aims different than the best that Christians know and hope for.

Is such a diversity in human destiny consistent with Christian convictions? Plainly Christian sources, from scripture on, tend to stress a twofold distinction (the saved and the lost). With time, however, consideration arose for at least some diversity among the saved. And such diversity was often also imagined among the lost, as in distinctions made between the destiny of unbaptized infants and others of the lost. . . . That is, within the overall twofold pattern, distinctions were made in each category. The possibility of alternative religious fulfillments can be viewed as a third division, a category that could be classed on one of the two sides or the other, depending on whether the emphasis is on the absence of the distinctive end Christians seek or on the intrinsic character of the alternative.

The possibility of a more thoroughgoing diversity in the future of humanity is in some measure authorized by the trinitarian vision of God and a notion of the divine plenitude. That is, it rests on the conviction that the most emphatic no of the human creature to the end of loving communion with God meets always some variation of God's merciful yes to creation.

Plenitude and Trinity

. . . From such a revised Christian perspective three types of religious option appear rather than two: lostness, penultimate religious fulfillments, and communion with the triune God. The real possibility remains that a person may not actualize any viable religious end, may find not an alternative fulfillment but rather none at all. There are human conditions, contemporary or eschatological, that no valid religious view claims as consistent with its end. On this point there is ample room for common cause among the faiths: spiritual and practical cooperation to overcome these conditions, even from differing perspectives.

There is an enormous difference between this lostness from all religious fulfillment and the achievement of *some* religious fulfillment. Christians can affirm an eschatological plenitude whereby, for instance, those who give themselves to the "'divine abyss" of emptiness can be seen to have realized a facet of the divine plenitude. From my Christian view this is a secondary good, since I believe that communion with God in a fuller range of God's being is possible. But the end is neither unreal nor evil; it does truly offer release from the round of human suffering. Our place in the great tapestry of the consummation is alterable, but each one glorifies God in some measure. This Christian conviction would be analogous to a Buddhist's confidence that a Christian's spiritual fulfillments could only uphold and be consistent with the dharma.

Is the realization of such diversity necessary to the fullness of the divine glory? Eschatological plenitude consists in the *range* of such fulfillments available to creation, not in any requirement that each one be realized in some fixed ratio. Human freedom shapes the diversity of fulfillment the eschaton exhibits. If all human beings eventually participate in the triune life in a network of relation among unique created selves, this would constitute a variety at least as deep in its richness as that represented by the panoply of various religious ends. And surely Christians believe the divine plenitude would be diminished if none were saved in the Christian sense. But no fixed proportion between these possibilities is necessarily specified by Christian eschatological hope.

Within Christian tradition there were debates over God's obligation to save humanity: Is God's justice or love compromised if some are not redeemed? Our new framework casts this question in a changed light. We could certainly affirm that God would be just if all the world attained a Buddhist religious end rather than a Christian one, even though what Christians believe a fuller opportunity for humans was not realized. Communion with the triune God is thought to encompass dimensions of other fulfillments, to be better because more consistent with the nature of the ultimate, and so more inclusive.

We cannot deny that other religious fulfillments have something, in their intensity and exclusivity, that is not present by definition in the end Christians seek. Christian religious fulfillment cannot be inclusive of an exclusive focus on either a feature of created being or a divine facet to the point of eliminating others. The divine love which overflows with such plenitude also sustains the diversity of ends that can flow from it. Persons who individually or communally fix upon a real aspect of divine creation or being and make their universe revolve about that center are "let be" by the divine love. There is no invocation of an arbitrary end to such pluralism.

This continuing conviction on the part of Christians that theirs is a distinctive and preferable religious end is itself a ground for the recognition of distinctively different religious fulfillments in other traditions. The two go together. This reinforces the arguments on behalf of an orientational pluralist outlook which I offered earlier. Christians may and should continue to argue that the patterns of life and thought relating to communion with the triune God can be crucial sources for developing perspectives on *common* areas of human life, whether political or economic. Religious convictions are of public and not only private significance.

Michael Amaladoss

The South Indian Jesuit theologian Michael Amaladoss (b. 1936) has taught theology at Vidyajyoti Theological College in Delhi, and has served as president of the International Association for Mission Studies. Amaladoss sees mutually transformative encounter with religious others as a fact of life for Christians in Asia. Whereas Western Christian theologians speak from what is (or was until very recently) a predominantly Christian context, Asian Christians work in, and are the products of, socio-cultural-political contexts that have been shaped by other religious traditions (which in the case of Amaladoss include Hinduism, Buddhism, Islam, and the various primal religions of south India). As a result of what he calls Asian Christians' "ongoing dialogue of life," they have gained a new respect for their religious neighbors: "We respect and read with profit their scriptures and other sacred writings. We learn from their sadhana, methods of prayer, and religious experience."

In the following essay Amaladoss sketches the groundwork for an Asian theology of interreligious dialogue; this in turn assumes and implies an underlying theology of religions, in which four major points can be emphasized. First, rather than seeing religions as "ways of salvation" (as does John Hick), Amaladoss stresses the experiential dimension of the divine-human relationship. God reaches out to humans, and religions are "expressive mediations" of their experience of God's outreach. He writes:

If we believe with the Second Vatican Council that the Holy Spirit offers to every one the possibility of participating in the paschal mystery in ways unknown to us; if we are aware that more than 80 percent of humanity are not Christian (including among the non-Christian community all those who are Christians in name only); and if we do not continue to play with concepts like "implicit" and "explicit" that come not from experience but from a priori argumentation, then we can make space for other religions.

Second, the concept of the Reign of God plays a key role in Amaladoss's theology of religions. He understands God's Reign in two senses simultaneously. On the one hand, it is "the wider reality of God's mystery, not merely eschatologically, but also in history, which serves as a counterpoint to the reality of the church as a visible, institutional community." On the other, it is "the common human community of freedom, fellowship, and justice, toward the building up of which all believers are invited to collaborate." Crucially, the Reign of God is not purely ecclesial for Amaladoss. Though related to church, the Reign of God transcends it: the church does not have a monopoly on the presence and action of God in the world, which extends to communities beyond the boundaries of the church. While proclamation witnesses to the divine mystery as it has been manifested to Christians, "[d]ialogue reaches out to the mystery of God active in others." Accordingly, while the church is called to proclaim God's Reign, it first should listen to religious others, so that its proclamation will be relevant to the context and respectful to God's action in the world.

A third feature of Amaladoss's theology of religions involves Christians' affirmation of the centrality of Jesus Christ, which is often seen as a stumbling block to dialogue with religious others. It should not be, Amaladoss argues. The real problem is not Christ but "the attempt of the church to monopolize Christ." Too often, he argues, the church's arguments for the uniqueness of Christ are in fact veiled arguments for the uniqueness of Christianity. "If we do not identify Christ with Christianity," he writes, "then Christ need not be an obstacle to dialogue between religions."

Finally, Amaladoss, like Fredericks, argues that dialogue can precede theology, at least in some areas. Addressing the question of how salvation in Christianity is "mediated to people through other religions or even no religion at all," he suggests, "the practice of interreligious dialogue need not wait for a clear answer to these questions and explorations. Perhaps interreligious dialogue may throw further light on some of these mysteries." In other words, a theology of religions may flow from interreligious dialogue, rather than being the prerequisite for it.

Source: Michael Amaladoss, "Interreligious Dialogue: A View from Asia," *International Bulletin of Missionary Research*, January 19, 1995: 2-5. (ATLA0000896639)

For us Asian Christians, Hindus, Buddhists, Muslims, and others are part of our life. We share a common culture and way of life. We belong to a common economic and political system. We have a common history. Our religious differences have cultural, political, and even economic implications. In this ongoing dialogue of life we have begun to appreciate the believers of other religions. We respect and read with profit their scriptures and other sacred writings. We learn from their sadhana, methods of prayer, and religious experience. We regard positively their moral conduct. We collaborate with them in the promotion of common human and spiritual values like freedom and justice, love and service. We do not feel superior to them. On the contrary, some mystical, nondualistic traditions in Asia consider our

Christian communities as being at a stage of inferior spiritual development, still busy with rituals and symbols. We are often sought after more for our social and educational services than for our spiritual example or leadership.

At least for some of us, interreligious dialogue is also an interior, personal search for our own religious roots, which we want to rediscover and integrate. . . .

While theologians tend to speak of the religions as systems or as ways of salvation, we prefer to speak of people and of God reaching out to them. Religions do not save; God does. Religions are only expressive mediations of divine-human encounter. What is important is the experiential and personal aspects of this encounter, not the rituals in which it is celebrated and the systems that organize, express, and reflect on it. . . .

One of the starting points of an Asian theology of interreligious dialogue is the acceptance of the reality and legitimacy of other religions as social-symbolic mediations of divine-human encounter. This perception of other religions is based not on an evaluation of them as systems but on the experience of people who practice them and of the action of God in those people as shown by their moral and spiritual action. It is not helpful to isolate and reify the religions as systems in themselves, set apart from this experiential complex. As systems, they are limited expressions; they may have sinful elements too, because they are human expressions. But they are also symbolic mediations of divine action and human response in freedom. . . .

To look at other religions in this manner has consequences for the way we look at our own. Though we speak of the church as pilgrim and think of ourselves as sinful, we tend to think of the church institution itself as somehow escaping all historical and cultural conditioning. We give the impression that inspiration and revelation are used as absolute qualities of the Christian Scriptures, though we accept the need for interpretation. . . . I do not in any way deny or minimize the authenticity and absoluteness of the action of God in and through the social-symbolic structures of the church. I only question the attribution of such authenticity and absoluteness to institutional aspects and practices of the church. . . .

The Second Vatican Council spoke of the church as a sacrament—that is, symbol and servant of communion with God and of unity among all peoples. This is the reality of the reign of God. Starting with this, the Asian theologians speak of the church as the symbol and servant of the reign of God. Sacrament affirms a symbolic and social dimension. It speaks of a real, but a nonexclusive, relationship. The reign of God is larger than the church. This difference between the church and the reign of God makes space for other religions. It gives the church not a dominant but a servant role. The church is not focused on itself but on the reign of God. It does not proclaim itself but Jesus and the reign of God that Jesus himself proclaimed. It welcomes people as disciples of Jesus to continue fulfilling the church's role of service of the reign of God in the world. But its primary aim is building up the reign of God. It builds itself up only in view of its service to the reign. It thus discovers a wider field of service and mission. The church and the reign of God must not be separated, neither should they be confused. The church has its existence and meaning only in the context of the reign of God. The reign of God, in God's plan as we know it, is related to the church, though it transcends it.

One important element of this complex awareness is that the church does not monopolize God's presence and action in the world. . . . God also continues to act in the world, outside the church, in other peoples. Some theologians speak of this as the mission of God. Others talk about the work of the Spirit. Still others suggest the cosmic Christ. . . . The church is called to proclaim the good news revealed to it. But perhaps it should listen first, so that its proclamation may be relevant to the situation and respectful of God's own continuing action there. . . .

. . . Asians tend to use the phrase "reign of God" in a double sense. On the one hand, it indicates the wider reality of God's mystery, not merely eschatologically, but also in history, which serves as a counterpoint to the reality of the church as a visible, institutional community. On the other hand, it refers to the common human community of freedom, fellowship, and justice, toward the building up of which all believers are invited to collaborate. Believers individually find inspiration and motivation for their commitment in their own religion. But they try to develop a common human vision and project through dialogue. Part of this common project is also the harmony among the religions themselves. Some seem to think that an effort at building a common human community is disloyalty to the project of building the church. Is it not possible to promote both the church and the reign of God, neither identifying them nor opposing them one to the other? . . .

Where is Christ in this whole process? The uniqueness of Christ is often presented as a burning issue in the context of dialogue. I think that in Asia the person and role of Christ is not a problem. The real problem is the attempt of the church to monopolize Christ. I have the impression that what is often presented as the question of the uniqueness of Christ is actually the problem of the uniqueness of Christianity. If we do not identify Christ with Christianity, then Christ need not be an obstacle to dialogue between religions. The ghost of the claim "There is no salvation outside the church" often takes new forms in formulas like the "necessity of the church for salvation." The church then becomes the visible part of a mysterious, ahistorical entity, identified as the mystical body of Christ, and every person who is saved becomes an anonymous Christian. To call a believing Hindu an anonymous Christian is offensive, unless one is also ready to be considered an anonymous Hindu. . . . What seems clear to us today is that God's universal salvific will does not depend on the historic-symbolic mediation of the visible, institutional church alone. . . .

We believe in the centrality of the paschal mystery of Christ in God's saving action. But we need not adopt the sacrificial, juridical, and onto-logical theories developed in a different cultural and philosophical context. Considering universality as the universalization of a historical particularity also depends on a particular view of history and its relation to mystery. We also believe that this mystery is linked to the church in a special, but not an exclusive, way, provided this specificity is spelled out not triumphalisti-cally but in terms of kenosis and service. To our traditional questions we may add a new one: How is salvation in Christ mediated to people through other religions or even no religion at all? But the practice of interreligious dialogue need not wait for a clear answer to these questions and explora-tions. Perhaps interreligious dialogue may throw further light on some of these mysteries. . . .

In concluding these reflections, I would like to point to two principles of Asian theology that are relevant to the area of interreligious dialogue. The first is the need to go beyond physical and conceptual categories to personal ones like freedom and relationships. This is the basis for pluralism. Without personal categories, unity in pluralism can be thought of only in terms of hierarchy. I am also wary of easy and neat classifications like exclusivism and inclusivism, theocentric and Christocentric, and so forth. I think that the development in Asia of a theology of harmony is worth pursuing.

The second principle that seems to be guiding Asian theological reflec-tion, consciously or unconsciously, is that of the advaita, or nonduality. The principle of advaita, explained in various ways by the philosophers, tries to hold together two realities that are experienced as neither one nor two. It resists the temptation to solve the problem by identifying them. . . .

The spirit of dialogue is the ability to live with difference, accepting ten-sions but overcoming them through human relationships converging toward harmony. We have to discover today that one of the goals of evangelization is the promotion of reconciliation and harmony in the world in view of God's plan for the unification of all things.

James L. Fredericks

The Catholic theologian James Fredericks has emerged as one of the most important proponents and practitioners of comparative theology. His *Faith among Faiths: Christian Theology and the Non-Christian Religions* (1999) sets out the case for a comparative theology. *Buddhists and Christians: Through Comparative Theology to Solidarity* (2004), excerpted below, offers a rationale for comparative theology, and illustrates the comparative method by placing Thomas Aquinas in conversation with the second-century C.E. Buddhist phi-losopher Nagarjuna.

Fredericks regards comparative theology as a fundamental departure from the theology of religions approach, since it "does not start with a grand theory of religion in general that claims to account for all religions," nor does it "look for some abstract lowest common denominator or essence that all religions, including Christianity, share."[57] Indeed, Fredericks contends that a complete and satisfactory theology of religions is not possible prior to in-depth dialogue with other religions. For one thing, the more Christians learn about other religions, the less plausible those "grand theories" appear. For another, the fact of religious diversity makes it imperative that Christians learn from the real differences in the beliefs and practices of their non-Christian neighbors. By flattening out religious differences to some common core, the theology of religions approach "can be used to inoculate Christians against the power and novelty of other religions traditions."[58]

Comparative theology, on the other hand, begins with both "a commitment to Christian tradition" and "an openness to the truths of non-Christian religions."[59] According to Fredericks, comparative theology is a kind of "doing before knowing": "Instead of using theology as a theoretical basis for dialogue, [Fredericks proposes letting] dialogue be the basis, or praxis, of doing theology." Comparative theology, thus, is "a theology that arises *through* dialogue," "a Christian theology done by means of dialogue with those who follow other religious paths."[60]

The goal is to keep the tensions "creative" in order to achieve "a spiritual transformation of Christian believers."[61] Fredericks argues, "By exploring the truths of Christianity in dialogue with the teachings and traditions of other religious believers, Christians will come to embrace their own cherished beliefs in new ways. In the process, Christianity will be enriched and Christians will forge new bonds of respect and even admiration with their non-Christian neighbors."[62] For example, "The aspects of the [Buddhist] Dharma that differ most starkly from the Gospels may constitute the most valuable truths Buddhists have to teach Christians."[63]

What does a Christian comparative theology look like? Fredericks gives an admittedly limited yet nonetheless helpful illustration of the approach in *Buddhists and Christians*. The approach of Fredericks is characterized by four main features. First, it is self-consciously rooted in the Christian tradition and seeks to serve that tradition.[64] While Fredericks's exercise in comparative theology requires a firm grasp of Buddhist teaching, and thus works to promote understanding between Christians and Buddhists, its goal is to help Christians better understand their own tradition.[65] Second, it attempts to avoid a priori theorizing about the nature of other religions or Christianity's relationship with them. Fredericks does not advance any theory about how Buddhism, for example, is or is not a product of the work of the Holy Spirit, or how Buddhist emptiness reflects the same "Real" to which Christians also witness.

Third, having eschewed grand theories, Fredericks sharply limits the scope of investigation, and (fourth) proceeds by means of comparison and contrast. The exercise in *Buddhists and Christians* compares Nagarjuna's teachings on emptiness with Thomas Aquinas's discussion of the incomprehensibility of God.

Fredericks's work, along with that of his fellow comparative theologians Francis X. Clooney and John P. Keenan, represents a fresh and innovative approach to theological reflection about religious others.[66]

Source: James L. Fredericks, *Buddhists and Christians: Through Comparative Theology to Solidarity* (Maryknoll, NY: Orbis Books, 2004), 25-27, 97, 103-4.

. . . In the twenty-first century Christians need to find an alternative to the entire project of a theology of religions. Preoccupation with a comprehensive interpretation of the other religious paths is neither necessary nor advisable for Christians committed to developing new forms of social and religious solidarity with those who follow other religious paths. Instead of a theology that attempts to account comprehensively for the religious lives of those who follow the other paths, Christians should set for themselves a considerably more modest goal. This will entail a shift from theory to praxis. . . .

. . . Christian theology needs to respond in greater depth to the contemporary turn away from hegemonic and homogenizing discourse like Rahner's notion of a "universal religious experience" underlying all the religions. Especially, there is increased suspicion of grand narratives that purport to explain all and account for all from a perspective that remains unaffected by what is explained. Theologies of religions, including those that measure up to the demands of the Christian tradition, are such grand narratives. This dissatisfaction with grand narratives poses a challenge to Christians. I also believe that it constitutes an opportunity for Christians. . . .

Now attention needs to be shifted from fulfillment theology as theory to inter-religious dialogue as praxis. . . .

. . . Comparative theology is not a theory that provides a foundation for praxis. Rather, the theology being proposed here is a critical reflection on praxis in the light of Christian faith. There has been much discussion in the debate over the theology of religions of the need to find a theoretical "foundation" or "basis" for dialogue. The problems attending theologies of religions make clear how dubious this project is. Instead of using theology as a theoretical basis for dialogue, I propose to let dialogue be the basis, or praxis, of doing theology. Doing theology in dialogue with the others is not an attempt to provide a foundation or rationale *for* dialogue. Rather, what is called for is a theology that arises *through* dialogue. This is not a theology about interreligious dialogue, or a theology that justifies dialogue, but rather Christian theology itself carried out in dialogue with those who follow other religious paths. . . .

Unlike a theology of religions, doing Christian theology comparatively does not hope to establish a comprehensive account, or grand narrative, based solely on Christian faith, in which Buddhism or Islam, Hinduism or Confucianism appear as mere examples of a truth more clearly visible in Christianity. Instead of erecting an encompassing theory, this theology proceeds by means of very limited acts of interpretation rooted in the praxis of dialogue. Instead of distorting the "other" by construing it within a grand narrative, Christian theologians encounter that other as a partner in a dialogue. By critically reflecting on this praxis, the other becomes a resource for Christians in thinking about their faith in new ways. In the process, the Christian community builds new forms of social and religious solidarity with other religious communities.

For example, the great Japanese Pure Land Buddhist teacher Shinran (1173- 1263) is renowned for his understanding of enlightenment as *shinjin*, which is often translated into English as "faith." A theology of religions asks: Is this Buddhist "faith" really the work of the Holy Spirit, despite what Shinran and contemporary Pure Land Buddhists might say about it? A theology rooted in the praxis of dialogue asks a different and more constructive question: How does Shinran's understanding of enlightenment as "faith" help Christians to think in new ways about their own religious lives? For Shinran, *shinjin* does not imply belief in a savior God. Neither is there a notion of a "Spirit" in this Buddhist teaching. Moreover, there is no need for Christians to impose this Christian view on Buddhism. Instead, by means of dialogue with Pure Land Buddhists, Christians may discover both similarities and differences that are theologically challenging. By reflecting on the praxis of dialogue with these Buddhists, Shinran's teaching becomes a theological resource for Christians for renewing and deepening their own understanding of faith. In the process, Buddhists and Christians in Japan will have become related in new forms of social and religious solidarity. . . .

Comparative theologians need to resist the temptation to absolve themselves of this tension between openness to truth and fidelity to a specific tradition. Losing a sense of fidelity to a specific religious tradition indicates that one is no longer engaged in doing theology in the proper sense. Theology is critical reflection on praxis done in service to a specific religious community. . . . On the other hand, losing a sense of the allure of teachings from outside the tradition, or what Francis X. Clooney, SJ, has called "vulnerability to the truth," means that one is no longer doing theology comparatively. By experimenting with the truths of another religious tradition, the comparative theologian is transformed and enriched. . . .

Comparative theology, I have said, is defined by a tension between fidelity to Christian tradition and openness to the teachings of other religious traditions. . . .

. . . [I]n order to become more creatively engaged with the other religions, Christians need to shift their energies from the theory of a grand theological narrative about other religious believers to the praxis of interreligious dialogue. Comparative theology is critical reflection on the praxis of that dialogue. . . .

Interreligious dialogue can be thought of as Christian practice in at least three ways. First, dialogue with other religious believers can become a concrete form of the church's pilgrimage toward the kingdom of God. As a guard against all forms of triumphalism, Christians need to find ways to resist the temptation to equate the church with the kingdom of God. Dialogue with other religious believers is helpful in this regard. Entering into dialogue with a Buddhist should leave a Christian with a deeper sense of Christianity's eschatological incompleteness. . . .

. . . [Second, dialogue] with other religious believers purifies Christian hope of its triumphalism by impressing on the Christian believer a renewed sense of eschatological incompleteness. Buddhist friends of mine have called this aspect of Christian discipleship "hard practice." I think they are correct. Discipleship is the "hard practice" of a life completely oriented to a radically eschatological hope. Dialogue with other religious believers is a helpful way to realize this radical hope and carry out this "hard practice."

There is a third way in which dialogue with other religious believers may be thought of as Christian practice. For Christians, interreligious dialogue is a form of service to the world. . . . Dialogue with other religious believers should be motivated by a great desire for service to the dialogue partner, in keeping with the evangelical commandment to love. Thus, the practice of the church includes not only preaching the good news and ministry to word and sacrament. Christian practice also includes a continuing search for truth and service to the world. Interreligious dialogue should be embraced as an important opportunity for the Christian community to carry out its mission of service in the world.

Notes

1. Clements goes on to cite as exemplars of this approach Søren Kierkegaard, Albrecht Ritschl, Adolf von Harnack, Ernst Troeltsch, Rudolf Bultmann, and Rudolf Otto. See Keith Clements, *Friedrich Schleiermacher: Pioneer of Modern Theology* (San Francisco: Collins, 1987), 36.

2. Friedrich Schleiermacher, *The Christian Faith*, ed. H. R. Macintosh and J. S. Stewart (Edinburgh: T&T Clark, 1999), 42.

3. This is ironic, since as Richard Crouter notes, in the *Speeches* he criticizes the "cultured despisers" of religion for relying on deductive concepts of religion "without having taken the trouble to justify this understanding inductively through knowledge of particular instances of actual religion" (in Friedrich Schleiermacher, *On Religion: Speeches to Its Cultured Despisers*, trans. Richard Crouter (New York: Cambridge University Press, 1988), 88 n. 23. Of course, the present wealth of scholarship in religion studies was not available in Schleiermacher's day.

4. For example, when Schleiermacher refers to "the influence of the sensible upon the character of religious emotions" in Islam, he does not specify what he means, how this influence is manifested, or even where he gets this idea. Furthermore, although he

categorizes Islam as monotheistic, he associates this "influence of the sensible" with polytheism, implying that Islam is tainted by polytheistic elements. Given the Prophet Muhammad's uncompromising assertion of the oneness of God and the Qur'an's vigorous rejection of Arab polytheistic practices, it is difficult to regard Schleiermacher's characterization of Islam as built on anything other than prejudice.

5. Pages 12, 17-18, 26, 31, 33-35, 37-38.

6. Ernst Troeltsch, *Christian Thought, Its History and Application,* trans. Mary E. Clarke (New York: Meridian Books, 1957), 37.

7. Ibid., 38-39.

8. Ibid., 39.

9. Ibid., 42-44, 51.

10. Yet Troeltsch also notes that what is true for Christians "does not cease, because of this, to be very Truth and Life" (Troeltsch, *Christian Thought, Its History and Application*, 63).

11. For example: What is philosophy? What is religion? How do they differ? If they are not religions, why bring them up at all in a discussion of religion(s)? Interestingly, Troeltsch himself refers to Buddhism as a religion later in the talk.

12. These excerpts are from pp. 53-63.

13. Two points should be noted here. First, in the selection below, Barth understands only one revelation—that recognized by the church. In later sections of the *Church Dogmatics* [CD] (IV/3), he refers to "other lights," suggesting other revelations. However, he remains adamant that these only reflect the one (Christian) revelation. Second, Barth does not reduce this "revelation" to the Bible. In *Church Dogmatics* I/1, Barth takes care to distinguish the Word of God from scripture or from church proclamation by speaking of the "threefold form" of the Word: the Word revealed, the Word written, and the Word preached (CD I/1, §4). George Hunsinger comments on this threefold form: "Jesus Christ is viewed by Barth as the truth of the gospel. This truth takes secondary form in the written testimony of the scripture, and tertiary form, so to speak, in the verbal testimony of the church. Neither form of testimony occurs in such a way that the truth of Jesus Christ is simply a semantic feature of those sentences by which this testimony is expressed" (George Hunsinger, *How to Read Karl Barth: The Shape of His Theology* [New York: Oxford University Press, 1991], 171). However, Barth refuses to distance scripture and proclamation too far from the revealed Word: "the verbal form of this testimony is thought to be so indirectly identical with Jesus Christ that he continually discloses himself through it" (171) (Hunsinger cites CD I/1, 88-120).

14. It is true that in his discussion of the Incarnation, Barth links divine Otherness with humanity. Indeed, he later is able to speak of "the humanity of God" and to repent (to some extent) of his earlier tendency to sharply oppose the divine and the human (see his essay "The Humanity of God," in Barth, *Theologian of Freedom,* ed. Clifford Green [Minneapolis, MN: Augsburg Fortress, 1991], 46-66). Nonetheless, his discussions of revelation and religion rest on a fundamental opposition between the divine (revelation) and the human (religion), an opposition rooted in Barth's construal of the *externality* of the divine.

15. In the original German, Barth uses the term *Unglaube,* which translates roughly as "unfaith."

16. Barth admitted as much in his oft-cited response to D. T. Niles: "Karl Barth was asked how he knew that Hinduism was a form of unbelief, given the fact that he had never met a Hindu. . . . Hinduism can be known to be unbelief, according to Barth, a priori" (Fredericks, *Faith among Faiths: Christian Theology and Non-Christian Religions* [Mahwah, NJ: Paulist, 1999], 21). Peter Harrison contends that "religion" is for Barth

purely formal and "devoid of any intrinsic significance": "It serves only as the backdrop against which a positive understanding of revelation—Barth's primary concern—may be projected. As Aagaard rightly observed: 'Religion thus remains for him [Barth] without any connection with actual religions and religious phenomena'" (Peter Harrison, "Karl Barth and the Nonchristian Religions," *Journal of Ecumenical Studies* 23, no. 2 [Spring 1986]: 215).

17. Charles T. Waldrop summarizes Barth's stance as follows: "The Christian religion, with all its concepts and practices, is a creaturely reality, while God is wholly other than anything and everything human" (Charles T. Waldrop, "Karl Barth and Pure Land Buddhism," *Journal of Ecumenical Studies* 24, no. 4 [Fall 1987]: 590).

18. Alan Race and Paul Knitter cite Barth as an example of the exclusivist approach to religious diversity, and many other scholars agree, including Fredericks, *Faith among Faiths*, 16. For a survey of other representatives of this position, see Peter Harrison, "Karl Barth and the Nonchristian Religions," 209). It should be noted, however, that this view is not universally accepted. For an opposing view, see Joseph Di Noia, "Religion and the Religions," in *Cambridge Companion to Karl Barth*, ed. John Webster (New York: Cambridge University Press, 2000), 243-57.

19. As discussed in "New Testament Precedents," above, the witness of the New Testament regarding religious others may be more complex and multivocal than Barth suggests.

20. See David R. Brockman, "Turning to Religious Others: Visions and Blindspots in Modern Christian Reflection about Non-Christians" (Ph.D. diss., Southern Methodist University, 2006), 271-75.

21. The following selections are from pp. 280-81, 294-95, 297-301, 302-3, 314, 325-27, and 344.

22. [Ed.] That is, in Barth's earlier examination of revelation.

23. Since the concept of anonymous Christian turns on whether or not a given person knows or realizes the source of grace and salvation, some readers mistake Rahner's stance for a kind of Gnosticism. It is not. Unlike the Gnostics, Rahner does not claim that salvation comes through special knowledge. Quite the contrary: it comes exclusively through divine grace, whether the recipient knows it or not.

24. Paul F. Knitter, *Introducing Theologies of Religions* (Maryknoll, NY: Orbis Books, 2002), 104. Noting Pope John Paul II's inclusivist call for dialogue with religious others in which Christians can be "'enriched,' 'challenged,' 'transformed,' perhaps even 'converted,'" Knitter puts the question this way: "Just how deep can enrichment or challenge or conversion go when Christians are convinced that in Jesus they have God's full, final, and fulfilling Word?" (103).

25. The following excerpts are from pp. 118-23, 125, 128, and 131-34.

26. [Ed.] Note the similarity to Barth's sense of Christianity as true religion only when it recognizes its own status as unbelief.

27. Hick, "Is Christianity the Only True Religion, or One Among Others?"; http://www.johnhick.org.uk/article2.pdf. Accessed 1 August 2007.

28. The "axial age," a term borrowed from the philosopher Karl Jaspers, occurred between 800 and 200 B.C.E. (Hick dates it to "the first millennium B.C.E."). Under the heading "post-axial faiths" Hick includes Hinduism, Judaism, Buddhism, Christianity, and Islam.

29. John Hick, *An Interpretation of Religion: Human Responses to the Transcendent* (New Haven, CT: Yale University Press, 1989), 240.

30. Ibid., 235-36.

31. In a sense, Hick's noumenal Real is similar to the "Wholly Other" of Karl Barth.

32. Hick, *An Interpretation of Religion*, 300.

33. Ibid., 89.

34. Knitter, for example, argues that Hick's view is in danger of "creeping relativism": "John Hick's 'Real' that hides within all religions is certainly as vague and amorphous as it might be real. It can oblige just about any image of the Divine or of God that the human imagination can come up with. His notion of the 'divine *noumenon*' that is beyond the reach of any of the religious phenomena we encounter in history is so far beyond reach that it can adapt to anything that we might ever encounter. After all, Hick himself can make room in his 'Real' for both personal and impersonal understandings of the Ultimate or for views that claim that this world is real and those that say it exists only in our imagination. Is there any image of the Divine or of the world that Hick's Real could not accommodate?" (Knitter, *Introducing Theologies of Religions*, 162-63).

35. See, for example, chapter 15 of *An Interpretation of Religion*.

36. Paul Knitter takes a similar approach in *One Earth Many Religions* (Maryknoll, NY: Orbis Books, 1995).

37. The following excerpts are from pp. 87-88, 107-10.

38. Pieris uses the term *metacosmic* for "religions that postulate the existence of a transphenomenal Reality immanently operative in the cosmos and soteriologically available within the human person either though agape (redeeming love) or through gnosis (redeeming knowledge)." He includes under this term Judaism and Christianity, as well as monastic forms of Hinduism, Buddhism, and Daoism. Pieris contrasts metacosmic religions with *cosmic* religions, in which he includes tribal or primal religions (Pieris, *An Asian Theology of Liberation* [Maryknoll, NY: Orbis Books, 1988], 54).

39. Joseph-Marie Ndi Okalla, "The Arts of Black Africa and the Project of a Christian Art," *Mission Studies* 12, no. 2 (1995): 277-84. This article also contains a bibliography of Mveng's works.

40. The following excerpts are from pp. 26-29.

41. Mveng refers to the declaration issued by the 1977 congress in Accra, at which the Association Oecuménique des Théologiens Africains (Ecumenical Association of African Theologians) was formed.

42. Interview in *Zion's Herald*, 177, no. 5 (Sept./Oct. 2003): 14.

43. The following excerpts are from pp. 59-61.

44. S. Mark Heim, *The Depth of the Riches: A Trinitarian Theology of Religious Ends* (Grand Rapids, MI: Wm. B. Eerdmans, 2001).

45. Ibid., 3.

46. Ibid., 18.

47. Knitter, *Introducing Theologies of Religions*, 193.

48. Heim, *The Depth of the Riches*, 181.

49. Ibid., 167.

50. Ibid., 184, 185, 181. Two examples illuminate Heim's approach. Buddhism's realization of "emptiness" (*śunyata*) is grounded in one dimension of the life of the Trinity, the *impersonal* flux of the divine life. By contrast, Islam's unswerving affirmation of God "as a free, transcendent, and personal creator over against whom humans stand as responsible individuals and communities" is grounded in the *personal* dimension of the life of the Trinity (Heim, *The Depth of the Riches*, 219, 194-95).

51. "The only truly unique component of the Christian identity is communion [with God and others] in Christ" (Heim, *The Depth of the Riches*, 213). But note also 213-14 n. 3.

52. Ibid., 253.

53. Thus, Heim argues, "A trinitarian perspective can affirm diverse religious ends as real, and the traditions that offer them as valid ways to relation with God. Any of these is preferable to no realized relation with God" (Heim, *The Depth of the Riches*, 181-82).

54. Ibid. Heim's sense of "loss or damnation" is not punitive or retributive, but is analogous to the circles of Hell and Purgatory in Dante's *Divine Comedy*, which he uses as a kind of template authorizing his vision of multiple religious ends (96-117).

55. For example, in his treatment of Hinduism and Islam he writes: "The aim is to indicate how what makes these faiths different from Christianity can be understood as valid in its own terms, and yet how Christians may view those differences as deficits, open to Christian witness, as well as realized relation with God" (ibid., 220).

56. The following excerpts are from pp. 129-30, 144-47, 149, 158, 160-63, and 165-66.

57. Knitter, *Introducing Theologies of Religions*, 173; Fredericks, *Faith among Faiths*, 167-68.

58. Fredericks, *Faith among Faiths*, 166-67.

59. Ibid., 169. This reflects Fredericks's two criteria for evaluating Christian responses to religious diversity. First, they must be responsible to the Christian tradition; second, they must help Christians "live creatively with their non-Christian neighbors" (19-20, 21).

60. James L. Fredericks, *Buddhists and Christians: Through Comparative Theology to Solidarity* (Maryknoll, NY: Orbis Books, 2004), 26.

61. Fredericks, *Faith among Faiths*, 170-71.

62. Ibid., 162.

63. Ibid., 163.

64. Fredericks, *Buddhists and Christians*, 98. Fredericks writes that "The deepest aspiration of comparative theology is a spiritual transformation of Christian believers" (171).

65. For example, Fredericks writes that "By means of this play of similarity and difference, emptiness proved to be of service to Christians as a resource for thinking about God in new ways" (Fredericks, *Buddhists and Christians*, 97).

66. For an appreciation and a critique of comparative theology, see Brockman, "Turning to Religious Others," 99-117.

Readings

Church Documents on Relating
to Religious Others

Roman Catholic Church

The Second Vatican Council (1962-1965), convened under Pope John XXIII and continued after the latter's death during the papacy of Paul VI, marked a new era for Roman Catholics in terms of their self-understanding and understanding of their mission in the world. Moving away from a narrow interpretation of the dictum *extra ecclesiam nulla salus* ("no salvation outside the church") that characterized the Roman Catholic exclusivist stance vis-à-vis others (including Christians outside the Roman Catholic fold) for centuries, the documents of the Council urged Catholics toward an attitude of openness and listening to the world as the field of divine grace and activity. In particular, *Gaudium et Spes* (Pastoral Constitution on the Church in the Modern World),[1] and *Nostra Aetate*, the conciliar document on non-Christian religions,[2] considered a Magna Carta for constructive relations with members of other religious traditions, are of note and are excerpted below. For the full text of these documents, see the Vatican's Web site.

Nostra Aetate *(Second Vatican Council, 1965)*

(2) Throughout history, even to the present day, there is found among different peoples a certain awareness of a hidden power, which lies behind the course of nature and the events of human life. At times there is present even the recognition of a Supreme Being, or still more of a Father. This awareness and recognition results in a way of life that is imbued with religious sense. The religions which are found in more advanced civilizations endeavour by way of well-defined concepts and exact language to answer these questions. So . . . religions which are found throughout the world attempt in their own ways to calm the hearts of men [and women] by outlining a programme of life covering doctrine, moral precepts, and sacred rites.

The Catholic Church rejects nothing that is true and holy in these religions. She regards with sincere reverence those ways of conduct and of life, those precepts and teachings which, though differing in many aspects from the ones she holds and sets forth, nonetheless often reflect a ray of that Truth which enlightens all men [and women]. Indeed, she proclaims, and ever must proclaim Christ "the way, the truth, and the life" (John 14:6), in whom men [and women] may find the fullness of religious life, in whom God has reconciled all things to Himself.

Gaudium et Spes *(Second Vatican Council, 1965)*

(76) With loyalty to the Gospel in the fulfillment of its mission in the world, the Church, whose duty it is to foster and elevate all that is true, all that is good, and all that is beautiful in the human community, consolidates peace among men [and women] for the glory of God.

(92) Our thoughts go out to all who acknowledge God and who preserve the precious religious and human elements in their traditions; it is our hope that frank dialogue will spur us all on to receive the impulses of the Spirit with fidelity and act upon them with alacrity.

For our part, our eagerness for such dialogue, conducted with appropriate discretion and leading to truth by way of love alone, excludes nobody; we would like to include those who respect outstanding human values without realizing who the author of those is, as well as those who oppose the Church and persecute it in various ways. Since God the Father is the beginning and end of all things, we are all called to be brothers [and sisters]; we ought to work together without violence, and without deceit to build up the world in a spirit of genuine peace.

Redemptoris Missio *(Encyclical of John Paul II, 1990)*[3]

John Paul II's papacy is marked by bold steps in interreligious ventures. This encyclical is only one among many official documents issued during his tenure which offer a glimpse of the manifold ways he reached out toward peoples of other faith traditions, informed by a deeply spiritual sensitivity to the demands of the Christian gospel.[4]

Dialogue with Our Brothers and Sisters of Other Religions

55. Inter-religious dialogue is a part of the Church's evangelizing mission. Understood as a method and means of mutual knowledge and enrichment, dialogue is not in opposition to the mission *ad gentes*; indeed, it has special links with that mission and is one of its expressions. This mission, in fact, is addressed to those who do not know Christ and his Gospel, and who belong for the most part to other religions. In Christ, God calls all peoples to himself and he wishes to share with them the fullness of his revelation and love. He does not fail to make himself present in many ways, not only to individuals but also to entire peoples through their spiritual riches, of which their religions are the main and essential expression, even when they contain

"gaps, insufficiencies and errors." All of this has been given ample emphasis by the Council and the subsequent Magisterium, without detracting in any way from the fact that *salvation comes from Christ and that dialogue does not dispense from evangelization.*

In the light of the economy of salvation, the Church sees no conflict between proclaiming Christ and engaging in interreligious dialogue. Instead, she feels the need to link the two in the context of her mission *ad gentes.* These two elements must maintain both their intimate connection and their distinctiveness; therefore they should not be confused, manipulated or regarded as identical, as though they were interchangeable.

I recently wrote to the bishops of Asia: "Although the Church gladly acknowledges whatever is true and holy in the religious traditions of Buddhism, Hinduism and Islam as a reflection of that truth which enlightens all people, this does not lessen her duty and resolve to proclaim without fail Jesus Christ who is 'the way, and the truth and the life.' . . . The fact that the followers of other religions can receive God's grace and be saved by Christ apart from the ordinary means which he has established does not thereby cancel the call to faith and baptism which God wills for all people." Indeed Christ himself "while expressly insisting on the need for faith and baptism, at the same time confirmed *the need for the Church*, into which people enter through Baptism as through a door." Dialogue should be conducted and implemented with the conviction that *the Church is the ordinary means of salvation* and that *she alone* possesses the fullness of the means of salvation.

56. Dialogue does not originate from tactical concerns or self-interest, but is an activity with its own guiding principles, requirements and dignity. It is demanded by deep respect for everything that has been brought about in human beings by the Spirit who blows where he wills. Through dialogue, the Church seeks to uncover the "seeds of the Word," a "ray of that truth which enlightens all men"; these are found in individuals and in the religious traditions of mankind. Dialogue is based on hope and love, and will bear fruit in the Spirit. Other religions constitute a positive challenge for the Church: they stimulate her both to discover and acknowledge the signs of Christ's presence and of the working of the Spirit, as well as to examine more deeply her own identity and to bear witness to the fullness of Revelation which she has received for the good of all.

This gives rise to the spirit which must enliven dialogue in the context of mission. Those engaged in this dialogue must be consistent with their own religious traditions and convictions, and be open to understanding those of the other party without pretense or close-mindedness, but with truth, humility and frankness, knowing that dialogue can enrich each side. There must be no abandonment of principles nor false irenicism, but instead a witness given and received for mutual advancement on the road of religious inquiry and experience, and at the same time for the elimination of prejudice, intolerance and misunderstandings. Dialogue leads to inner purification and conversion which, if pursued with docility to the Holy Spirit, will be spiritually fruitful.

57. A vast field lies open to dialogue, which can assume many forms and expressions: from exchanges between experts in religious traditions or official representatives of those traditions to cooperation for integral development and the safeguarding of religious values; and from a sharing of their respective spiritual experiences to the so-called "dialogue of life," through which believers of different religions bear witness before each other in daily life to their own human and spiritual values, and help each other to live according to those values in order to build a more just and fraternal society.

Each member of the faithful and all Christian communities are called to practice dialogue, although not always to the same degree or in the same way. The contribution of the laity is indispensable in this area, for they "can favor the relations which ought to be established with the followers of various religions through their example in the situations in which they live and in their activities." Some of them also will be able to make a contribution through research and study.

I am well aware that many missionaries and Christian communities find in the difficult and often misunderstood path of dialogue their only way of bearing sincere witness to Christ and offering generous service to others. I wish to encourage them to persevere with faith and love, even in places where their efforts are not well received. Dialogue is a path toward the kingdom and will certainly bear fruit, even if the times and seasons are known only to the Father (cf. Acts 1:7).

World Council of Churches

The World Council of Churches, which brings together 349 churches, denominations, and church fellowships active in more than 110 countries, representing roughly 560 million Christians, has, for several decades, taken many initiatives and has encouraged its members to engage in interreligious dialogue and cooperation with people of other faith traditions. The document below, promulgated in 1979 following a meeting in Chiang Mai, Thailand, set the tone for the WCC's subsequent stance on the matter, reaffirmed again and again at its periodic Assemblies and other official gatherings.

Guidelines on Dialogue with People of Living Faiths and Ideologies (1979)[5]

18. Dialogue, therefore, is a fundamental part of Christian service within community. In dialogue Christians actively respond to the command to "love God and your neighbour as yourself." As an expression of love engagement in dialogue testifies to the love experienced in Christ. It is a joyful affirmation of life against chaos, and a participation with all who are allies of life in seeking the provisional goals of a better human community. Thus "dialogue in community" is not a secret weapon in the armoury of an aggressive Christian militancy. Rather it is a means of living our faith in Christ in service of community with one's neighbours.

19. In this sense dialogue has a distinctive and rightful place within Christian life, in a manner directly comparable to other forms of service. But "distinctive" does not mean totally different or separate. In dialogue Christians seek "to speak the truth in a spirit of love," not naively "to be tossed to and fro, and be carried about with every wind of doctrine" (Eph. 4.14-15). In giving their witness they recognize that in most circumstances today the spirit of dialogue is necessary. For this reason we do not see dialogue and the giving of witness as standing in any contradiction to one another. Indeed, as Christians enter dialogue with their commitment to Jesus Christ, time and again the relationship of dialogue gives opportunity for authentic witness. Thus, to the member churches of the WCC we feel able with integrity to commend the way of dialogue as one in which Jesus Christ can be confessed in the world today; at the same time we feel able with integrity to assure our partners in dialogue that we come not as manipulators but as genuine fellow-pilgrims, to speak with them of what we believe God to have done in Jesus Christ who has gone before us, but whom we seek to meet anew in dialogue.

20. Christians engaged in faithful "dialogue in community" with people of other faiths and ideologies cannot avoid asking themselves penetrating questions about the place of these people in the activity of God in history. They ask these questions not in theory, but in terms of what God may be doing in the lives of hundreds of millions of men and women who live in and seek community together with Christians, but along different ways. So dialogue should proceed in terms of people of other faiths and ideologies rather than of theoretical, impersonal systems. This is not to deny the importance of religious traditions and their inter-relationships but it is vital to examine how faiths and ideologies have given direction to the daily living of individuals and groups and actually affect dialogue on both sides.

29. In a world in which Christians have many neighbours, dialogue is not only an activity of meetings and conferences, it is also a way of living out Christian faith in relationship and commitment to those neighbours with whom Christians share towns, cities, nations, and the earth as a whole. Dialogue is a style of living in relationship with neighbours. This in no way replaces or limits our Christian obligation to witness, as partners enter into dialogue with their respective commitments. . . .

. . . In many places people of different living faiths interact not only with each other, but also with people of various ideologies, though sometimes it is difficult to make a clearcut distinction between religions and ideologies, for there are religious dimensions of ideologies and ideological dimensions of religions, Christianity included. The emergence of new religious groups in many countries has brought new dimensions and tensions to inter-religious relationships. With all this diversity in mind, the following guidelines are commended to member churches for their consideration and discussion, testing and evaluation, and for their elaboration in each specific situation.

1. *Churches should seek ways in which Christian communities can enter into dialogue with their neighbours of different faiths and ideologies.*

2. *Dialogues should normally be planned together.*

3. *Partners in dialogue should take stock of the religious, cultural and ideological diversity of their local situation.*

4. *Partners in dialogue should be free to "define themselves."*

5. *Dialogue should generate educational efforts in the community.*

6. *Dialogue is most vital when its participants actually share their lives together.*

7. *Dialogue should be pursued by sharing in common enterprises in community.*

8. *Partners in dialogue should be aware of their ideological commitments.*

9. *Partners in dialogue should be aware of cultural loyalties.*

10. *Dialogue will raise the question of sharing in celebrations, rituals, worship and meditation.*

11. *Dialogue should be planned and undertaken ecumenically, wherever possible.*

12. *Planning for dialogue will necessitate regional and local guidelines.*

13. *Dialogue can be helped by selective participation in world interreligious meetings and organizations.*

Joint Statement by the Federation of Asian Bishops' Conferences and Christian Conference of Asia (1987)

Asia, as a region marked by a wide diversity of religious traditions since ancient times, is an area where Christian leaders have been particularly sensitive to the tasks of interacting with their neighbors from other religious traditions. The following is a statement endorsed by both the Roman Catholic Bishops' representatives and the WCC-related Christian Conference of Asia, who gathered together in Singapore in 1987 for a consultation on collaborating with people of other faiths, which offers pastoral recommendations for interreligious tasks.[6]

... The urgent need to seek new relationships with neighbors of other religious traditions brought together representatives of the member churches of the Christian Conference of Asia (CCA) and of the member conferences of the Federation of Asian Bishops' Conferences (FABC) to consider the theme "Living and Working Together with Sisters and Brothers of Other Faiths in Asia." The first such CCA/FABC initiative, this gathering involved fifty-five participants from fourteen countries. All were conscious of the significance of this historic event, giving thanks to God for his gift in Jesus Christ who brought them together. Many insights emerged from our common deliberations. From them we highlight a few which we believe to be particularly significant for our churches.

1. Asia's dominant reality is, on the one hand, the massive presence of diverse religious traditions and ideologies, and, on the other, its widespread poverty and political oppression. Further, with the increasing politicalization of religions and the frequent clashes between religious communities, there is an increasing awareness that peace within and between nations is not possible without peace between religions. Conscious of their respective spiritual resources, people of all traditions share a responsibility to work for a new society (2 Cor. 5:17). In such a context, dialogue becomes an urgent priority for the churches.

2. Dialogue, then, is not primarily a matter of talking. It is, in the first instance, an attitude, an openness to the neighbor, a sharing of spiritual resources as people stand before the great crises of life and death, as they struggle for justice and human dignity, as they yearn for peace (John 14:27). In this, Christians have a contribution to make. In dialogue, Christians and their neighbors enter into a reciprocal relationship which becomes a process of mutual learning and growth.

3. We enter into such relationships of dialogue on the basis of our faith in God through Jesus Christ, conscious that the Holy Spirit is guiding us toward an enrichment of human life and deeper appreciation of truth. This faith gives us our identity as Christians and empowers us to share with the neighbors our faith and vision, our words and silence.

4. As "mission," "evangelism" and "evangelization" have different nuances for Christians of different traditions, so too has the relation between dialogue and mission. However, we affirm that dialogue and mission have their own integrity and freedom. They are distinct but not unrelated. Dialogue is not a tool or instrument for mission and evangelization, but it does influence the way the church perceives and practices mission in a pluralistic world. Mission invites us to participate in God's continuing activity through the Spirit to mend a broken creation, to overcome the fragmentation of humanity and to heal the rift between nature, humanity, and God. God's recreating activity is prior to and more comprehensive than the church's mission, and it directs our attention beyond the church to the Kingdom.

5. Dialogue offers opportunities for Christian witness. Christians, while sharing insights from their faith, will be attentive to the insights of sisters and brothers of other religious traditions. Thus, the way is open for mutual criticism and mutual enrichment among all those who bring a religious perspective to the human quest. All life has a pilgrim character, and neighbors of other religious traditions are our fellow pilgrims on the way. In humanity's shared pilgrimage, the church is called to be an effective sign and symbol of the Kingdom of God. Dialogue is a lifestyle, which can be learned only by doing. At the same time interreligious dialogue has theological underpinnings.

The following pastoral recommendations are made:

i. It is important that persons in leadership positions in the churches take the theological understanding of, and participation in, interreligious dialogue seriously.

ii. The theological basis of interreligious dialogue and courses on religions outside Christianity should be included and strengthened in the curriculum of the seminaries and other houses of formation. Not only seminarians but bishops and clergy as well as lay people should at this point be given opportunities to update themselves.

iii. Christian institutions like schools and hospitals could become centers for interreligious dialogue, not for the sake of evangelism, but within an enlarged theological-religious framework. The public schools, too, in some areas, could become places where interreligious understanding may be furthered.

iv. A commission on interreligious relations could be established or activated at the local, regional, and national levels to work alongside other religious bodies so as to foster interreligious understanding and cooperation. Insofar as possible, these efforts should be carried out in an ecumenical spirit.

v. Christian groups (youth, women, and men) and their counterparts in other religions should be encouraged to visit one another, cooperate in community development, and participate in people's movements for human rights issues and promotion of justice and (dialogue of life).

vi. Interreligious gatherings for prayers and meditation on important national and international days, as well as occasions of religious festivals, should be encouraged.

vii. Guidelines for interreligious dialogue (such as those which have been prepared by CCA and FABC, and other national and international Christian bodies) should be widely distributed, studied and used, revised and adapted if necessary.

viii. Careful thought should be given by the proper religious authorities to the pastoral problems of mixed religious marriages and funeral services for a multireligious family.

ix. Attention should be given through the appropriate channels to the religious phenomena of fundamentalism and fanaticism.

x. The mass media should be used to promote interreligious understanding and harmony.

Ecumenical Resources for Interreligious Ministry

Many mainline churches, denominations, and institutions have taken steps to partner and share resources on different aspects of church life, including interreligious dialogue and cooperation. Among these include the Evangelical Lutheran Church of America, the Episcopal Church, the United Methodist Church, the Presbyterian Church (USA), the United Church of Christ, the Alliance of Baptists, Christian Churches (Disciples of Christ), the Church of God, the Society of

Friends, the Mennonite Central Committee, the Reformed Church of America, the National Council for the Churches of Christ, and the Society for Pentecostal Studies. Their documents reflect the particular ways in which their communities approach the question of relating to the religious others in our midst, based on their own spiritual heritage and specific charisma.[7]

Below are two selected examples of two mainline churches that have set clear guidelines on engaging members of other traditions in the spirit of mutual respect, dialogue, and cooperation.

United Methodist Church

Resolution #3142, *The Book of Resolutions*, 2008 (Nashville: United Methodist Publishing House, 2008), 280-89.

> "Dialogue" is the word which has come to signify an approach to persons of other faith communities which takes seriously both the call to witness and the command to love and be neighbors. To be engaged in dialogue is to see witnessing and neighborliness as interrelated activities. Rather than a one-sided address, dialogue combines witnessing with listening. It is the intentional engagement with persons who hold other faith perspectives for purposes of mutual understanding, cooperation, and transformation.
>
> "Dialogue" may be as informal as a conversation in the marketplace or as formal as the leader of one religious group explaining to others its belief or worship life. Dialogue is more than an individual or academic enterprise. It also involves groups or communities of people holding different convictions who reach out to one another. This community orientation gives a practical bent to interreligious dialogue.
>
> In dialogue, one individual or group may seek relationship with another in order to expose misunderstandings and stereotypes and to break down barriers that separate and create hostility and conflict. Ethnic or religious communities may approach each other in dialogue in order to resolve particular problems or to foster cooperation in dealing with a local, national, or even global situation of human suffering. At its deepest level, dialogue is both learning about and sharing our faith through its stories and images. Each partner learns from the rich store of wisdom of the other, and each expresses his or her own deepest conviction in the faith that it has truth worth sharing with the other.
>
> Through dialogue with persons of other faith communities, new insights are received regarding God's activity in the world today, the divine purpose for humankind as a whole, and the place of the Christian community within these purposes. It is also a common experience for Christians to feel the need to express their own faith with greater clarity. We trust in the Holy Spirit to make known new and different insights through such encounters.

Episcopal Church of the United States of America

Following up on the Lambeth Conference of 1988, a gathering of Anglican bishops and ecumenical partners, which encouraged "dialogue with people of other faiths as part of Christian discipleship and mission, with the understanding that . . . dialogue depends upon mutual understanding, mutual respect and mutual trust," the Episcopal Church of the United States endorsed this statement at its 76th General Convention in 2009.

Statement on Interreligious Relations

> We affirm the foundational Gospel proclamation that "Jesus is Lord" (1 Corinthians 12:3 NRSV here and hereafter) and therefore [Jesus'] Summary of God's Law: "love the Lord your God with all your hearts, with all your souls, and with all your minds, and to love your neighbor as yourself" (Mark 12:29-31; BCP, Catechism, page 851). For this reason we reach out in love and genuine openness to know and to understand those of other religions.
>
> Therefore, we commend to all our members: dialogue for building relationships, the sharing of information, religious education, and celebration with people of other religions as part of Christian life,
>
> 1. dialogue begins when people meet each other
> 2. dialogue depends upon mutual understanding, mutual respect and mutual trust
> 3. dialogue makes it possible to share in service to the community
> 4. dialogue is a medium of authentic witness by all parties and not an opportunity for proselytizing.
>
> We believe that such dialogue may be a contribution toward helping people of different religions grow in mutual understanding and making common cause in peacemaking, social justice, and religious liberty. . . .
>
> 27. Professing salvation in Christ is not a matter of competing with other religious traditions with the imperative of converting one another. Each tradition brings its own understanding of the goal of human life to the interreligious conversation. Christians bring their particular profession of confidence in God's intentions as they are seen in and through the incarnation, death and resurrection of Jesus Christ. . . .
>
> 28. Claiming Jesus as the Way . . . requires us to "respect the dignity of every human being" (BCP, p. 305). This grounds our expectation that we shall discover new insights and develop new relationships through interreligious dialogue. In mutual encounters and shared ascetic, devotional, ethical, and prophetic witness, we dare to hope that God will reveal new and enriching glimpses of a reconciled humanity.

Notes

1. http://www.vatican.va/archive/hist_councils/ii_vatican_council/documents/vat-ii_cons_19651207_gaudium-et-spes_en.html.

2. http://www.vatican.va/archive/hist_councils/ii_vatican_council/documents/vat-ii_decl_19651028_nostra-aetate_en.html.

3. For full text, see http://www.vatican.va/holy_father/john_paul_ii/encyclicals/documents/hf_jp-ii_enc_07121990_redemptoris-missio_en.html.

4. See Byron L. Sherwin and Harold Kasimov, eds., *John Paul II and Interreligious Dialogue* (Maryknoll, NY: Orbis Books, 1999).

5. http://www.oikoumene.org/en/resources/documents/.

6. This statement is reprinted in Don Pittman, Ruben L. F. Habito and Terry Muck, eds., *Ministry and Theology in Global Perspective: Contemporary Challenges for the Church* (Grand Rapids: Wm. Eerdmans, 1996), 503-5.

7. See the Web site of the Evangelical Lutheran Churches of America, which includes a list of the Ecumenical Partners for Interreligious Dialogue, also giving access to their documentation: http://www.elca.org/Who-We-Are/Our-Three-Expressions/Churchwide Organization/Ecumenical-and-Inter-Religious-Relations/Inter-Religious-Relations/Resources-and-Organizations.aspx.

PART II

Christian Ministry, Theology, and Spirituality in Interfaith Dialogue

Introduction

RUBEN L. F. HABITO

THE FIRST PART OF THIS VOLUME FOCUSED ON CHRISTIAN ATTITUDES toward religious others in the light of the Gospel, in the context of our global community marked by severe woundedness on many levels, and wherein religious differences have contributed to the aggravation of this woundedness. Amidst the variety of Christian theological perspectives and differing angles in approaching the matter, there is an underlying consensus that emerges from the voices heard, whether it be that of individual thinkers or of official church bodies. This involves an affirmation of two poles that seem to be in mutual tension. First, Christians are called to a firm commitment to their own faith tradition, centered on living the Good News in their own lives and also accepting the mandate to witness to it and share it with all people. Second, Christians are called to relate to their neighbors (read: people of other religious communities and traditions, and also people who reject religion altogether) with mutual respect and love, as prospective allies in our shared task of healing our Earth. This latter affirmation not only entails accepting religious others *as* other, but also seeking to understand them as they understand themselves, that is, learning *about* them, learning *from* them, learning *with* them.

What happens when Christians committed to their faith and to the gospel interact with people of other religions also committed to their own respective traditions, in a spirit of respect, mutual learning, and cooperation? The essays in this latter section of this volume offer glimpses based on testimonies and reflections of Christians who have engaged in such interreligious interaction.

We can map out three areas in this regard. One relates to renewed perspectives and initiatives in Christian mission and ministry. A second area has to do with fresh directions for theological reflection on key doctrinal, liturgical, and practical issues in Christian faith. A third area relates to reinvigorated initiatives and new horizons in spiritual practice and Christian life.

Andrew Wingate's "Mission as Dialogue: A Contextual Study from Leicester, UK" is an excellent account of various initiatives and renewed perspectives in Christian mission and ministry taken on by a local church congregation, spurred by the influx and ongoing presence of people of other faiths in the same local community. It may hopefully inspire local pastors and congregants and inform them of what they may also take up in their own churches given their own resources.

Jeanne Matthews Sommers's "Jesus Loves Me, This I Know, for the Buddha Tells Me So" describes one kind of Christian response to a Buddhist challenge by someone entrusted with educating youth. Teaching at a college founded by Christian missionaries in the Appalachian region of the United States, Sommers gives an account of how a visit by Ajarn Sulak Sivaraksa, a prominent lay Buddhist from Siam (Thailand), challenged the students and the faculty to examine the ills of their own North American consumeristic society, and, while learning from Buddhist approaches, also to turn to their own root Christian tradition for ways to address the situation and work together toward transforming society in the practice of justice and compassion.

The essay by Joseph Stamer considers the question "Can Christians and Muslims Pray Together?" Noting reservations and expressions from both sides of the divide, and also outlining points of caution and consideration, the author suggests possible ways Christians and Muslims might be able to bridge the divide and find some precious though limited ground to share in worshipping the one God who is creator of all the Earth.

The next set of essays focuses on Christian theological themes that can be seen in new light through the encounter with other traditions.

Timothy Tennent's "Trinity and Saccidananda in the Writings of Brahmabandhav Upadhyaya" is a carefully crafted piece on how Hindu scriptural accounts, notably Upanishadic texts, can open to Christian theologians some unexplored horizons in considering the basic Christian doctrine of the trinitarian God. This kind of theological endeavor is especially significant in presenting the Christian message in the context of a culture wherein the working concepts and worldviews of the people are informed by the spiritual riches of the Hindu tradition, a cultural context which differs in many respects from the Graeco-Roman and medieval European culture that served as the matrix for key formulations of Christian doctrine.

John Keenan's "Mahayana Theology of the Real Presence of Christ" is a particularly illuminating essay that throws fresh light on a hallowed Christian doctrine that has sparked controversy and caused division among Christians for centuries. Keenan begins by describing how the term "transubstantiation," taken by the Roman Catholic Church in its official statements, is based on a conceptual framework that assumes the Aristotelian notion of "substance," and thereby is no longer theologically adequate to convey the significance and import of the doctrine that Christ is "truly present" in the Eucharist, especially for those with a worldview wherein the Aristotelian category of "substance" is no longer operative. Keenan goes on to explore the Mahayana Buddhist notions of "non-self" and "interdependent arising," and, taking a cue from these notions, suggests a coherent, meaningful, and also inspiring and empowering theological expression for this hallowed Christian belief. In his excursion into Buddhist modes of thinking, he opens the way for possibly overcoming the lines of division that have separated Christians and prevented them from sharing the Lord's table through the ages.

Addressing in particular the adherents of the world's religions, Paul Knitter, in "A Common Creation Story? Interreligious Dialogue and Ecology," considers a theme of tremendous import for all of us as inhabitants of this endangered Earth. Of late, more and more Christian theologians are coming to see the importance and seeking to unpack the implications of the ecological dimension of the Christian gospel message. A dialogue between science and religion becomes imperative in this regard. (See the supplementary bibliography at the end of the essay.) Knitter pursues this multilayered theme in the context of an ecumenical dialogue not only among Christians but, more significantly, among members of the world's religions who seek ways of harnessing the resources of their respective traditions toward our common task of healing Earth's wounds.

Amos Yong's "Toward a Pneumatological Theology of Religions" is taken from the concluding chapter of his book on the same theme. Yong argues for a contextualization of the Christian message in a way that people whose worldviews are shaped by the world's religions, including the Buddhist, Hindu, Muslim, Taoist, Confucian, indigenous, and other traditions, would, taking their own cultural and religious values into account, find affinity with the gospel message. An important task for Christians especially in our globalized and religiously pluralistic society is to be able to present the gospel message in terms that people from other faith communities are able to understand and resonate with, in the light of the values and perspectives cherished in their own traditions. This means that precisely in order to be true to the mission of witnessing to the gospel to all peoples in an adequate and effective way, it is imperative for Christians to have solid knowledge and understanding of the different faith traditions that inform the values and perspectives of people around them.

The essays in the last section give readers a prospectus of new horizons in spirituality forged in an encounter with other religious traditions.

James L. Fredericks's "Masao Abe: A Spiritual Friendship" is an insightful and inspiring account of how his own Christian faith and understanding came to be deepened in and through his lifelong friendship with a Japanese Buddhist philosopher well-known in Western circles, and endearingly called "Mr. Sunyata (Emptiness)," because of his work elaborating on this central Mahayana Buddhist notion in dialogue with Western philosophical and religious concepts.

Frances Adeney, guided by a Catholic priest trained by a Buddhist master, shares her own experience of engaging in contemplative practice and describes the profound enrichment for her own Christian praxis, spiritual life, and vision.

Maria Reis Habito goes a step beyond the previous authors, and relates some highlights of her own spiritual journey in her essay "Bridging the World Religions: On Being a Buddhist-Christian Woman." Reis Habito's account may shed light on a question being posed by more and more individuals living in our multireligious world: Can one profess adherence and commitment to more than one religious tradition at the same time? Her essay is not a theoretical and systematic response to the question, but a very personal testimonial of what can happen when a committed Christian opens oneself to the riches of the Buddhist tradition.

These essays in part II are not necessarily to be taken as models to be followed by others, nor do they presume to provide any definitive answers. They are simply presented here as indications of new avenues and pathways forged by those who have wrestled with questions relating to how Christians are called to live out the implications of the Gospel as they engage with their neighbors in our multireligious world.

The epilogue is a short piece by Yossi Klein Halevi, published in the *New York Times* barely one month before the tragic events of September 11, 2001. It can be read as a testament of hope and an earnest invitation for all of us to go beyond our own comfort zones and venture to cross traditional boundaries that separate us from the religious other, to find common ground that we can share, as we open ourselves together to the presence of the Holy in our midst.

Readings

Ministry in Interfaith Settings

Mission as Dialogue:
A Contextual Study from Leicester, UK

*Andrew Wingate**

THE CONCEPT OF "DIALOGUE" HAS ENTERED OUR MISSION vocabulary comparatively recently. When I studied theology in England in the early 1970s, it was a word that never entered our minds. Nor did the presence of vast numbers of Muslims, Hindus, and Buddhists in our world. There was an awareness of Jews, largely because of the Holocaust. What was to the fore was Marxism, with the cold war at its height. Yet at the same time, large numbers of Indians, Pakistanis, and others were arriving in Britain. They were known as "immigrants," though they were taking up work that local people were not willing to do. They were not known as Muslims, Hindus, or Sikhs, and they worshipped behind closed doors in converted houses or factories.

"Dialogue," meanwhile, had been taking place in the Asian sub-continent for centuries. An excellent study by Kenneth Cracknell, *Justice, Courtesy and Love*,[1] shows how leading British missionaries in the nineteenth century were changed, as they encountered Hinduism and Buddhism in India and China. Great figures of mission history like Henry Martyn, and in the twentieth century, Kenneth Cragg[2], George Appleton, and David Brown, were key figures in the transformation of attitudes toward Islam, as they communicated its spirituality. The increasing influence of South Asians at the WCC led to the 'official' discovery of dialogue, with a dedicated desk established in the 1970s. Perhaps more important was Vatican II, and its document *Nostra Aetate,* which, at a stroke, revolutionised attitudes in the largest church in the world, from a strict Catholic exclusivism, to a generally accepted Catholic form of inclusivism.

---

* The author is advisor in Inter-Faith Relations to the bishop of Leicester, and canon theologian and director of the St. Philip's Centre for Theology and Ministry in a Multi-Faith Society. His publications include *Celebrating Difference, Staying Faithful: How to Live in a Multifaith World* (London: Darton, Longman & Todd, 2005).

I will be looking here at the contemporary situation in Britain, and considering how understanding of dialogue matches local experience, and how local experience helps to mould that understanding. Though I am writing about Britain, much is common to Scandinavia and the rest of Europe. Overall, I will want to show that "dialogue" is not something "wishy-washy" and vague, nor a betrayal of Christian faith. Rather it is an adventure full of vigour, where Christian faith can be affirmed as well as much learnt from the other faiths. Moreover, it is vital for the future of our increasingly multi-religious continent, now excitingly linked together in an expanded European Union.

DIALOGUE, INFORMAL AND INTENTIONAL

Dialogue begins when people meet people. This may happen by chance or by intention. All kinds of interfaith conversations happen in an entirely informal context, between neighbours, friends, work colleagues, fellow students, and so on. These are the most natural of experiences, and can quite transform attitudes. An elderly Christian told me recently that it was through talking regularly to her Muslim neighbour, Mrs. Ahmed, that she had come to the conclusion that there is much more in common between religious persons from different faiths, than there is between a Christian and a person of no faith, even if of the same culture.

This is the kind of transformation illustrated by Jesus' encounter with the Samaritan woman in John 4. By going to her place, the well of Jacob, and by asking something of her, water, Jesus opened up a dialogue across faith, as well as across gender and caste. The result was that she gained living water, and he expressed a new truth, that God is Spirit, and those who worship should worship in Spirit and in Truth. The location, whether Mount Gerizim or the temple in Jerusalem, does not matter. This story is an outstanding biblical example of dialogue in practice, with respect, directness, and expectation from both sides.

However, there are contexts when sustained interfaith dialogue can best be organised through a group encounter. This nearly always, at least at the local level, comes out of a prior friendship between at least two persons from two faiths. Such a friendship will have taken time to develop, and trust will already have been established. Clarity will also be needed about intentions that neither party is attempting to convert the other. This question may be best directly confronted. My Muslim Imam dialogue partner in Leicester was very happy to clarify this issue. He wrote an article on how he saw dialogue, for the Diocesan magazine. He included the statement, "I would like Andrew to become a Muslim, and I am sure he would like me to become a Christian. Both are highly unlikely. Acknowledging this, we talk and work together for a more understanding society."

It may be helpful to make such a statement to a new group, to reassure those who attend. Probably it is better to leave this implicit, provided the leaders are seen to be acting within this spirit. If anyone tries to use the group for proselytising, such a person should be politely confronted. If the group includes Hindus, this needs special care. Hindus have deep suspicions of Christian mission. Not normally being missionary themselves, they feel vulnerable. They will need special reassurance that this is not "the same old Christian missionary thing." The same applies with Jews, who have suffered enormously from Christians in the past. Their present fears include anxiety about Christian mission. Their numbers are dropping because of other factors, especially marrying out, and they have an understandable fear of Christian movements, which target them.

There is often a pressure to establish aims for a group before things start. What will it achieve? Such an exercise should probably be resisted. The group itself will work that out implicitly or explicitly as it progresses. There needs to be a degree of open-endedness. The members will themselves decide whether something useful is being achieved or not. If it is not, the group may die. This should not be seen as a disaster or failure. If people from two faiths have met for a time, and learnt from each other, then that is an achievement, and there may be a ripple effect of which we may never know the extent. Aims, too, may change as time passes. We should hope there will be surprises; Christians may centre their thinking on the Spirit, who blows where the Spirit wills, as we are led into all truth. What is essential is persistence. Understanding takes time to develop. Frustrations will come, and probably misunderstandings. But if there is an underlying commitment, then transformation may come to all concerned in different ways. . . .

I will outline here experiences with the several different groups that I am involved in. They are only examples, and the reader must consider their own context and what may be possible. If they live in a large city, these kinds of programmes may seem easier to achieve. But there are significant centres in many places less obvious than Leicester or Birmingham or Bradford or London. Hindu and Buddhist communities often exist in rural or suburban areas, and they may very well welcome contact and dialogue. Numbers need not be large. A few committed people can start a useful conversation. There are also wider groups, not locally based, such as one of my examples here.

THE CONTEXT OF LEICESTER

Leicester is a city of 289,000 people, 100 miles from London. It has become the most multi-religious city in Britain, outside London. The census of 2001 showed that 36 percent are of black or Asian background, and by far the majority of these people are of Indian descent, either direct from India, or via East Africa. The proportion of white children in city schools was only 51 percent in 2001, and probably is now a minority, with the younger populations from within Asian and Black communities. More than 14 percent of the population is Hindu, and 11 percent Muslim. Hindu numbers are declining as the more affluent move outside the city. Muslim numbers are certainly underestimated . . . with the large numbers (probably about 8,000) of recent immigrants from Somalia, and the many asylum seekers. Those affirming they are Christians are 44 percent.

On the whole, the Leicester social situation has been stable in recent years, with a strong sense of pride in the multicultural dimensions of the city, and a high level of expectation, in terms of education. Most are employed, though wages are not of the highest. There has been a Council of Faiths since the mid-1980s, and Faith Leaders' Meetings for the last three years. There is increasing faith involvement in the regeneration of the city, with a young Muslim employed as Faiths Regeneration Officer, with half his salary from church sources, and working from the Diocesan offices.[3] A recent national report stressed the importance of dialogue/friendship groups. Leicester is highlighted there.[4] I outline here these groups.

The Leicester Muslim-Christian Dialogue Groups

I came to Leicester from Birmingham in May 2000. I had been involved in Muslim-Christian dialogue for many years, and had written a book based on our experiences.[5] I met with local Muslims much influenced by Sufism, and involved theological students whom I was teaching. We decided to live in Leicester within an area largely Muslim, and I have special responsibility for relations between Christians and people of other faiths across the city. I am a priest at St. Philip's Church, which is a small Christian community, largely elderly, whose church has been refurbished and is excellent as a centre used by people of all communities. Soon after we arrived, a major new mosque was opened across the road from the church, with adherents perhaps twenty times those of the church. This provided both threat and opportunity. I decided to use my growing friendship with a local Muslim leader, not only to make myself well known in that mosque, but also to join with friends in establishing a dialogue group. This group first met in a neutral office space over three years ago, but soon began to meet every six weeks, in St. Philip's Church meeting room, or in a Muslim venue.

Membership is open to all. The majority are men, and include clergy from both faiths, as well as lay people. A minority are women, and we make every effort to keep some within the group, though we realise that the Women's Group described below is an easier place for the majority. Normally we have an input from a Muslim and a Christian, and then open the meeting to general discussion. Until now, unlike in the Birmingham group, we have not had any explicit prayers, though we have had silent prayer around certain topics. We have now begun opening with an appropriate prayer from one faith, and ending with another prayer from the other tradition. The meetings will last one and a half hours, and after the two inputs, there will be a chaired discussion, enabling all who wish to contribute, and allowing those who prefer to listen to do so.

Subjects covered were at first the obvious doctrinal areas: God, Jesus, Muhammad, prophethood, prayer, justice, etc., and this involved particular attention to scriptures. However, we have increasingly considered a wider variety of issues, some of them around events beyond our group. These have included 9/11, the wars in Afghanistan and Iraq, the Bali bombings, Palestine/Israel, Gujarat. All these conflicts potentially had local repercussions, and the kind of leadership shown by a group like this has perhaps played a small part in helping to avoid problems. On Bali, for example, we issued a statement, proposed by a Muslim member, deploring the violence there, for which there could be no excuse. Drawing on the wisdom of several members of the group, I wrote a full-page article in a national Christian newspaper, affirming that Muslims had spoken consistently against terrorism, locally, nationally, and beyond, in answer to an article complaining that Muslims did not so speak.

We have also discussed significant local community issues: Muslim and Christian schools, for example. We have heard from a Religious Education teacher, a Christian, who teaches in a school which is over 90 percent Muslim, and from a Muslim, who is head of Religious Education in a Christian High School. We have discussed racism, and it was a Muslim who challenged us all to accept that racism was potentially there with all of us, Asian or white. Another Muslim challenged his fellow Muslims, as to why Bosnian Muslims had been accepted by their community in Leicester, as refugees, but that had not happened easily with the Somalis, also Muslims. Was this racism? We discussed conversion in general, a contentious topic, but then had the trust to listen to converts either way. We have also each shared our understandings of the divisions within each of our communities, and what they mean, as well as positive mutual learning about Sufism, Christian mysticism, and the Wesley brothers as spiritual giants.

We are at present engaged in a series of three meetings related to the law. In the first, we looked at *sharia,* and at the Christian concept of law. Both the excellent introductions made a considerable impact, and showed how stereotypes such as Islam is a religion of law and Christianity of grace are just that, stereotypes. The popular view among non-Muslims, is that *sharia* law is all about chopping off hands for stealing, and worse. The talk showed us what a richly nuanced concept *sharia* is, and how much it is at the heart of a Muslim's religious faith, even though there is no wish or expectation that it could become part of British law. We considered how British law operates in two difficult contemporary fields—that of the anti-terrorism act, and asylum regulations. A meeting then followed when two senior representatives of the local police attended, and they responded openly to the issues that had been raised. Another meeting will follow related to the prison system, and its impact on the communities, addressed by significant players in the field from both faiths. What can be seen here are two stages of building up trust, the first related to the religious concept of law, the next to the operation of the law in practice. What is also shown is a trust from the police side, that this will be a constructive dialogue, within the difficulties under which they operate as they try to apply deeply unpopular laws, which only serve to increase the Muslim sense of victimhood.

These encounters have also had practical outcomes. In face of the war in Afghanistan, we considered what we could do, once the war started. We decided on a joint appeal for Save the Children, which raised £6000. A similar sum was raised the following year for two projects, one Christian and one Muslim, and the money was given to a joint fund, and then divided. We have held fast days in common, in Ramadan, each year, when the fast has been broken together, in the local mosque. In the Christian Holy Week, we held a joint fast with one or two Jews, and broke the fast in the church hall, as we each read from our scriptures. We held a joint prayer, again the three faiths, in the face of the threat of the

Iraq war, and shared a common prayer. Some of us joined in an enormous demonstration in London, and three of us Christian priests travelled in a bus with Muslims, and enjoyed both the common experience, much dialogue, and what seemed almost like sacramental sharing of food, on the return journey. At one level, all these things are just signs of what could be. No more than forty have been involved, with an average of twenty on any occasion. Continuity, as with all groups in modern life, is a difficulty. We have recently established a steering group. This is not because the two who initiated the group cannot manage. But sharing responsibility will also share leadership commitment. We need to speak of what has been happening, not that it is great, but that it can become infectious. Muslims and Christians can live alongside each other, and more than that, can develop friendships and trust that allow much to happen, that we believe is led by the one God whom we own together, and are guided by together. It was out of the fruit of the experience of this group that three of us Christians were privileged this year to be invited to the great Eid celebrations in Leicester, and to sit in a vast tent, with about 1,500 Muslims. Such an experience is the fruit of the kind of long-term journey we have been able to make together in this group.

The Muslim-Christian Women's Group

I offer here what has been offered from the women leaders. I suggested that such a group should be convened, and clearly have had no part in it, except to rejoice that it is happening. Diane Johnson, the priest who initiated things, is an encouragement for all readers who may have had no experience of this kind of challenge. She herself had no prior background, unlike me with more than two decades of it. It is not necessary to be a specialist to launch a group, just some qualities of leadership, some personal skills, confidence in one's own faith and the ability to articulate it, and above all, a sense of common humanity.

Diane Johnson writes: the group started in May 2002, as a result of a friendship between myself and two young Muslim women, one of whom had been in church when I was licensed to my present post at St. Philip's, Leicester, and the other whom I met at a Muslim women's group which I visited not long after my arrival in the parish. We each invited people who we felt were secure enough in their faith to be able to find out more about the *other* faith without feeling threatened. We started with about twenty people, equal numbers of Christians and Muslims. We shared something of our own faith, and identified aspects of the other faith, which we found good. In other words, we started with the positive.

Early on, we identified some of the issues we would like to explore together, such as marriage, *jihad*, the way in which our scriptures had come to be written down and what the texts meant for us, women and leadership, and the way in which the media presented faith communities. We also agreed to have at every meeting a reading from the Qur'an and from the Bible, selected by one member of each faith, who would explain why this passage was important to her. To begin with, we prayed in the same room, but separately, but after a few meetings, we decided to try to pray together in ways that did not compromise one another.

And we agreed that at every meeting there should be a significant time to sit and talk informally over a cup of tea or coffee.

We have met for two hours approximately every month, and always at St. Philip's Church. We have visited Launde Abbey, the Diocesan Retreat House, together. We had a splendid party in my garden in the summer, and recently we had the cameras of MATV, the Asian TV channel, with us, and we shared a meal together. We heard at a recent meeting about the work of an organisation, which provides clothes, basic toiletries, food and supermarket vouchers to women asylum seekers, and we decided that after several months of talking, we ought to *do* something together. So we collect items and bring them to the meetings, to be passed on to the project, and at some stage we hope to visit the centre. A few of us joined in the Muslim fast for a day during Ramadan, and broke the fast with our Muslim sisters. And we have as a group been invited to several Muslim dinners, and one fashion show! I have been invited to a Muslim wedding, and on two occasions have been asked to write a reference to enable Muslim children to be admitted to the local Church of England primary school.

We find that we have a great deal of shared experience as women and particularly as mothers. We also feel that we know and trust one another sufficiently to begin to explore issues that divide us. We can only do that from a basis of real friendship. Most of us feel far more comfortable in this women's group than in the largely male main dialogue group, which seems to us more defensive and wary. [Andrew's comment: this is probably right, and also comes from the lack of clergy in the women's group, or of representative community persons.]

The group has enabled Christian women from an area of Leicestershire where there is little experience of Islam to meet Muslim women in a gentle, non-confrontational way, a way which knocks down stereotypical preconceived ideas. It has also enabled Christian women in our area of Leicester, where the Muslim presence is most evident, to meet their Muslim neighbours as individual people. We cannot know or measure what tangible benefits this will bring. Who can say what effect it will have on other people when friendships between Muslim and Christian women are made at the school gates, for example, as a result of the building up of trust and understanding between young mothers in and beyond the group? Who can say what effect it will have on the children, especially the boys, to have Christian friends?"

I suppose one could say that this group is not typical of either community. But this begs the question, what is typical? We are mostly a group of quite highly educated and articulate women: teachers, a pharmacist, two Ph.D. students, nurses, a lecturer. But we have to start where dialogue is possible, rather than where it is not. There are now nearly fifty people on my mailing list, which speaks for itself. And we are increasingly being invited, both within Leicester and further afield, to share our experiences, and encourage others to take steps in their own context.

The experience of Miallem al Rawi, a Muslim member of the group. She is a young mother of two, of Iraqi background, and writes: I had been involved in Muslim-Christian dialogue before and had assumed that the meetings would be the usual highly intellectual, highly theological speaking that they normally are, but to my relief I found that this group offered an entirely different experience. While we do discuss theological issues and sometimes delve into controversy, it is the personal friendships that have developed which sustain this group and make it the success it is. These friendships have enabled us to speak with each other openly and honestly and discuss issues of controversy with ease and comfort. We often share personal stories and this shows the confidence and trust we have in each other.

In the meetings we share a lot of information about each other's faiths but what makes the meetings so good is that they are great fun, as well as praying together we laugh together and while our initiatives may not save the world they do a great deal for us as individuals and we take that back with us to our families and our communities. We have also shared many religious and social experiences together, from Ramadan to retreats and family picnics to fashion shows. We have more or less done it all, and these are invaluable experiences. When we first started the group, no doubt many of us viewed the other only as a Muslim or a Christian but now we see the human in each other, the mother, the wife, the teacher, and the nurse. As a Muslim I know we still face many struggles in society particularly overcoming the negative stereotypes which fan the flames of prejudice and hatred, but what the women's group shows me (contrary to what the doomsayers may think) is that we can and should coexist in a state of mutual understanding and friendship.

The fact is that, if we are to understand Britain as it is today, and if we are to understand society as it is today, it is vital that we look around us and learn more about the diverse faiths and cultures, ethnicity and creed of others. It is only then that we will learn to respect and appreciate each other . . . it is only then that we can live together in true peace and harmony and God says,

> O Mankind We created you from a single (pair) of a male and female and made you into nations and tribes, THAT YOU MAY KNOW EACH OTHER. Verily the most honoured of you in the sight of Allah is the one who is most righteous. And God has full knowledge and is well acquainted (with all things). (Quran 49:13)

Leicester Hindu-Christian Forum

This started with a significant underpinning of goodwill within the city, which in a way has become the "Hindu capital" of England. Hindus are seen as colourful people, hospitable and committed to Britain. They are in the forefront educationally and in terms of business. Their religion is full of festivals, which now come onto the streets. Most notable is Diwali, which is promoted by the City Council as an occasion for all, part of the annual round of events by which the city advertises itself. The inner workings of the religion are hard to understand, but it seems a good-enough faith to live by, and its adherents are law-abiding model citizens. It is true that things may be rather different in India, with the violence that breaks out occasionally. But Muslims are the main victims and that only compensates for the many other places where they seem to be the perpetrators. Christians who think more deeply may find the whole area of idol worship, the many gods, and the caste system distinctly unattractive, or more so. But caste is only obviously prevalent in India, and there is a sense of the oneness of God behind the idols or images. It is therefore possible to put aside such doubts in the interests of harmony. Not all can do this, particularly those who know India well in terms of caste, and those for whom idol worship is fundamentally against one of the ten commandments. But such persons are a minority and seem to be causing trouble, if they raise their voice.

With this background in mind, we decided to initiate a forum for Hindus and Christians to learn more of each other. This was not difficult to do. But it has proved harder to reach any of the depth that we have experienced with Muslims. The format has not helped, though there are reasons for how we proceeded. We meet in temple or church premises. We begin with a meal, and then we have prayers from both communities, which have included observing the Hindu *puja* and saying the late night compline service. A rather formal opening follows, with chairs and speakers at the front, which is mirrored at the end with formal votes of thanks. There are then two "lectures," followed by cross-faith groups, which report back by asking a question of each of the two speakers. Speakers have been asked normally from outside Leicester, rather than from within the group, which has added to the formality. There have been an average of forty persons present on each occasion, which is good. But it has been difficult to ensure continuity. Topics covered have been so far "safe" ones—festivals and what they tell us of the understanding of God, non-violence, use of scriptures, comparison between icons and images, living within two religions through interfaith marriage, those who have lived religiously across faith, what makes a saint in each faith. There has been a good feel, and it has provided an example of two different faiths looking at common themes. It has not yet reached a point of depth or of real integration within the group. This has happened to some extent within the organising group. What we have not yet discovered is whether we can begin to tackle more difficult subjects.

Hindu-Christian UK Forum

Parallel with this local experience, I have been involved as co-chair of a national forum. This was established in 2001, and the aim was to provide a place where Hindus and Christians could talk at a fairly sustained level on issues they faced within the community. There have been some stops and starts. What did not help was that we began with difficulties. This immediately brought to the fore questions of mission and conversion. This became the touchstone issue, as we struggled to agree on a common statement of goodwill. This common statement happened only with difficulty, but was eventually achieved. In the process, we agreed to three ground rules for the group. The first was that this was a group about Britain. We would only talk about India, in so far as issues there affected life here. Another was that there needed to be a settled membership. This was not the case at first, and new agendas were raised each time. Another was that each organisation or denomination would be represented by two named persons.

Alternates were not encouraged. This has ensured wide participation, from five or six groups each, and prevented a kind of entryism, which could enable one group or agenda to dominate. The result is that we have been gradually building up trust, so that we can tackle the difficult issues. What has helped is that in two successive meetings, the main item has been personal faith sharing from three or four of each faith. This enabled those of the other faith to hear of the variety of faith journeys and faith positions held.

The statement of goodwill is a useful document to enable groups of Hindus and Christians to talk together without unnecessary suspicion. It is a compromise document wherein Christians have obtained a clear statement that conversion is, within this country, a step that someone may legitimately take, while Hindus are clear that they do not wish to be targets for explicit evangelism, or for any kind of inducements which will weaken the fabric of their faith or put pressure upon individuals. Misunderstandings have arisen. One member, from an evangelical organisation, wrote a popular article in which he was quoted as saying that the Christian task was to rescue Hindus from spiritual darkness. The Hindus felt this was a breach of trust. I wrote a critical article about *Hindutva* (the philosophy behind the BJP political party) in an academic journal. The goodwill statement as previously quoted was invoked. This questioning did allow me to have a two-hour private meeting with my fellow chair, who is President of the *Vishwa Hindu Parishad* (VHP) of the UK, the leading religious backer to Hindutva and the BJP. It enabled us to clear the air, and move forward, not agreeing, but understanding where each comes from.

Both the national and local group was much encouraged by a visit of the Archbishop of Canterbury, Rowan Williams, to Leicester. He spent the day in the biggest Hindu temple here, and also meeting Christians involved with Hindus. These included the national group, where, in a closed meeting, Hindus and Christians were able to put direct questions to him. A call for a greater concentration on theology, from one of the Hindus, much warmed the heart of the Archbishop.

Leicester Family of Abraham Group

This group illustrates the need for long-term commitment when things grow difficult. This group of Jews, Christians and Muslims, called *Family of Abraham,* at the suggestion of an Imam, was formed after a visit from the Israeli Ambassador. He asked to meet with a group of Christian leaders, and I requested him also to meet with some Muslim leaders. There was a frank, though good-willed, discussion which inevitably centred on Israel-Palestine. In the light of a large amount of polite disagreement, he challenged us to send a group of Muslims and Christians to Israel, to investigate the historical and ground realities. We decided first to get to know each other, Jews, Muslims, and Christians, better in Leicester. Hence a group was formed. The ground situation has never allowed the visit to be made, but the group has continued.

There have been several phases to this journey. The first two meetings were dominated by the Israel-Palestine issue. Open disagreement was to the fore.

This was between the Orthodox Jews in the group, and the Muslims, most of whom are members of *Friends of Al Aqsa*, a support organisation for the freeing of Jerusalem for the worship of all faiths, and seen with deep suspicion by most of the Jews. At the same time, there were Progressive Jews from the Just Peace organisation, who by no means followed their Orthodox counterparts. Christians hovered in the middle. We then called a moratorium on such discussion. We agreed to concentrate on building trust in Leicester, which we could do something about, rather than talking of a situation about which we could do nothing. Three good meetings followed, where we visited each other's places of worship, followed by discussion. It is very different going to a mosque with Jews, than going just as a Christian group. They were thrilled with how well they were received, and remarked on how close they found the religious practices, which they observed. The same in reverse was seen in the visit to the synagogue. So also, we learnt much when they came to the church. Here, we used the architecture and stained glass windows to explain much, and also through showing the eucharistic vessels and vestments we were able to talk of the fundamental events of the Christian story. We also said compline, and the Jews were struck by how much the words were like their Bible words. The Muslims remarked upon the continual references to the Trinity, which jarred within what were common religious ideas within the psalms and readings. This is a thoroughly helpful way of making visits within a dialogue programme.

We planned three further meetings, around festivals, young people's concerns, and common issues for Muslims and Jews, such as Halal meat/Kosher food, issues of circumcision, and burial needs. Unfortunately, we then faced a major setback. The *Jewish Chronicle*, the national paper, sent a reporter to research the group, and a favourable article was published. However, within it, one of the Jewish members was quoted as saying that he respected greatly the Muslim members, except those who were members of *Friends of Al Aqsa*, who wanted, de facto, to wipe Israel off the map. The article was read by Muslims nationally and locally. Trust disappeared, since it was pointed out that all the Muslim members of our group were in this organisation, including its Secretary, as were most Muslims in the city and beyond. More than sixty e-mails had to be answered, and libel action was threatened against the *Jewish Chronicle*.

The two sparring parties asked me to call a meeting in the church. I chaired a very tough meeting between five Jews and five Muslims. After a long meeting, and considerable honesty and tension, the Jewish friend, very committed to the group and to interfaith in Leicester, agreed to withdraw his accusation, if it was wrong, and write accordingly to the *Jewish Chronicle*. The Muslims demanded to see his statement, but I said he should sleep on it, and write it the next day. He then sent it to the *Chronicle* and to me. There was a further problem about this, but I defended his right to send it to whomever he wished. A first attempt to begin again was to have two further meetings, in a progressive synagogue and mosque. The first meeting could not tackle the agreed subject, because the key Orthodox leader read out a long statement saying why he could not continue in the group, because he had problems of trust. The leading Muslim, who is Secretary of the Friends of Al Aqsa, in response, offered to resign, so that trust could be restored. Clearly this was not a good basis for going forward, though the Orthodox leader appreciated a local expression of solidarity. He and others had been insulted when walking from the synagogue on a Friday, seemingly by Muslim youth. Two members of the group, an Imam and the above Secretary, offered to walk home with him each Friday. They also agreed to continue to work together on other common issues in Leicester. When the Muslim burial ground was desecrated soon afterwards—not by Jews but by vandals—a message of sympathy was immediately sent by Jewish leaders. There was also a fine Holocaust Memorial Day evening, supported by all concerned from the three faiths.

The next hurdle was when it was decided—by me—that we would postpone a meeting, in order to support a request from Just Peace, to go to see a film, and partake in a discussion, related to the West Bank and Gaza. This was seen as politicising the group again! We have now begun again, encouraged by the arrival of a new Progressive Rabbi. There will now be clergy leadership from the three faiths. The next three meetings are to be occasions when we talk of our personal faith journeys, and how that impacts on how we approach community and wider issues. The Jewish evening provided four testimonies, each very different from the other, and included both Orthodox and Progressive.

This may all sound hardly worthwhile. It is an important story illustrating the complexity of dialogue groups, particularly when more than two faiths are involved, and in particular, these three faiths. They are hostages to events quite outside our control. Their very success leads to expectations of trust, which are perhaps unrealisable. But they need to continue. Conflict resolution has had to be to the fore, as we search for a place where it can be a "win-win" situation. We should be modest in what we can achieve. It is unrealistic to think that Palestine will never arise in our discussions. But the focus on the local, and on the traditions of our faith, needs to be central, if we are to make meaningful progress.

As Christians we (also) have a possible role here of facilitation, of being a bridge across communities. We have to be wary to be no more than that. We cannot be arbiters in the affairs of two separate communities. We have to tread a narrow tightrope in being even-handed with both communities. It is often felt that Muslims are a favoured community, and we have to make clear that this is not so. At the same time, we do not always need to go along with the stereotype that Hinduism is a religion that never causes trouble. Because it rightly has a very eirenic profile in this country, this does not mean that what has happened in India can be ignored, nor the age-long effect of caste be bypassed, because it is not apparent here.

GROUND RULES/PRINCIPLES OF DIALOGUE

(The author summarizes the guidelines for dialogue published by the World Council of Churches in 1979. See pp. 141 of the present volume for a list of these guidelines, also available at http://www.oikoumene.org/en/resources/documents/.)

In the following, I offer my own points for Christians, about establishing and sustaining a dialogue group.

1. Two people from two faiths are enough to begin. It is on the basis of such a friendship that most dialogue groups begin, and can be sustained.

2. A sense of freedom is needed about time, and direction. Agendas will not always be followed as expected, people may come and go, and what takes place after meetings may be as important as within the more formal part.

3. Perseverance and stability are vital. We should not give up easily, and there may need to be considerable work between meetings, with networking between key persons. This can be on the telephone, and mobiles are ubiquitous. But such means of communications should be undergirded by personal meetings.

4. We need to be very clear which faiths are involved, what can be expected from each, and where the sensitivities are likely to be. (See the above list of dialogue groups and the varying experiences). Dialogue with Muslims is very different from dialogue with Hindus.

5. Questions of hospitality are important, and will vary. Hindus and Sikhs assume this is part of any occasion, and indeed it is a religious duty to offer hospitality. If we are entertaining Muslims or Jews, there are the issues of what is *kosher* or *halal*. It is better to stick to Bombay mix or biscuits, checking they are *halal,* or fruit, or vegetarian food of some kind. The minimum is tea, coffee, and biscuits.

6. We must expect to do things that are uncomfortable for us. This may include sitting on the floor, drinking very sweet tea, receiving sweet meats in a temple (even if we do not eat them for conscience's sake; see elsewhere).

7. We must be sensitive to Christian women and their perceptions, without being unrealistic about what other faiths will allow, or in practice happens.

8. Group dynamics are very important, and become more complicated when we meet across faiths. Can we enable those who are lay people, for example, to speak in the presence of an Imam, or juniors in front of seniors?

9. The quality of *empathy* is fundamental. Can we enter into the world of the other, and understand their feelings, even if we cannot share them? Only so can we learn what it means for a Hindu to celebrate the birth of Krishna, a Muslim to go on Hajj. Only so can we expect others to share the experience of what Easter can mean.

10. Listening needs to be total, not just a waiting till we can speak. And that listening needs to cover whatever the other presents.

11. In time we should not be reticent about challenging—"telling the truth in love"—rather than allowing misconceptions to continue. This can

be termed "caring confrontation," and shows when there is a maturity in the dialogue. We should not try to defend the indefensible within the practice of our faith or our faith communities. Dialogue is about conflict as well as about harmony. It may end in conflict resolution, it may not, but hopefully the personal relationships will be maintained and we can agree to differ.

12. We should remember that we meet as persons of faith and prayer. At the same time we meet as common citizens of our city or country. A group needs to be ready to range widely in its concerns, but be prepared to give a chance to people to express their personal faith, as well as the issues within society.

13. We should not worry over much about results. Our very meeting regularly is an effective demonstration within our easily divided society, and polarised religions. But we should be prepared to be surprised by where we end up, under the guidance of the Holy Spirit, in Christian terms. And we may never know the ripple effect of those who are touched in a group, and then touch others.

14. Our groups should normally be open. Numbers do not matter in themselves, and we should remember what twelve persons achieved as they followed Jesus. How a group operates, will depend upon its size. One of the best ways to increase a group's numbers, is through regular members being invited to bring a friend. This insures those who come fall within the ethos of the group.

15. Where we sit is important. It may be easier to sit with a Christian friend, but we can do that every Sunday. A real breakthrough comes in a group, when we find ourselves agreeing on a particular point with someone from the other faith more than with someone from our own.

CONCLUSION

I began by affirming that this is a *kairos* time for dialogue. It is not just an optional extra for a small but keen minority group. It is a necessity for the survival of our communities, as they learn to live together, particularly in the post–9/11 world, where echoes of world crises in Afghanistan, Iraq, Israel/Palestine, Gujarat, and many parts of Africa, find echoes in Europe. Europe is pivotal politically, but also increasingly religiously. Dialogue in many other parts of the world is fraught with difficulties. An article from Peshawar, on the North Western frontier of Pakistan, records (Summer 2004) a brave attempt at a dialogue for peace seminar. It ends, "To speak of interfaith dialogue at this stage might be on the grandiose side, but at least there is a new readiness to look and listen to one another, and a pleading to correct the distortions in the name of justice and truth." It is heartening to see recorded that we are on a common journey with Christians in one of the hardest parts of the world. Nor can we be complacent in Britain or Europe. As I write, the *Sunday Observer* has an article (May 30, 2004) headlined *British hostility to Muslims "could trigger riots,"* and continues by suggesting a report is about to come out from the Commission on British Muslims and Islamophobia, saying that Britain is "institutionally Islamophobic." It is a gloomy, or perhaps, realistic report. This makes it all the more urgent that we pursue the kind of dialogues recorded above.

I asked a group of educated Muslims what they thought Christians thought of them. They said things like "Terrorists," "Extremists," "Fanatics," "Women abusers." I said that I thought of Muslims as "People of prayer," "People of discipline," "People who have taught me about fasting," "People who take faith to be over the whole of life." An urgent task for dialogue, in Sweden or Norway, as well as in Britain, is to help Christians to move from the first list of stereotypes, to the second. This, I said to that group of Imams, is a common task, for you as well as for us. Perhaps that is the most urgent task for us in dialogue. The future religious cohesion of our continent may depend on it.

Notes

1. (London: Epworth, 1995).
2. For example, Kenneth Cragg, *The Call of the Minaret*, 3rd ed. (Oxford: Oneworld Publication, 2000).
3. Riaz Ravat, ed., *Embracing the Present, Planning the Future* (Leicester, 2004).
4. *Local Inter-Faith Activity in the UK* (London: Inter-Faith Network for the UK, 2003).
5. *Encounter in the Spirit: Muslim-Christian Dialogue in Practice* (Geneva: World Council of Churches, 1991).

Jesus Loves Me, This I Know, for the Buddha Tells Me So

*Jeanne Matthews Sommer**

ONE NIGHT, AS PIOUS AND FAITHFUL RABBI EISIK SLEPT, HE HAD a dream; the dream enjoined him to proceed afar to the Bohemian capital Prague, where he should discover a hidden treasure, buried beneath the principal bridge leading to the castle of the Bohemian kings. The Rabbi was surprised, and put off his going. But the dream recurred twice again. After the third call, he bravely girded his loins and set forth on the quest.

Arriving at the city of his destiny, Rabbi Eisik discovered sentries at the bridge, and these guarded it day and night; so that he did not venture to dig. He only returned every morning and loitered around until dusk, looking at the bridge, watching the sentries, studying unostentatiously the masonry and the

---

* The author teaches at Warren Wilson College in Swannanoa Valley near Asheville, North Carolina, and is an ordained Presbyterian minister.

soil. At length, the captain of the guards, struck by the old man's persistence, approached, and gently inquired whether he had lost something or perhaps was waiting for someone to arrive. Rabbi Eisik recounted, simply and confidently, the dream that he had had, and the officer stood back and laughed.

"Really, you poor fellow!" the captain said. "Have you worn your shoes out wandering all this way only because of a dream? What sensible person would trust a dream? Why look, if I had been one to go trusting dreams, I should this very minute be doing just the opposite. I should have made such a pilgrimage as this silly one of yours, only in the opposite direction, but no doubt with the same result. Let me tell you my dream."

He was a sympathetic officer, for all of his fierce mustache, and the Rabbi felt his heart warm to him. "I dreamt of a voice," said the Bohemian, Christian officer of the guard, "and it spoke to me of Cracow, commanding me to go thither and to search there for a great treasure in the house of a Jewish Rabbi whose name would be Eisik son of Jekel. The treasure was to have been discovered buried in the dirty corner behind the stove. Eisik son of Jekel!" The captain laughed again, with brilliant eyes. "Fancy going to Cracow and pulling down the walls of every house in the ghetto, where half of the men are called Eisik and the other half Jekel! Eisik son of Jekel, indeed!" And he laughed, and he laughed again at the wonderful joke.

The unostentatious Rabbi listened eagerly, and then, having bowed deeply and thanked his stranger-friend, he hurried straight-way back to his distant home, dug in the neglected corner of his house and discovered the treasure which put an end to all his misery. With a portion of the money, he erected a prayer house that bears his name to this day.[1]

It was 1997 when Ajarn Sulak Sivaraksa first wandered into my life and the life of our community at Warren Wilson College. A phone call from a new friend of mine—an old friend of Ajarn Sulak's by the name of Elmer Hall— brought an invitation to host a "Buddhist social activist, Nobel Peace Prize nominee" from Thailand who would soon be visiting the area. Since Thailand and Buddhist social activism were not topics with which I was very familiar and a part of me hoped that Buddhism might be free of some of the hypocrisy I was seeing within my own Christian tradition, I welcomed the opportunity to host this stranger. What began during that visit was a friendship that has simultaneously opened me and many others within our college community to the beauty, complexity, and suffering within Siamese culture and to a deeper exploration of our own Christian roots and influences, both personally and as an institution.

I teach in a small liberal arts school, Warren Wilson College, begun by Presbyterian women missionaries in 1894 as a high school for impoverished farm boys in the Appalachian mountains of North Carolina. For over 100 years, the school—in its various incarnations as a high school, junior college, and now a liberal arts college—has endeavored to embody an alternative educational philosophy that combines liberal arts academics with work and service-learning. As part of a consortium of six "work colleges" in the nation, we offer what we call the "Triad" approach to education. This means our nearly 800 students study, work 15 hours per week on one of over 100 different work crews that sustain the life of our community, and complete a minimum of 100 hours of community service and reflection.

We continue to farm and nurture over 1,100 acres of land, including cattle and pig farms, a sustainable garden, and over 700 acres of forest. Students have created and implemented the idea of a vegetarian restaurant on campus, ironically called "The Cow Pie." The college has undertaken one of the most extensive environmental reviews and campus "greening" policies of any college in the nation, as stewardship of the natural environment in which we live continues to be one of the mainstays of our philosophy and practice as a community. We also continue to wrestle, as a college community, with whether or not these values of care for the earth, for the dignity and value of labor, and the sharpening of the life of the mind should be attributed, at least in part, to our Christian roots or if we should content ourselves with more generic language of spirituality; for the schools who most often identify themselves as "Christian colleges" in the United States tend to be institutions that are theologically fundamentalist or evangelical.

Ajarn Sulak is intensely familiar with the complexities that colleges like my own encounter. Many of the ideas and practices that Ajarn Sulak has been urging his country to consider with regard to alternative education, through his SEM (Spirit in Education Movement), are ideas and practices that Warren Wilson College has been experimenting with for over 100 years. He is certainly one of our school's "good friends." Because of his own Buddhist commitments and his work in Siam on behalf of education movements that include spirituality as a core principle of personal and social transformation, Ajarn Sulak understands the impulses that encouraged those 19th century Christian missionaries to found our school, impulses that we may be in danger of forgetting.

The Christian missionaries who founded our college were men and women whose beliefs compelled them to live out a life of service and care for the land, for they knew that the heart of America's strength, both economically and spiritually, was connected to the health of those who suffered most in the rural areas. The missionaries came to our valley from the northern portion of the USA, in the days when the Presbyterian Church was separated into northern and southern denominations after the Civil War. These missionaries were "longtermers" who tended to stay for more than five years and were, as a result, as affected by the culture in which they immersed themselves as were those whom they came to serve. This is perhaps one reason why the college has maintained a long history of appreciation for diversity and a commitment to its continued cultivation, particularly in relation to international students, many who hail from Asia.

There is a bit of irony, however, that—despite our founding by Presbyterian missionaries and our continued affiliation with the Presbyterian Church (U.S.A.)—our students, according to a 1995 survey I conducted on campus, are most interested in the Buddha Dhamma and indigenous cultures and religions. Many, if not a majority, of our students also express a mild to sharp disdain for Christian traditions. Interest in Christianity ranked, in that survey, below Orthodox Judaism and Islam. What began as a school for poor Appalachian farm boys, has metamorphosed into a college for students—a majority women—who come from relative wealth, who hail from all over the United States and a good portion of the world community, and who are—more often than not—either ready to resign themselves from Christian faith and practices with which they were raised or who come from families who have consciously raised them according to other traditions or ethical views.

In the face of such conditions, what, if any, relevance can or should we find in our earliest Christian roots? This is one of the main questions that our community is currently exploring as it takes itself into the new millennium. Into a period of time in our college's history when we are debating to what degree, if any, Christian language should be present—either implicitly or explicitly— Ajarn Sulak stepped again in the winter of 2002.

To our students, he reminded them, as he did on his first visit with us in 1997, to explore the roots of their own cultures, including the Christian traditions—warts and all—which shape our consciousnesses even when we are raised within another religious tradition, are in the process of rejecting Christianity, or are trying to find some way to claim the Christian path with integrity and with real concern for social justice, not just individual salvation. To the college, he urged us to find language that can direct the school's mission into the 21st century in ways that will enable our community to take relevant and compelling stands within a nation that appears, increasingly, to use Christian theological language to justify imperialist policies in support of the new religion of Consumerism. This new religion has a mantra that sounds more and more like "Buy, buy, buy, throwaway, throwaway, throwaway, buy more, buy more, buy more." Its litany is deafening and deadly.

Upon Ajarn Sulak's last visit, I was reminded again of how many liberal Christians and the institutions associated with them have failed keenly to articulate a compelling word that speaks to the de facto religion of Consumerism that is exported with American foreign policy on a daily basis and is coming to dominate developing peoples' consciousness as well as our own. I came to understand, in a much more painfully poignant fashion, that there is a direct correlation between my/our inability to articulate a compelling voice that includes Christian language and the dehumanization of the people of Siam, of others, and of the earth. Because of Ajarn Sulak's visit to our campus and my recent travels to Thailand where I was able to witness first hand the new city temple, The Mall, I saw the "truth" of America's new religion, the "Middle Way" of Consumerism.

American culture finds itself poised between two extremes: the way of fundamentalism and the way of secularism. As one of my students wrote in her journal after Ajarn Sulak's visit this fall:

> It also kind of feels like the world is at a turning point. So are we going to stay where we are on the boat as it starts to capsize? Or are we going to drop everything and run to the other side to try and counterweight the overturn? What would be the Buddhist response? In my opinion, it is going to take

a lot of what Sulak would call "good friends" to come with us to stop the boat from overturning.[2]

The religion of Consumerism is America's "Middle Way" response between the extremes of Christian fundamentalism and secularism. It is keeping the boat afloat, for now, but its efforts are not sustainable. Both extremes, either intentionally or unintentionally, enable the religion of Consumerism. Christian fundamentalism does so by promising a kind of "gospel of wealth"—in this life for the wealthy and in the next life for the poor—as reward for obedience. Secularism does so by dethroning all sacred religious values. According to Ajarn Sulak,

> One of the characteristics of the new secular intellectuals is their eagerness to scrutinize religion and its protagonists. These intellectuals examine how far the great systems of faith have aided or harmed humanity and to what extent religious leaders have lived up to their precepts of purity, truthfulness, charity, and benevolence. Then they issue harsh denouncements against both churches and clergy. Over the last two centuries as the influence of religion has declined, secular intellectuals have played an ever-increasing role in shaping our attitudes and institutions.[3]

Posed between secularism and fundamentalism, I began to recognize a Buddhist response, a true "Middle Way" which seems to be recalling us to our roots in hope that the spiritual biodiversity of our nation and its exported values can be rescued from the mono-crop consumerist spirituality that is colonizing our culture and providing a deluded and temporary solution. Ajarn Sulak came to us and called us to explore, even claim, our Christian roots, as individuals and as a college. Currently, many institutions of higher education in the United States continue to remove explicit Christian language from their mission statements.[4] They oftentimes retain some language that recalls their historical relationship to the denomination that founded them and opt either to emphasize their commitments to a more vague exploration of "spirituality" or to no religious education at all, perhaps in obeisance to secularism or out of fear of being associated with the fundamentalists. The debates, in my opinion, are not just about the words. They are about deep questions of institutional identity and what role, if any, academic institutions should take in the religious education of students. The removal of explicit Christian language seems related in my mind to the degree which institutions can offer compelling alternatives to secularism, fundamentalism, and the "Middle Way" of Consumerism.

If our college and others like it follow this trend, we will continue to bolster the "Middle Way" of Consumerism. In our case we will do so because we will be educating students who do not really understand how to have compassion for and interact with the majority of Americans who have not questioned the ways in which their faith or secular views support this new religion. We will continue to concede the word "Christian" and the tradition itself to those fundamentalists who would do dishonor to the tradition in its very name and who see American soil as suitable to only one kind of planting. As the world becomes more dominated in the coming years by absolutists and religious extremists of all sorts, successive generations of our students will have less access to the knowledge that there is another viable, religiously committed and open path within the Christian tradition because progressive and compassionate Christian individuals and the institutions to which they are related remain silent.

Because of the silence, the de facto religion of Consumerism—along with the Christian fundamentalism that parodies this de facto religion and the arrogant secularism that enables it—will continue to be exported around the world. As Ajarn Sulak writes:

> You cannot walk down the streets of Bangkok, for example, without being bombarded by billboards touting the benefits of various soft drinks. Streets here are jammed with expensive, foreign cars that provide the owners with prestige and the city with pollution. Young people define their identities through perfumes, jeans, and jewelry. The primary measure of some one's life is the amount of money in his or her checkbook. These are all liturgies in the religion of consumerism.[5]

If higher education in America fails, in word and deed, to demonstrate how Christian language and praxis can serve as a door to genuine and deep pluralism, not just toleration, and how the tradition can help us to ascertain and address the real sources of conflict and healing in the world, the palette of theological acumen from which we can draw will become increasingly pale in America. It is necessary that we find a way to demonstrate this because our complex future will include (whether we like it or not) many theological discussions about how Christianity contributes to the good society. My main concern is with regard to who will be equipped to guide these discussions and how thoughtful and compassionate these discussions will be. Institutions like ours have a great responsibility to shape this dialogue effectively. We owe it to ourselves and to the future not to take ourselves out of this conversation prematurely.

What, if any, is the correlation between our students' eagerness to explore the Buddha Dhamma as it is practiced in America, Thailand, and around the world, and our need to explore—perhaps even to reclaim—our own Christian spiritual roots? I have found that—just as some have suggested that the Buddhist awakening that is occurring in the west may be one key to the recollection of Buddhism in the east toward its own compassionate roots—the opportunity to explore Buddhist philosophy and practice may be one of the keys to recovering the teachings of compassion and social justice that are at the heart of the Christian tradition.

When Ajarn Sulak first visited our college in 1997, he made the distinction, as he does in *Seeds of Peace*, between big "B" Buddhism and small "b" buddhism. The former is a Buddhism that allies itself with state power and multinational corporations while the latter focuses on the original, reformist teachings of the Buddha. He writes:

If we Buddhists want to redirect our energies towards enlightenment and universal love, we should begin by spelling Buddhism with a small "b," Buddhism with a small "b" means concentrating on the message of the Buddha and paying less attention to myth, culture, and ceremony. We must refrain from focusing on the limiting, egocentric elements of our tradition. Instead we should follow the original teachings of the Buddha in ways that promote tolerance and real wisdom.[6]

When Ajarn Sulak spoke of this distinction, he challenged us at the college and within America in general to do the same thing with regard to the Christian (little "c") tradition: not to abandon the language or praxis of the tradition itself, but to reclaim it on behalf of the radical, non-violent intent that informs its core teachings. Perhaps we would, in the process, begin to find our own "Middle Way." This Christian middle way would not be a watered-down version between two extremes, as is Consumerism, but the real way of the cross that calls us to live in the center between the intersecting, often contrary claims upon our lives which call us to practice both justice and compassion.

When Ajarn Sulak gave us this challenge, I began to understand that this stranger was not coming to our campus to call us to be Buddhist—for it is not the Buddhist way to say that "if everyone practiced Buddhism the world would be a better place"—but to point us to our own resources, hidden as they are within an increasingly secularized or fundamentalist culture. I found myself going to sleep that night singing, "Jesus loves me this I know, for the Buddha tells me so." Just as Rabbi Eisik entered into the foreign territory of Bohemia and found there some insight that enabled him to return to his home and find what was buried there all along, so my own sojourn and that of many of our students into the Buddha Dhamma may lead us back to our own hidden, spiritual treasures at home. Ajarn Sulak's insights and the Buddhist teachings of wisdom and compassion can be key resources on our campus for discovering wisdom and compassion within and for Christianity and for the elimination of hatred and disdain. Hatred and disdain, even a relatively benign "dismissal"—whether such attitudes originate on the "right" or the "left"—are never postures with which we should content ourselves.

I wish to thank Ajarn Sulak—who has had the courage to explore alien territory with grace and compassion—for pointing me, and others, toward the dirty corners of our own spiritual territory that we may find long-forgotten treasures of loving-kindness. Over 100 years after our founding, another missionary, this time a Buddhist one, came to our lovely Swannanoa valley and helped us to nurture the seeds of peace—including the Christian seeds—planted in this fertile Appalachian soil.

Notes

1. Wendy Doniger O'Flaherty, *Other Peoples' Myths* (New York: Macmillan, 1988), 137-38; citing Zimmer, *Myths and Symbols*, 219-21; citing Martin Buber, *Die Hassidischen Bucher* (Hellerau, 1928), 532-33.

2. Kate Reese, *Socially Engaged Buddhism Journal*, December 17, 2002.

3. Sulak Sivaraksa, *Seeds of Peace: A Buddhist Vision for Renewing Society* (Berkeley: Parallax, 1997), 59-60.

4. There are many church-related colleges in the United States but the colleges who emphasize that they are "Christian" colleges tend to be those schools that are fundamentalist or evangelical.

5. Sivaraksa, *Seeds of Peace*, 3.

6. Ibid., 68.

Can Christians and Muslims Pray Together?

Joseph Stamer＊

A FEW PRELIMINARY REMARKS ARE IN ORDER REGARDING THE possibility of common prayer between Christians and Muslims. First, there cannot be a single response to the question "Can Christians pray with Muslims?" Situations and social and cultural contexts are so diverse that what seems possible and even demanded in one place may be totally inappropriate in another. Without wishing to fall into total relativism, we must say it is evident that the various reflections and suggestions have to be understood in their own contexts.

Second, the question of the possibility of common prayer with Muslims is part of the larger effort for Islamic-Christian dialogue. True dialogue eventually leads naturally to a desire to turn together toward God by means of approaches discerned in mutual discussion. Common prayer between Christians and Muslims is an integral part of our wider spiritual encounter. Therefore, the question of praying together should be treated not in isolation but within the whole context of the dialogue. Moreover, we cannot restrict our attention to the comparatively simple matter of how to organize common prayer. There has to be prior theological reflection. If we are to achieve an authentic encounter in prayer, we must have reflected first on what unites us and what divides us, and on the special meaning of prayer in Christianity and in Islam: in short, we must operate on the level of faith. Is our common faith in the One God a sufficient basis for common prayer?

Finally, there is the question of *opportuneness* in moving toward common prayer, and this practical question too can be answered only in the context of the specific Islamic-Christian situation.

Only when we have carried out these indispensable preliminaries are we in a position to reflect on the precise form and content of an approach to common prayer.

＊ The author is a Catholic priest who works with the Episcopal Commission for Relations between Christians and Muslims in West Africa.

DIVERSE INITIATIVES

The inquiry prompted a great variety of initiatives and efforts to bring Muslims and Christians together in common prayer. It also revealed strong resistance on the part of certain Christian communities and their leaders, as well as a paucity of initiatives coming directly from Muslim communities.

There is no lack of opportunity for Christians and Muslims to meet for prayer in communities where both groups share the same culture. As would be expected, the situation is different where the members of one or the other group are simply tolerated as outsiders. In this regard, one may distinguish between officially-organized prayer meetings and more informal gatherings. In a number of countries, the national life has a religious dimension. Feasts and major events are celebrated with common prayer, whether the occasion is one of thanksgiving or of prayer for peace and national prosperity. The prayers are conducted by leaders of the different religious communities. In recent years the international life and various situations of conflict have influenced relations among religious communities and are generating more and more meetings to pray for peace. The great Prayer Meeting for Peace in Assisi in 1986 has been an inspiration for similar meetings more or less throughout the world. We can also think of the more formal meetings in many places between Christians and Muslims which usually include a time for recollection and prayer.

In addition, the common experiences of daily life offer many opportunities for people to come together as praying believers. One may think of neighborly visits on occasions like births, marriages, sickness, and bereavement. Common misfortunes such as drought may also bring people together, as may encounters in hospitals or prisons. The inquiry revealed innumerable opportunities for common prayer when Muslims and Christians live together and get to know one another. Reservations on both sides, however, prevent full exploitation of all these opportunities.

Besides a variety of occasions, there is diversity in forms of prayer. Sometimes the members of a community practice "spiritual hospitality," assisting at the worship of another community either out of friendship or by virtue of civic functions. This might be seen as an opportunity to welcome in a special way the presence of another faith without necessarily making the occasion one of common prayer.

In actual attempts at common prayer, the Assisi model is sometimes followed: Christians and Muslims assemble in the same place for prayer, each group leading the prayer in turn according to its own tradition. When there is a genuine effort to share forms, words, and external attitudes, all kinds of possibilities arise: readings, meditation, shared commentaries on a text of scripture or of a spiritual author; silence as an expression of inability truly to share "God's space" in prayer; prayers of praise, thanksgiving, and petition expressed in traditional formulas such as blessings, litanies, psalms, hymns, or recitation of poetry. In certain cultural situations there may also be sacred songs and instrumental music.

RESERVATIONS ON BOTH SIDES

Perhaps one of the most surprising facts revealed by the inquiry is that Muslims very rarely take the initiative in inviting Christians to common prayer. On the other hand, they nearly always respond positively to Christian invitations and initiatives. When Muslim religious leaders find it difficult to take part officially in common prayer, they may send representatives. However, in regions where the Sufi influence is strong, Muslims are more likely to take the initiative. It is especially in emotional situations like wars and natural catastrophes that Muslims ask Christians for prayers, and they may also invite them to common prayer. Reluctance in this matter is not, however, confined to Muslims. Until quite recently, Christians had rarely envisaged the possibility of common prayer with Muslims—even Muslims deeply committed to Islamic-Christian dialogue.

The fairly widespread reluctance on both sides, and the fact that most of the initiatives for common prayer come from Christians, are matters calling for further reflection and research. Many people who take collaboration with Muslims in general as a matter of course do not seem to regard common prayer as a natural part of such collaboration.

Expressions of Respective Faiths

Any approach to common prayer must take account of the specific character of prayer in both the Muslim and Christian traditions. Do we Christians really understand the meaning of prayer for Muslims? And of course the converse applies as well. Only when we know what we are talking about are we in a position to assess the particulars of a given initiative in the direction of common prayer. We have to understand and, in a sense, make our own the deep attitudes of the other at prayer. Only then can we look for precise formulas for ensuring the success of a common effort and avoid the danger of ill-considered experiments.

Christianity and Islam represent differing approaches to the same God, and these differences are reflected above all in our respective ways of prayer. It is especially in liturgical prayer—the prayer which expresses community identity—that these different approaches are manifested. When a Muslim hears the word "prayer," he or she thinks immediately of *salat*, ritual prayer performed five times a day according to fixed gestures and formulas. Any other form of prayer is regarded by Muslims as inferior and of secondary importance.

It is through ritual prayer that Muslims bear witness to faith in the transcendent God. They wish to obey an explicit command of God in the Qur'an, "Be faithful to prayer and almsgiving, bow down with those who bow down" (Qur'an 2, 43, and in many other places). Good Muslims consider themselves '*abd* in the double sense of the root of that word: "slave" and "adorer." Muslim prayer is therefore essentially an act of praise and adoration due to God alone. Based on God's absolute right to praise and adoration, the Muslim tradition has always shown a preference for "non-personal" prayer. When a Muslim continually repeats a prayer-gesture, it is to recognize God's absolute sovereignty and to acknowledge that he or she can add nothing to it. The sober simplicity of ritual prayer reflects the acceptance that God is all. What we Christians are tempted to call "ritual formalism" is for the Muslim an idea which expresses in praise and adoration the utter centrality of God. In essence, it is God praising God through the self-effacing gestures of the believer. We can understand, then, why the Muslim attaches so little importance to the words of formal prayer. Indeed, since most Muslims do not know Arabic, they do not understand—at least not fully—what they are saying when they pray.

Another aspect, though secondary, is that when Muslims carry out ritual prayer they are acting as witnesses (*shahid*). Ritual prayer is a public affirmation of one's membership in the *umma*, the community of those who submit and bear witness. Even when the ritual is carried out in private it has a community dimension, if only because the person praying turns toward Mecca, the center of the *umma*.

Apart from this fundamental ritual, Islam knows other forms of prayer:

1. The recitation of, and meditation on, the Qur'an in the silence of the heart renders the word of God present in life. On the basis of this theory, Muslim piety has developed one of the loveliest forms of prayer and the one most accessible to non-Muslims: meditation on the Most Beautiful Names of God. This can be done in private or in community, using a rosary of 99 beads.

2. The various stages of pilgrimage to Mecca are also marked by prayers of praise and request for forgiveness which often reflect great spiritual profundity.

3. The daily life of the Muslim is punctuated with formal prayers of praise, blessing, petition. Everything takes place under the kind and merciful gaze of the creator and master of all things.

4. Finally, Muslim piety is expressed in deeds as well as in words: charity toward the poor, justice, fidelity to one's word: "Piety does *not* consist in turning your face to east or west. The good man is he who believes in God . . . he who, for the love of God, gives of his substance. Those who carry out their commitments . . . are the ones who fear God" (Qur'an 2, 177).

For the Christian, prayer means above all praying like Jesus, with Jesus, and in Jesus, in whom God has made himself present in the world in a unique and unheard-of manner. For the Christian, God is simultaneously the Transcendent One, the Wholly Other, and the Immanent One, *not* only profoundly involved with humanity but actually one with all humanity in Jesus. All Christian prayer attempts to reflect this double dimension of transcendence and immanence, and this makes Christian prayer fundamentally different from the ritual prayer of Islam.

The model for Christian prayer is the teaching of Jesus and his own life of permanent union with the Father during his time on earth. It is, in fact, the Spirit of Jesus that prays in each Christian and makes up for the human inability to pray (cf. Rom 8:26). The Christian unites in prayer with Jesus within the church. This is particularly evident in the Christian prayer par excellence, the Eucharistic celebration. The Mass is, first, the community listening to the Word of God and, second, the sacramental participation in the sacrificial act of Christ, who gave his life for God and for his human brothers and sisters. Finally, the Eucharist is communion, the mysterious source of the whole Christian life.

The Christian tradition, especially in monasteries, has instituted a daily rhythm of prayer for the sanctification of the day. The Divine Office is an ancient practice in which many lay Christians now take part, reliving, over the course of a year, the stages of the mystery of salvation, God's extraordinary intervention in the history of humanity. This continual prayer constitutes at the same time praise, adoration, and thanksgiving, as well as intercession and a prayer for forgiveness.

The wealth and diversity of Christian liturgical prayer may give the impression that in Christianity the ordinary Christian—the private person—is neglected; however, this is not so. As official prayer seeks to sanctify and bring to God the whole life of the church, so the life of the Christian is supported by key moments of encounter with God, although these may not be regulated in detail: morning and evening prayer, grace before and after meals, and prayers (such as the Angelus) at other important moments of the day.

The originality of Christian prayer is that it is above all "incarnate" prayer, finding expression in words, signs, symbols, and a variety of gestures. Beyond these various expressions, it has many points of contact with Muslim prayer: adoration, praise, a profound sense that what we do adds nothing to God but benefits the one who prays. Thus we may raise an important question:

Are Muslims and Christians capable, on each side, of accepting each other and our respective approaches to God in prayer? For Christians in particular, we may ask whether the ritual formalism that the Muslim sees as an integral part of faith, is simply a "non-value" or, rather, is felt as a challenge to leave more space to the mystery of God. Are we ready to accept with respect the prayer of the other and to carry "the suffering of difference"?

Whatever the real differences, both the Christian and the Muslim at prayer are *shahid*, witnesses to God in a world that seems to be moving farther and farther away from God. The prayer of the believer should be an inoffensive witness.

IS COMMON PRAYER POSSIBLE?

It is clear that the specific characters of ritual prayer in Islam and of the Eucharistic celebration in Christianity make it impossible for the members of each community to take an active part in the central public prayer of the other. It would make no more sense for the Christian to join the ranks of praying Muslims during *salat* than for the Muslim to participate at the Eucharistic table.

Such conduct would amount to putting one's faith and religious loyalty at the disposal of the other. Yet alongside these "foundation actions" of the two communities, there remains open the whole field of the search for God under other forms. Would it not be possible for Muslims and Christians to encounter each other and encourage one another in "seeking the face of God"? What must be considered in regard to such a procedure, and what weight should be given to the different arguments on either side?

Islam's View of Christianity

The traditional Muslim attitude toward Christianity has its roots in ancient and restrictive interpretations of certain Qur'anic texts. To a Muslim, Christians are certainly believers since they possess a divine scripture. They have, however, corrupted what they have received: their faith in one God is contaminated by *shirk*, human association. Christians are at least partly in error because of their attitude toward (perhaps invasion of) "the space of God." How can Muslims share this space without contaminating it and thus becoming contaminated themselves?

At the same time, we can find in the Qur'an, the tradition, and the Qur'anic commentaries another, more positive way of looking at Christianity. For example, there is plenty of evidence that the first Muslims had no scruples about carrying out the ritual Islamic prayer in Christian places of worship; despite the statues, icons, and other items found in these places, they still represented "holy space." A verse in the Qur'an says that "hermitages, synagogues and other places of prayer are, like mosques, places where the Name of God is invoked" (22, 40b). (Later commentaries, however, were at pains to limit the extent of this recognition.) Two well-known Qur'anic passages, the "verse of light" (24, 35-36) and "the well-furnished table" (5, 112-15), also suggest that the first Muslims were at least passive witnesses at Christian liturgical celebrations. Conversely, Muslim tradition speaks of the prayer of the Christians of Najran in the Prophet's mosque at Medina.

Beyond this mutual frequentation of places of worship, sources show that the Muslim could have a very close relation with the non-Muslim in and through prayer. A series of Qur'anic texts shows how Abraham, the Muslim par excellence, interceded with God for "the idolators." His intercession for the people of Loth (cf. Qur'an 11, 74) takes the form of a sharp exchange with God. And what is affirmed of Abraham is also asserted, if less directly, about Muhammed himself, God's last envoy. All of this shows that Muslims, in their prayer of adoration, are allowed and even encouraged to have non-Muslims in mind when they pray.

Christians' Reluctance

The fundamental Christian objection to common prayer with Muslims derives from the close link between faith and prayer: we cannot pray together officially and liturgically because such prayer would ignore irreducible differences of faith. And for certain Christians the impossibility of common prayer goes beyond the sphere of liturgy, based on the conviction that any form of common prayer would be an offense against their Christian identity. How could it be a "prayer of truth" when the general climate is one of antagonism and insists on differences? There is also the fear of a kind of syncretic indifferentism. This is particularly true for children and less-well-instructed adult Christians. It is clear that any attempt at common prayer must be preceded by sound catechesis.

OVERCOMING DIFFERENCES

Though these various objections are serious, they are to be regarded as essentially superficial and temporary. All authentic prayer originates in a reality that transcends the person who prays—namely, in the Spirit of God. It is on the basis of this truth that Christians and Muslims can move beyond their differences and legitimate hesitations to share their experience of the living God in prayer.

No doubt the road to mutual knowledge and acceptance is long and full of difficulties, but once that goal has been reached it is clear that common prayer will give much greater depth and vigor to all efforts toward encounter and dialogue. Such prayer will purify hearts and help participants to overcome fixed and rigid positions by placing God and the search for his will at the core of dialogue.

The conclusion must be that, while attempts to bring about common prayer between Christians and Muslims cannot be imposed, this will come about of itself once both sets of believers are to walk together in full awareness of their respective riches and weaknesses. They will then be ready to unite to adore and give thanks, to offer common prayer in situations of distress, and to contemplate together the mystery which is both Justice and Mercy.

Possible Forms of Common Prayer

It is important first to answer the fundamental question, "What is it that we are seeking in these efforts toward common prayer?" Are we simply coming together, each group praying in its own style, or are we seeking a genuine unity, really sharing as equal partners in the words and gestures of prayer?

The different examples of "spiritual hospitality" are not to be regarded as occasions of genuine prayer in common. There are situations in which, for one reason or another, the Muslim comes to a Christian celebration as a respectful spectator, or the Christian may feel obliged to make the gesture of being silently present at Muslim ritual prayer. Though these are not examples of common prayer, there should still be prudent pastoral reflection on the rules that should govern such occasions of courtesy.

Some people believe that *silence* is the best form of common prayer between Christians and Muslims. It is possible in all contexts, even in situations of conflict in which words can easily be misinterpreted. However, it is normal for common prayer to be lived and expressed in words which can be heard and understood and, in principle, repeated and shared by all.

When Christians and Muslims pray *successively*, the reading of holy books plays an important part. The situation is more delicate when the prayer is to be shared by all, but our respective traditions do contain sufficient inspirational texts that are acceptable to both faiths—apart from the scriptures, which are often occasions of discord. An exception might be made for the Old Testament, especially the psalms, which constitute to some extent a common patrimony.

We have, then, a number of possibilities: readings, prayers taken from the respective spiritual traditions, meditation on the Most Beautiful Names of God, and responsorial prayers or litanies. The reluctance of Muslims to pray spontaneously in public has already been mentioned. In the same way, they prefer to express their *du'a*, or invocation, indirectly; they object to addressing God in, as it were, a conversational tone. These reservations must be genuinely respected in the planning of common prayer. And perhaps the most sensitive area of all is that of music, both instrumental and vocal. Differences of approach and attitude toward sacred music exist not only between Christians and Muslims but also among Muslim groups from various parts of the world.

We cannot expect everyone to have the same answer to the question of common prayer between Muslims and Christians, and we recognize that it raises fundamental issues in the whole Islamic-Christian dialogue. But this does not mean that those who believe in the one God may not meet for common praise and adoration. What we have to do is take the first step in that "competition for holiness" so often mentioned by John Paul II and already suggested in the Qur'an (cf. 5, 48). In his encyclical *Ecclesiam Suam*, Paul VI mentioned four somewhat paradoxical characteristics of dialogue which apply very well to the practice of common prayer between Christians and Muslims: *clarity* and *gentleness*, *trust* and *prudence*.

Readings

Theology in Interfaith Dialogue

Trinity and Saccidananda in the Writings of Brahmabandhav Upadhyaya

*Timothy C. Tennent**

INTRODUCTION

CHRISTIANITY IS THE ONLY WORLD RELIGION WHOSE PRIMARY source documents are in a language other than the language of the founder of the religion. The New Testament is written in Koine Greek, not in Aramaic, the language of Jesus. This is unique among all world religions and stands as a remarkable testimony to the translatability of the Christian message which has been enshrined in our most sacred texts. This linguistic translatability of the Christian message has been the inspiration for the translation of the New Testament into thousands of global languages. However, the gospel is not only linguistically translatable, it is culturally translatable. The gospel is not only delivered to us in the enscripturated text, but also in the proclamation and witness of a believing community, the members of which belong to a particular culture at a particular time in history. Indeed, the gospel must be made intelligible as it is announced in specific, local contexts. Authentic theology has been described as "reflecting on the faith in the light of one's historical context."[1]

The purpose of this study is to explore the work of an Indian Christian theologian who sought to communicate the Christian gospel to those in the Indian context who remain unfamiliar with western theological formulations and western church history. This study is representative of both the complex

---

* The author, president of Asbury Theological Seminary (since 2009), was long-time professor of World Missions and Indian Studies, and director of missions programs at Gordon-Conwell Theological Seminary. He is the author of *Building Christianity on Indian Foundations* (2000) and *Christianity at the Religious Roundtable: Evangelicalism in Conversation with Hinduism, Buddhism and Islam* (2002).

challenges the church has faced, as well as the creative solutions which have been offered as these Christians have tried to explore how the gospel can best address itself to the particular challenges posed by a religiously and culturally diverse world.

This study focuses on the writings of the 19th century Hindu convert to Christianity, Brahmabandhav Upadhyaya (1861-1907). He was a journalist, a theologian and, at the end of his life, an imprisoned leader of India's nationalistic movement, who earnestly sought to use the language of advaitic Hinduism as an interpretive bridge or hermeneutic whereby he might be able to better communicate Christianity to enquiring Hindus. This study will focus on his use of the advaitic doctrine of saccidananda (Sat-Cit-Ananda) to explain and expound the doctrine of the Trinity.

CAN THE HINDU UPANISHADS HELP US
EXPLAIN THE TRINITY?

Brahmabandhav Upadhyaya, the 19th century convert from Hinduism, has been called the "father of Indian Christian theology." Since many of our readers will be unfamiliar with Brahmabandhav Upadhyaya, we will begin with a brief overview of his life and work.[2]

Brahmabandhav Upadhyaya (1861-1907) was born Bhavani Charan Banerjea into a Bengali Brahmin family in 1861. In 1887, he was formally initiated into the Brahmo Samaj, a Hindu reform movement founded by Ram Mohan Roy (1772-1833). In keeping with the vision of the society, Upadhyaya worked hard during his years with the Brahmo Samaj to promote a version of Hinduism which was more consistent with monotheism. However, during this period he became increasingly attracted to the uniqueness of Christ and on February 26, 1891, he received Christian baptism, though he did not formally unite with the Catholic Church until September 1, 1891. In 1894, he declared himself a sannyasin (world-renouncer)[3] and thereafter was known as Brahmabandhav Upadhyaya.[4] Upadhyaya's conversion to Christianity marks the beginning of a series of journalistic efforts in which he sought to demonstrate how Christian theology, particularly neo-Thomistic thought, was compatible with indigenous thought forms in India. His writings are contained in several journals he founded, including *Sophia, The Twentieth Century,* and *Sandhya.*

Upadhyaya was dismayed at the inability of Christianity to flourish in India. He once described Christianity in India as "standing in the corner, like an exotic stunted plant with poor foliage, showing little or no promise of blossom."[5] He decided to dedicate his life to an expression of Christianity which was not Western, but was fully Indian in its expression. Over the course of his life, he made three major attempts to discover an appropriate foundation upon which the gospel could effectively take root and flourish in India. The first foundation upon which he attempted to construct a Christian proclamation was the foundation of natural theology based on general revelation and the universal knowledge of God which is present among all people. However, deficiencies in this foundation led him to re-examine the possibility of using the language and thought-forms of Hindu philosophy as a more appropriate foundation for establishing Christian thought in India.

Upadhyaya observed how Thomas Aquinas had boldly adopted the Aristotelian system of philosophy and effectively used it as the basis for constructing a Christian theology and philosophy which, in time, came to dominate the entire Middle Ages. Why, he reasoned, "should we Catholics of India now wage a destructive warfare with Hindu philosophy?" Alternatively, he argued, we should "look upon it in the same way as St. Thomas looked upon the Aristotelian system." He then declared,

> We are of the opinion that attempts should be made to win over Hindu philosophy to the service of Christianity just as Greek philosophy was won over in the Middle Ages. . . . The task is beset with many dangers. But we have a conviction and it is growing day by day, that the Catholic Church will find it hard to conquer India unless she makes Hindu philosophy hew wood and draw water for her.[6]

Upadhyaya was convinced that the 8th century Hindu philosopher Sankara (discussed in chapters two and three) could serve Christianity in India the way Aristotle served Aquinas. This project consumes much of Upadhyaya's writing during the next four years. It is his writings concerning the Trinity which emerge during this period that will be the focus of this case study.

While Upadhyaya never abandoned his desire to establish a philosophical foundation for Christianity in India, he did come to realize that many Indians who were committed to popular, village Hinduism did not respond to the sublime philosophy of the Upanishads. Thus, in his later years he attempted to find ways to build Christianity on a third foundation of Indian culture through a Christian interpretation of such common cultural practices in India as the caste system, idol worship, and the four life-stages. It was his attempt to affirm the value of India's cultural heritage that eventually placed him as a leader of India's nationalistic movement. He has the distinction of being the first Indian to publicly call for complete independence from Britain. In fact, his writings were considered sufficiently seditious by the British in India to warrant his arrest and imprisonment. However, he continued his protest against the British even from prison. However, while his trial was still on, Upadhyaya fell ill and was rushed to the hospital where he received a successful hernia operation. Tragically, he developed a tetanus infection and died in the hospital on October 27, 1907. Despite his untimely death, he left behind a remarkable collection of journalistic writings which continue to influence the debate today concerning the relationship between Hinduism and Christianity. This study will focus on only one aspect of his work; namely, his attempt to communicate the doctrine of the Trinity using the language of the Upanishads and the philosophy of Vedantic Hinduism.

UNDERSTANDING THE PROBLEM:
THE CLASSIC TRINITARIAN FORMULATION
AND THE INDIAN CONTEXT

The orthodox doctrine of the Trinity was formulated in response to heretical ideas such as modalism or Arianism. The Council of Constantinople in A.D. 381 issued a clear and explicit statement of the Trinity to articulate the beliefs, which had been held implicitly by the church until that time. The key formula which emerged from the affirmation that there is "one essence (ousia) in three eternal distinctions/persons (hupostasis)." All Western formulations which emerged in the centuries that followed were based on the Constantinople statement. Perhaps the most famous is the Westminster Confession formulated in the 11th century to provide doctrinal guidance for the church in the newly united kingdom of England and Scotland. The following statement concerning the Trinity was issued, clearly reflecting the orthodoxy of Constantinople:

> In the unity of the Godhead there be three persons, of one substance, power and eternity; God the Father, God the Son, and God the Holy Ghost. The Father is of none, neither begotten nor proceeding; the Son is eternally begotten of the Father; the Holy Ghost eternally proceeding from the Father and the Son.[7]

There are four technical terms in this brief statement: person, substance, begotten, and proceeding. All of these terms are immensely difficult to translate into Indian languages with the necessary precision. The word "person" for example is often translated as "individual" which it cannot mean in the orthodox statement. The word "begotten" will invariably utilize a word with sexual connotations. The word "substance" is often translated as something solid and material which is not at all what was meant by the Greek word *ousia*.[8] The word "proceeding" is invoked because of a long-standing theological and philosophical debate between the Eastern and Western branches of the Church. It is an important debate, but one in which the Indian church has not participated, so the terminology seems alien to them. In short, the orthodox formulations can be translated into Indian languages, but truly capturing the essence and heart of the formulation is exceedingly difficult.

Brahmabandhav Upadhyaya recognizes this problem and attempts to restate the same truths, capturing the essence of the Constantinople formulation, but using the language and thought forms more familiar to Indians. For Westerners, many of the terms and concepts utilized by Upadhyaya may be quite strange. Nevertheless, Upadhyaya is writing as an Indian for other Indians, and he is seeking to convey the Trinity in language and terms which they will understand. He does this through a restatement of Trinitarianism using as his starting point the Upanishadic and philosophic doctrine of saccidananda.

GOD AS SACCIDANANDA:
A RE-STATEMENT OF TRINITARIANISM

In the later Upanishads it is not uncommon to find Brahman described as sat (being or reality), cit (intelligence or consciousness) and ananda (bliss).[9] Thus, sat, cit, and ananda, often designated by the term saccidananda, is widely regarded as the most complete description of Brahman in all of Hindu sacred literature.[10]

The first Indian theologian to identify saccidananda with the Christian Trinity was Upadhyaya's mentor Keshab Chandra Sen. Sen used the picture of a triangle with Brahma of the Vedas at the apex. Brahma descends down as the Son, and then moving along the base of the triangle represents his permeation of the world. Finally, by the power of the Holy Spirit, he returns to the apex carrying degenerated humanity with him: the Still God, the Journeying God, the Returning God; Truth, Intelligence, and Joy.[11] However, this is only a first step, a bare sketch in terms of any comprehensive identification of the two great doctrines of saccidananda and Trinity. Sen's conception of the Trinity was modalistic and therefore could not serve as an effective model for the Christian Trinity.[12] It is Upadhyaya who provided the first detailed analysis of how the two doctrines could relate one to another without compromising Christian orthodoxy. Upadhyaya sought to restate the Trinity in a way which utilized the Upanishadic categories, but was faithful to the historic Christian position regarding the Trinity. The various components which Upadhyaya uses to construct this doctrine will now be examined.

INTERNAL KNOWLEDGE/RELATIONSHIP
WITHIN SAT, CIT, AND ANANDA

Upadhyaya begins by arguing that the three-fold distinction within the Upanishads of sat, cit, and ananda point to internal knowledge and relationships within the Godhead.

If, for example, God is cit, intelligence, as the Upanishads claim, reasons Upadhyaya, then he must necessarily know himself. To this end, "He must form to himself an inward word or image through which this self-knowledge is effected." However, the difference between the inner images we form and that of the Supreme Being is that our images are "accidental and transitory." For God, nothing can be accidental or transitory. Therefore,

His eternal self-comprehension or word is to be conceived as identical with the divine nature and still as distinct from the Supreme Being in as far as he by comprehending himself generates His word. God, knowing himself by producing or generating His own image and word, is called Father; and God as known by himself by this inward generation of the word is called the Word or the Son.[13]

This inner relation must be carefully distinguished from any necessary relationship external to himself. Upadhyaya writes, "The Supreme Being is absolute; he is beyond all necessary relationship with any object external to himself."[14] Thus, God has an eternal, necessary relationship within himself; but all relationships outside of himself are not necessary, but contingent (*vyavaharika*).[15] The idea of relating the relationship between sat, cit and ananda to the internal mystery of the three persons of the Trinity is completely unique to Upadhyaya and becomes the basic hermeneutic from which his whole argument proceeds. This argument by Upadhyaya is clearly an application of scholastic Thomism to the Indian context. However, Upadhyaya is not trying to explain the doctrine of the Trinity through reason alone. He says that the doctrine of the Trinity is a truth "which man can never find out, but [is] revealed by God himself or through his infallible messengers."[16] In other words, Upadhyaya believes that the revelation of God extends beyond the Bible because he sees fragments of divine revelation present in the indigenous scriptures of India in much the same way as Justin Martyr found fragments of revelation which he called "logos spermatikos" (seed of the word) present in Hellenistic philosophy.

GOD AS SAT, CIT, AND ANANDA

By December 1897, Upadhyaya is convinced that the seeds of the doctrine of the Trinity are present in the Upanishads. He credits the Vedantic philosophers with soaring so high as to "peep into the Essence of God [and] to contemplate His interior life."[17] What they realized is that God could not go outside of Himself to satisfy His infinite knowledge and bliss. If He did, He would not be absolute (*asanga*) and unrelated (*nirguna*). However, rather than recognize the internal relatedness of the Godhead, the philosophers either denied the reality of anything external to God, or declared that it was a mystery too great for the "undeveloped intellects of the common people . . . who must be satisfied with stocks and stones."[18] For Upadhyaya, this is the source of the idolatry which stands in stark contrast to the sublime heights which the Vedantic philosophers scaled.

Upadhyaya's understanding of Vedantism is profoundly influenced by his reading and study of the influential 14th century neo-Vedantic teaching manual Pancadasi by Vidyaranya.[19] The Pancadasi contains fifteen chapters divided into three sections known as quintads. Broadly speaking, "the three quintads have for their theme the three aspects of Brahman, sat (existence), cit (consciousness), and ananda (bliss).[20] Characteristic of Upadhyaya's own theological approach, the Pancadasi builds Vedantic revelation on the foundation of human reason, including the insight of Brahman as *saccidananda*.

Adopting the Pancadasi's three-fold framework of God as sat, cit, and ananda, Upadhyaya uses it as the basis for his Trinitarian theology. His application of this theology to each of the three persons of the Trinity will now be explored.

GOD THE FATHER AS SAT

In his journal Sophia Weekly, Upadhyaya launched a five-week series to demonstrate the philosophical underpinnings of his thought. Upadhyaya argues that Descartes' famous Cogito ergo sum is "beset with innumerable dangers" because it makes "human thought the measure of existence." Instead, Upadhyaya argues for Ens est ergo Cogito (Being is, therefore I think).[21] If Being is not posited first, then one risks falling into what Upadhyaya called the abyss of "nothingness" and "emptiness," an almost certain reference to Buddhism. For Upadhyaya, "Being is the ultimate foundation of all certitude, the foundation of thinking." Only God can be truly called sat, i.e. existence by itself which is eternal, immutable, and infinite. All other being has only a borrowed or contingent existence, enduring in time, and is both mutable and limited. To deny that true Being is self-existent "is to affirm that being and non-being are identical."[22]

For Upadhyaya, being (sat) implies not only relatedness, as explored earlier, but it also implies act. Two questions arise: What does an Infinite, self-existent, eternal Being act upon? How does it act? First, any form of dualism or polytheism is self-destructive, argues Upadhyaya, because "there can be only one self-existence; there is no room for a separate, co-eternal recipient of its influence" which is external to the self-existent Being. Thus, as before, the action must be necessarily inward, i.e., within its own self-existent Being, without ruling out the possibility of action with and upon contingently related finite beings. Second, the only way a self-existent being can act upon itself is through knowledge and intelligence; its act is self-knowledge: "The result of its self-act is an eternal distinction between its knowing self and known self without any division in the substance."[23] Thus, the presence of sat necessarily involves a self-related cit.

GOD THE SON AS CIT

We have already demonstrated that, for Upadhyaya, the object of God's knowledge is God. The consciousness (cit) of God must, of necessity, be distinguishable from the Subject (sat) because, he reasons, "a being cannot stand in relation to its identical self." Yet, as has also been demonstrated, God cannot go outside of himself for any necessary relations. Thus, Upadhyaya argues, there must be a "relation of reciprocity" without any division in the divine substance. This, according to revelation, is precisely what the Trinity provides: "God begets in thought his infinite Self-Image and reposes on it with infinite delight while the begotten Self acknowledges responsively his eternal thought-generation." Without compromising the unity of the absolute there is, nevertheless, a "variety of cognition and recognition, the subject and the object corresponding with each other in knowledge."[24] Upadhyaya has now established the ontological basis for the Second Person of the Trinity in a way consistent with advaitic thought.[25]

GOD THE HOLY SPIRIT AS ANANDA

The third and final radical making up the doctrine of saccidananda is the term ananda, translated as bliss or joy. The term ananda as joy or bliss sounds strange to the Western ear until it is recognized that it seals the internal joy of the triune Godhead apart from any external relationships, or, to use Upadhyaya's phrase, it celebrates "the beatitude of triple colloquy." All other sources of joy outside the Godhead must stand in only a contingent relationship to His eternal joy, lest the doctrine erode the doctrine of God as asanga (absolute).[26] Upadhyaya's development of ananda emphasizes three main areas. First, he seeks to demonstrate how ananda confirms the unrelated nature of the Absolute. Second, he seeks to make it clear that ananda is a person, a third, eternal distinction within the Godhead. Third, ananda protects the doctrine of God from slipping into a rationalistic abstraction, but clarifies that the Christian God is one, who out of joy, enters into direct, personal relations with humanity.

To begin with, Upadhyaya defines bliss (ananda) as "the complacent repose of a being upon its own self or its like."[27] He makes an important distinction between the Upanishadic use of ananda as a description of the Absolute, as opposed to vijnana. He argues that vijnana "cognises self through not-self" which implies that the Supreme Being knows himself through relations outside of His own eternal existence. The term ananda, in contrast, implies that the infinite is "self-sufficient, self-satisfied and not dependent upon relations which are not co-terminous with his substance."[28] For Upadhyaya any being which is "obliged to form alliance with something other than its own self cannot be essentially happy."[29]

Second, the three aspects of the Trinity are not qualities, but eternal, personal distinctions within the One Absolute Godhead. Indeed, as explored in chapter two, one of the great mysteries of Hinduism is the relationship between the "One and the many." Upadhyaya seeks to demonstrate that this ananda is distinct, yet One. The three eternal distinctions within the Godhead are not inconsistent with the unity of God. Upadhyaya says, "Sat, cit and ananda cannot be made to give up their distinctions though they are one in Brahman."[30] Ananda is distinct, yet it manifests "the infinitude of the Eternal Essence."[31]

Finally, Upadhyaya is convinced that the Upanishadic summary of the essence of Brahman as saccidananda separates God from the mere abstraction of the rationalists. While Upadhyaya repeatedly affirms his self-sufficiency and independence, this does not mean that God is unknowable or unapproachable. In a review of a collection of sonnets entitled Naivedya, published by his good friend Tagore, Upadhyaya writes:

> The keynote of the Sonnets is the direct, personal relation with the Infinite. There are some who argue that as the Infinite is not easily approachable, the finite should be worshipped tentatively as the Infinite by the less spiritually advanced. Is the Infinite really unapproachable? If it had been so, Reason would be an anomaly. The perception of the Infinite is the dawn of Reason.[32]

Upadhyaya views creation itself as "an overflow of bliss" (ananda). Vedanta teaches that "to know that the supreme being is bliss (ananda) and that the creation of the world (Ioka) is an outflow of that bliss, is the culmination of divine science (vidya)."[33] While it is not essential to His nature, the multiplicity of personal relationships nevertheless occurs as an overflow or abundance. Upadhyaya comments, "It is not a product of necessity, but of superabundance. But this overflow, this superabundance is a mystery which reason encounters as the very outset of religious enquiry."[34] God has endowed each person with a spiritual part, or sheath (anandamaya kosha) which "enables him to become a passive recipient of Divine grace and joy."[35]

Upadhyaya's development of God as sat, cit, and ananda is one of the most significant of his theological contributions. It is a bold attempt in contextualized theology which seeks to do theology "outside the gate" and, in the process, help to communicate the Trinity in language and thought forms which are familiar to those within his own context.[36] Ultimately, the Trinity remains a mystery which can only be grasped via revelation. It is beyond human comprehension to understand how "God begets in thought his infinite Self-image and reposes on it with infinite delight," never losing "blissful communication and colloquy within the bosom of God-head" without creating "any division in the divine Substance."[37]

CONCLUSION

Brahmabandhav Upadhyaya once said that the reason his Hindu friends could not understand "the subtlety and sanctity" of the Christian faith is "because of its hard coating of Europeanism."[38] This study has focused on an attempt by Upadhyaya to re-state the classic Trinitarian formulation in terms and thought-forms which may seem alien to those of us in the West, but are more familiar to Indians. Upadhyaya never claims that his use of saccidananda was able to capture the incomprehensible mystery of the Trinity. After all, every formulation must accept the limitations of human language. Nor did he believe that his re-statement of the Trinity using the language of Vedanta could ever become normative for anyone outside the Indian context. Rather, he was pioneering an experiment in contextualization which involved the re-statement of doctrines which continue, for the most past, to be stated around the world using the Latin and Greek conceptual framework. The fact that the church is now predominantly non-western, makes the kind of work by Upadhyaya and other non-western Christians impossible to ignore. We need a more vigorous discussion concerning the viability of these efforts, and it is hoped that this study will help us as we seek to find the proper balance between our commitment to the faith "once for all delivered to the saints" (Jude 1:3), as well as our calling to be faithful to the particularities of our local contexts.

WORKS CITED

Animanada, B. *The Blade*. Calcutta: Roy and Son, 1947.

Besant, Annie, trans. *The Bhagavad-Gita*. Wheaton: Theosophical Publishing House, 1998.

Boyd, Robin. *An Introduction to Indian Christian Theology*. Delhi: ISPCK, 1994.

Boyd, Robin. *India and the Latin Captivity of the Church*. Cambridge University Press, 1974.

Costas, Orlando. *Christ Outside the Gate: Mission Beyond Christendom*. Maryknoll, New York: Orbis Books, 1982.

Dabney, Robert L. *The Westminster Confession and Creeds*. Dallas: Presbyterian Heritage Publication, 1983.

Gispert-Sauch, Gilbert, S.J. "The Sanskrit Hymns of Brahmabandhav Upadhyaya." *Religion and Society* 19, no. 4 (Dec. 1972): 60-79.

Mahadevan, T. M. P., trans. *Pancadasi*. Madras: Sri Ramakrishna Math, 1967.

May, Peter. "The Trinity and Saccidananda." *Indian Journal of Theology* 7, no. 3 (July-Sept. 1958): 92-98.

O'Flaherty, Wendy, ed. *Hindu Myths*. New York, London: Penguin Books, 1975.

Radhakrishnan, S., ed. *The Principal Upanisads*. Delhi: Harper Collins, 1996.

Tennent, Timothy. *Building Christianity on Indian Foundations*. Delhi: ISPCK, 2000.

Upadhyaya, Brahmabandhav, trans. *Pancadasi*. Calcutta: Publisher Unknown, 1902.

Upadhyaya, Brahmabandhav. *Sophia: A Monthly Catholic Journal*, 1, 1-6, 3. Karachi: Phoenix Press (Jan. 1894-Mar. 1899).

Upadhyaya, Brahmabandhav. *Sophia: A Weekly Review of Politics, Sociology, Literature and Comparative Theology* 1, 1 (New Series)-1, 23 (New Series). Calcutta: K. C. Nan Publisher, (June 16, 1900-December 1, 1900).

Upadhyaya, Brahmabandhav. *The Twentieth Century: A Monthly Review* 1, 1-1, 8. Calcutta: K. C. Nan Publisher, January, 1901-August, 1901.

NOTES

*Diacritical marks for the Sanskrit terms in this essay are not incorporated in the printed format.

1. Orlando E. Costas, *Christ Outside the Gate: Mission Beyond Christendom* (Maryknoll, New York: Orbis Books, 1982), 3.

2. For a comprehensive study of the theology of Brahmabandhav Upadhyaya see my book, *Building Christianity on Indian Foundations: The Legacy of Brahmabandhav Upadhyaya* (Delhi: ISPCK, 2000).

3. In traditional Hinduism, Hindu life has four idealized stages, beginning with a student, followed by a house-holder, followed by a meditating forest dweller and finally, culminating in a world-renouncer or sannyasin.

4. It was customary for Brahmin teachers to take on a new name consistent with their life work. The word "Brahmabandhav" is the Sanskrit equivalent of the Greek name Theophilus, meaning, lover of God. His surname, Upadhyaya, means "teacher."

5. B. Animanada, *The Blade* (Calcutta: Roy and Son, 1947), Appendix 1, i.

6. *Sophia Monthly* 4, no. 7 (July 1897): 8, 9.

7. Westminster Confession 11.3. For a fuller text of the Westminster Confession see, Robert L. Dabney, *The Westminster Confession and Creeds* (Dallas: Presbyterian Heritage Publication, 1983).

8. For a fuller exposition of the problems of translating Latin doctrinal formulations into the Indian context see the excellent book by Robin Boyd, *India and the Latin Captivity of the Church* (Cambridge University Press, 1974).

9. Vajrasucika Upanishad, 9. S. Radhakrishnan, ed., *The Principal Upanishads* (Delhi: Harper Collins, 1996), 937-38.

10. Saccidananda is a religious formula similar to an adesa, i.e. a compact presentation of the truth, often contained in a single word or phrase, which summarizes the essence of a teaching. The formula saccidananda does not appear in the earlier Upanishads, but it was used by later Vedantists to summarize the essence of Upanishadic teaching regarding the Absolute as Sat, Cit, Ananda.

11. Ibid., 94.

12. Modalism refers to the ancient heresy of rejecting the three eternal distinctions in the Godhead and instead viewing the Father, Son, and the Holy Spirit as three, successive manifestations of the One God. According to Modalism, God has revealed himself in three names only. Sen also failed to relate the Trinity to nirguna Brahman, but only to precedents within Hindu literature identified with saguna Brahman.

13. *Sophia Monthly* 2, no. 4 (April 1895): 11. This is a summary of the position of "the Editor of Sophia" (Upadhyaya) as found in an article by A. Heglin, S.J., entitled "One God and Three Persons." Similar statements may be found in Upadhyaya's own writings, but this gives some insight into the early support, encouragement and, indeed, written defense, which he received in the early years from the Jesuit community in India.

14. *Sophia Monthly* 3, no. 2 (Feb. 1896): 5.

15. *Sophia Monthly* 4, no. 8 (Aug. 1897): 9.

16. *Sophia Monthly* 3, no. 3 (Mar. 1896): 4. In another article Upadhyaya writes of "the wonderful fitness of the Christian doctrine of the Trinity [which] illumines the darkness of that abode where dwells the Absolute in light inaccessible, [and] where human reason gets dazzled and blinded." See *Sophia Monthly* 4, no. 8 (Aug. 1897): 9.

17. *Sophia Monthly* 4, no. 12 (Dec. 1897): 2.

18. Ibid. This also sheds light on why Upadhyaya was unwilling to move closer to Ramanuja's position which, for his point of view, gives too much credence to the crude, exoteric worship of village Hinduism. A "stock" is a 19th century term for a block of wood.

19. For a modern English translation of the Pancadasi see, T. M. P. Mahadevan, trans., *Pancaadasi* (Madras: Sri Ramakrishna Math, 1967). Upadhyaya even attempted his own translation and verse-by-verse exposition of the Pancadasi, a portion of which was published in 1902. It is not known for certain how much of the Pancadasi he completed, as only the first fourteen verses (with commentary) are found in the archives of the Goethal's library in Calcutta. Unfortunately, the only extant copy stops in the middle of a sentence in his exposition of chapter one, verse 14. However, even in the small selection which is available, Upadhyaya clearly sets out his understanding in his opening exposition that the three divisions of the Pancadasi correspond to the three aspects of being: Sat, Cit, and Ananda. See B. Upadhyaya, translator, Pancadasi, 1902, publisher unknown, Goethal library archives, Calcutta.

20. T. M. P. Mahadevan, trans., ix. This is an editorial comment by Mahadevan who goes on to emphasize that though the three quintads carry these three themes, all three sections carry the essential teaching of Vedantism reflecting the common repetitious nature of this kind of teaching manual.

21. *Sophia Weekly* 1, no. 2, New Series (23 June, 1900): 8.

22. Ibid.

23. *Sophia Weekly* 1, no. 7, New Series (28 July, 1900): 7.

24. *The Twentieth Century* 1, no. 1 (Jan. 1900): 6, 7.

25. Although space does not permit a full development of Upadhyaya's development of the Son as cit, he seeks to establish it not only on epistemological grounds, but also on religious grounds through the application of logos theology to the advaitic context and a hymn of Christian worship to the Son of God using the language of Vedanta. For a full exposition and discussion of this advaitic hymn and the application of logos theology to the Indian context see my *Building Christianity on Indian Foundations.*

26. As the discussion concerning ananda will make clear, Upadhyaya's initial emphasis on the "unrelated nature" of God only means that God is not related to His creation out of necessity.

27. *Sophia Weekly* 1, no. 7, New Series (28 July, 1900): 6.

28. *Sophia Weekly* 1, New Series (Sept. 1900). Upadhyaya's identification of ananda and reason is based on his study of the Pancadasi which affirms that "inanimateness manifests his being, sentiency his intelligence and rationality his bliss." In the October 27 issue of *Sophia Monthly* 3, no. 2 (Feb. 1896): 5, Upadhyaya translates ananda as "unalloyed joy" to reinforce that His joy is not related by necessity to any contingent being to make His joy complete or full.

29. *Sophia Monthly* 5, no. 8 (Aug. 1898): 119. This clearly means that humans have no intrinsic or self-grounded ability to be joyful apart from a relationship with the living God.

30. *Twentieth Century* 1, no. 6 (June, 1901): 12.

31. Ibid.

32. B. Animananda, *The Blade*, 101; Robin Boyd, *An Introduction to Indian Christian Theology* (Dehli: ISPCK, 1994), 71.

33. As quoted in *Sophia Weekly* 1, no. 7, New Series (28 July, 1900): 6.

34. *Sophia Weekly* 1, no. 8, New Series (4 Aug., 1900). A similar statement is found in Upadhyaya's personal translation of a portion of the first chapter of the Pancadasi. He comments on verses 8 and 9 of the first chapter saying, "This eternal Samvid is bliss transcendent . . . it is its own object of supreme love. Its love of self is independent of its love of dependent objects; and its love for objects other than self proceed from superabundance of its love of the self-object. It is not in need of being correlated with the finite for the purpose of maintaining its bliss. It is pure self-act." See Pancadasi, translation with commentary by B. Upadhyaya, 1: 8, page 14; Goethal's library archives, St. Xavier's College, Calcutta.

35. *The Twentieth Century* 1, no. 1 (31 Jan. 1901): 10.

36. *Sophia Monthly* 5, no. 1 (Jan. 1898).

37. *Twentieth Century* 1, no. 1 (Jan. 1901).

38. Gilbert Gispert-Sauch, S.J., "The Sanskrit Hymns of Brahmabandhav Upadhyaya," *Religion and Society* 19, no. 4 (Dec. 1972): 74.

A Mahāyāna Theology of the Real Presence of Christ in the Eucharist

*John P. Keenan**

MAHĀYĀNA THEOLOGY IS AN APPROACH TO THINKING ABOUT THE Christian faith within the philosophical context of the great Mahāyāna Buddhist thinkers: philosophers of emptiness such as Nāgārjuna, Āryadeva, and Candrakīrti in the Mādhyamika tradition; and philosophers of consciousness such as Maitreya, Asaçga, Vasubandhu, Sthiramati, Paramārtha, and Hsüan-tsang in the Yogācāra tradition. The advantage of employing Mahāyāna philosophy in the doing of Christian theology is that this philosophical tradition developed with the dual purpose of supporting and encouraging faith and practice while eliminating absolutist claims for metaphysically fixed and unalterable ideas.

Mahāyāna is deconstructive without any of the aloofness that modern French philosophers apparently feel they must adopt vis-à-vis theology and the Church. Just as Plato did for the Fathers of the early church and Aristotle did for Aquinas, Mahāyāna opens avenues of thought and questioning for contemporary theologians that will gift our cultures with the grace of new theological insight into the meaning of Christ's presence to and among human beings.

And so I would like to do some theology here, demonstrating how a Mahāyāna thinker like myself might envisage the real presence of Jesus in the Eucharist.

THE REAL PRESENCE OF CHRIST

The theology of the real presence of Jesus in the Eucharist has had a long and fascinating development. For the first eight centuries, the issue did not arise with any doctrinal insistence.[1] Christians were content to see Christ's presence in the performance of the Eucharistic rite as a medicine of immortality that would heal their souls and embody for them the reality of the risen Christ. It was only later, in the condemnation of the theologian Ratramnus[2] and the development of the doctrine of transubstantiation, that the classical formulation took shape.[3] That doctrine was expressed in philosophic terms that were then current, concepts that were accepted as clear and valid frameworks for thinking.

Medieval theologians, especially the great St. Thomas Aquinas in the thirteenth century, had just rediscovered Aristotle and gloried in the subtle intricacies and vast overviews that this "new" learning provided them.[4] They philosophized by seeking insight into and defining the very act of existence

---

* The author, an Episcopal priest, taught at Middlebury College, and has written many noted volumes on Christian theological themes in dialogue with Mahayana Buddhist thought, including *The Meaning of Christ: A Mahayana Theology* (Maryknoll, NY: Orbis Books, 1990); *The Gospel of Mark, A Mahayana Reading* (Maryknoll, NY: Orbis Books, 1995); and most recently, *Grounding Our Faith in a Pluralist World* (Eugene, OR: Wipf and Stock, 2008).

itself, discussing the "essences," or "substances" of things as the underlying realities that we encounter in our life and in our faith. In this view, Christ "subsists"—that is, he really exists—as the substance of the bread and wine in the Eucharist. This is the philosophic view that is stressed even today in the Roman Catholic Church. . . .

The disputes about the real presence of Christ in the Eucharist hinged precisely on this issue—what is the inner reality of the sacrament?

My claim would be that it is no longer "fitting" to apply a little-understood medieval metaphysics of being to our understanding of faith in the real presence of Christ in the Eucharist. This approach is no longer a skillful way of teaching. For in order to comprehend the doctrine of transubstantiation, one first must be trained at least in the rudiments of the underlying philosophical framework it presupposes. It is not that people no longer believe that the substance of bread and wine is changed into the substance of the body and blood of Christ. They simply do not think in terms of substance and accidents at all. "Substances" refer to illegal drugs, and "accidents" to automobile crashes. Bread is just bread and wine is just wine—no inner substances are holding them in existence.

In an age when substance was the most real of real things, the explanation of the real presence of Christ in the Eucharist was well served by the doctrine of transubstantiation. Indeed, for people who have been graced with long years of training in that medieval philosophy, it remains a deep, penetrating, and true theology. To them, the appearances of bread and wine, their texture and taste, and so forth, are no more than the accidents, while the reality present is the very presence of the body and blood of Christ. This is not just a symbol. It is not like the barber pole that symbolizes the barber—who may or may not be present.

However, most people are not now trained in classical medieval thought, and one can no longer assume that somehow a cultural trickle-down will occur. What does trickle down in postmodern cultures is skepticism and doubt, and in this context metaphysically fixed doctrines find it difficult to maintain their stable and unchanging status.[5] For many in our time, the concept of transubstantiation brings to mind little more than a magic show.[6] Does Jesus actually come spiritually from somewhere else to be (substantially) present under the (accidental) guise of bread and wine? Where was he before that? And does he stay there afterward? These are all traditional questions, with varied and sophisticated answers, all couched in the language of medieval ontology.

There is another angle that must be considered. We are speaking not just about presence, but about the presence of a person. What is a person and how is personal presence brought about? Especially when that person is confessed to be the Christ, the Second Person of the Trinity?

The Presence of the Person of Christ

It is not just the presence of Christ that is encountered in the Eucharist, but his very person, his reality as a person. Christ himself becomes present to the eyes of faith. Saint Thomas of Aquinas explains that a person is "a distinct subsistence in an intelligent nature" (*subsistens distinctum in nature intellectualis*). This means that "a person, therefore, is that which subsists (stands under) as distinct in an intelligent nature."[7] Here the focus is on the person of the Second Person of the divine Trinity, whose very essence is described by St. Thomas Aquinas as "the very act subsistently to be" (*ipsum esse subsistens*), and whose three "persons" are defined only in terms of their shared mutuality and mutual relations.[8] The person of Christ is the Divine Logos, in two natures, his divine nature and his human nature. So Jesus was present as a human and so he continues in the Eucharist, as the human who died and was raised from the dead.[9] So in the act of the Eucharist and in our participation in that liturgy, we encounter, as Schillebeeckx insists, the dynamic presence of the primordial sacrament of Christ in forming, maintaining, and directing the Church. This is the Christ who, in taking upon himself our human nature, enables us by grace to become "divinized." Still, the definitions, once again couched in terms of medieval ontology, glory in notions and vocabulary scarcely accessible even to students of theology. What indeed is a person? Are the terms that are usually employed to explain this adequate? More to the point, do they still carry meaning?

Here once again we should pause to observe that, no matter how difficult and obscure the language, its point is to insist that in the Eucharist we actually do encounter the risen Christ, beyond death, but not beyond history. This is the same historical Christ who lived, taught, was executed, and rose, who has a history, and we are bidden to remember that history in the words that immediately follow the consecration: "Do this in remembrance of me." That is, recollecting how he lived, what he said, how he continued to direct the Church, how he breathes through the tradition ever since and into the future. This is the point, not the philosophical underpinnings of the doctrine. "Theologians continued to recognize that the fundamental content of the dogma of transubstantiation was the doctrine of the real presence, rather than a particular philosophical definition of substance and accident."[10]

The problem is that Christian theologians often simply equate "substantial" with true and real, and insist that these words must be repeated, learned, and treated as if they still possess semantic vigor. In fact, often they are of interest only to students of ancient and medieval Western thought. In a philosophic world accustomed to thinking in terms of interconnectedness and complexity theory, there simply are no real substances anywhere. Contemporary thinkers should not, I would argue, be excluded from the theological discourse that we so cherish because they do not embrace one particular metaphysics of being. True, both the Council of Trent and the 1994 *Catechism of the Catholic Church* say that the Church has "fittingly and properly" described the real presence in substantialist terms and the change that is wrought by the Eucharistic blessing "transubstantiation." It is indeed a question of what is fitting and appropriate, but I would suggest that what was fitting during the time of the Council of Trent is no longer apt or fitting today. God is immutable. Philosophies change.

And so I would like to sketch another option, an option that I hope will enunciate the dynamic presence of Christ in the Eucharist in terms that are more skillfully adapted to this culture and this time.

A MAHĀYĀNA UNDERSTANDING OF THE REAL PRESENCE

A Mahāyāna theology eschews a philosophy of substances. It refutes such a philosophic view simply as mistaken, as driven by human attachment to self-bolstering ideas. In a Mahāyāna understanding, transubstantiation describes an event that is not intelligible, since there are no substances in the first place. All things are empty specifically of substance. They exist in mutual dependence and construct their identities from a cluster of causes, genetic and historical. However, this does not mean that a Mahāyāna theology of the Eucharist must dispense with the real presence, only with its philosophical underpinnings. Indeed, many years ago in theology class at St. Charles Borromeo Seminary in Philadelphia, hardly a bastion of radical theology, I was taught that the hylomorphic framework (that things are constituted by matter [*hylê*], and form [*morphos*], i.e., essence) employed in sacramental theology was not itself a part of revealed truth, just a convenient format in which to present that truth. If it were proved to be mistaken (and indeed no physicist today talks in those terms of matter and form or considers them relevant), it would affect theology only on the periphery.

Let us then attack that underlying philosophy, so as to reclaim with vigor the doctrine of the real presence. Perhaps we not only can, but are called to, rethink these ancient traditions, not to "update" them from some misguided sense of modernity, but perchance to reclaim for them some of their ancient power and dynamism. We should not put extra burdens on people, demanding that they accept not only the doctrine of the faith, but its traditional philosophical scaffolding. One need not be Greek or European to confess Christ as truly and really present in the Eucharist.

What is Jesus doing at that Last Supper? He takes bread and wine, says that these are in fact his body and blood, and gives them to his friends to eat and drink. He does so in the context of a Jewish blessing of thanksgiving and tells his followers to repeat that supper in his memory.[11]

Who is this Jesus who acts thus? A first-century Jew, a prophet, a cynic philosopher, a messiah who will deliver his people, an anti-messiah who will die on a cross, the Son of God. There are many contemporary definitions, and many theologically driven definitions. Here in this context of meditating on the scriptural accounts of the Last Supper, I suggest that the central issue is indeed the identity of Jesus Christ. By doing just what he did, he drew the boundary lines that formed his identity around the bread and wine to be shared. Indeed, Jesus identified his historical self with those elements. He redefined himself, away from the single physical body about to be executed, and toward the cosmos itself in its supportive and nurturing dimension—the bread and the wine, the life-giving sustenance for human beings. It is not that he took his already set and firmly delineated identity and transferred that to the bread and wine, as if the historical world in which he lived, died, and rose were not crucially important, as if it were merely the backdrop to really important and substantial entities, each contained within specific and enclosed limits, and each identifiable. Christ lived and lives in time, not in static viewpoints.

As Schillebeeckx writes, the very being of Christ was to be transparently open to the Father.[12] He is, in the words of St. Ignatius of Antioch, "the voice of the Father from silence," the speaking of God (sermo dei).[13] In Zen Mahāyāna terms, Jesus is the finger constantly pointing to the Father, and then turning to point at the sufferings and injustice we find everywhere in our world. We are properly concerned, creatively so, to delineate his historical person. But in the texts upon which we base our faith, Jesus is more slithery, slipping out of our intellectual grasp, described only in broad terms, and not focused upon his own consciousness, but upon the mind of his Father—the rule of justice and peace for all humans. At the end of his earthly life, he does delineate his own identity, but there is no "Here I stand! This is Me!" Only "Forgive them!" and "It is finished!" In the earliest layers of the gospels Jesus does not affirm his supernatural identity. Nor does he hide himself away within the bread and the wine. Rather, he declares his very personhood open to and encompassing the entire sustaining world. When he says, "This is my body. . . . This is my blood," we wonder what the meaning of "is" is. To a Mahāyānist, these statements signify that now and henceforth Jesus is present in and identified with the sustaining world, in and with the bread and wine. This is why sharing in that meal is the medicine of immortality, the meal in which we share in the life-giving sustenance of Jesus, so that we too might depart from all too rigid definitions of our own identities, that we too might realize no-self. This is not a meal that Jesus puts on by himself, but by its very nature is a shared experience, an experience that Jesus shared with his closest friends and shares again with ever-new friends. Participation in the Eucharist does not invite us each to intensify our own identities, to define more clearly who we think we are. Rather, it draws us to incorporate ourselves within his mystical body, to practice insight into the no-self of all our deluded, self-enclosed identities, and to take as our portion mystical identification of Jesus with the world as sustaining all sentient beings.

The community of Christians as the Body of Christ, an image first used by Paul, is an apt and skillful metaphor, which tells more truth than any literal statement. It does not mean, pace Bernard Cooke, that "individuals retain their identity, and yet there is truly a vital principle that unites them into one life."[14] We are attached to our self-constructed identities, to who we think we are. But our human life, permeated with the grace of the Eucharist, courses through the entire cosmos. The Fathers teach that in assuming human life, Jesus takes up all creation in his Body, of which we are members. Paul cries out that "I live now, not I, but Christ lives in me!" We become integral and functional parts of a larger whole that renders Jesus present again and again in all the deeds that benefit and gladden sentient beings. And this is healing precisely because it enables us, following the Master, to broaden our identity boundaries and serve as a saving community that is the body of the risen Christ.

Of course, "the mystical body of Christ" is a metaphor. We clearly each do retain our physical bodies, with their obvious functionings and disfunctionings. But the definition of self as bounded by the skins of these bodies is emptied of any final being. The self has no abiding essence (anātman). It exists essence-free in dependence upon a host of historical, genetic, and cosmic causes and conditions: our families, our parents, our path through this life, our genes, the very being of the universe, and—most especially—our memories, which lead us back to the time of Jesus and incorporate our self-identities within his identity. There is no final need to carve up the real into units of self and not-self. Rather, we live by passing through "the great doubt"—that we have no firm hold on being, that we do not control the flux and change that swirls through our veins—and into an assured and confident identification with Christ, mixing our memories and sharing his experiences. This is what the Greek Fathers meant by teaching that by the Eucharist, through participation in the Eucharist, we are "divinized," sharing by the uncreated grace of the indwelling Spirit in the very being of God. We are by grace what God is by nature, they declare. That is indeed a radical reorientation of anybody's sense of identity.[15]

It is not that what had heretofore been but bread and wine is now become Jesus. This explanation, taken in today's cultural context, encourages us to think of a Jesus hidden beneath the coverings of the bread and wine. It is a supernaturalist, almost alchemical, image of Christ's presence as secreted away and reduced to miniature. Supernatural essences function here the same way as any essences, placing boundaries around presence and defining realities. Yet these supposed realities are most ethereal, based as they are on misunderstood philosophies of being. They tempt us to erect entire orders of supernatural entities existing above and apart from our everyday world. The discouraging corollary to this supernaturalist theory is that, in that everyday world, Christ is not present at all. In this misunderstanding, his reality stands opposed to our cultures and our lives, ready to break in with supernal force, erupting into our proud and arrogant lives, constructed as they are upon sin, delusion, and doubt. In actual fact, all that is happening is that an outlived metaphysics of essence and definition is facing new and different patterns of philosophic thinking that focus on interdependence and complexity. Despite the wishes of fundamentalists, it is not Christ against culture, but one culture against another. In their view, the medicine of the Eucharist would effect radical surgery to eliminate culture, to amputate its ability to think in less substantialist terms about God and things divine.

It is not that bread and wine transmute into Jesus, but the other way around: through his wisdom of no-self, Jesus identifies his very being, his real presence, with the bread and wine, and thereby with the cosmos, as nurturing all sentient beings. Paul, having encountered the presence of the risen Christ on the road to Damascus and in his ecstasy while praying in the Temple in Jerusalem, knows that he too has been redefined, that he no longer is alive at all, but that his life force is now the life force of Christ. It is Christ who lives in him; for he has realized no-self (*anātman, ātmaśūnyatā*). Such redefinition, whether by Jesus or by Paul, is not a matter of adding something to an already well-delineated self. The mystical body is not just a Pauline metaphor but the very practice of Christian no-self: it is, like Jesus, to abandon all sense of self-enclosed identity to become one with the world and with all its creatures.

Our identities slacken, our self-affirming images and notions weaken, and we no longer remain encased within or circumscribed by some supposed core of being that we possess uniquely—no role, no rank, no status; no longer my body, my self, my faith, my religion. Perfect love casts out all fear, and our identities are defined now, not by the conventions of deluded primal ignorance, but by the conventions and practices of pilgrimage into Christ. All identities are conventional, all selfhood exists only dependent on clusters of causes and conditions. We are empty selves following a lord who emptied his very self, becoming the transparent mirror of the Father. With Christ, we too enunciate that voice of the Father from silence. Christians then are the words spoken by that voice. Metaphors become more central to who we are and how we are to practice.

The metaphysics of presence can be shunted to the sidelines as an apt tool for those who need to cling to metaphysical viewpoints, but that is very dangerous.[16] Indeed, the danger to the Christian theologian or apologist is not the encounter with new and unfamiliar theologies, but rather deluded attachment to old, unskillful philosophies. It is not Mahāyāna Buddhism that we need to fear, but rather our own squeamishness about moving out into the world of our culture, there to proclaim Christ in as many languages as there are tongues. To repeat the same ideas ad nauseam is to cause nausea. This habit tends to substitute our own cherished ideas for authentic Christian experience, drawing us away from practice and toward spurious claims that God is thus and such, or speaks only so and not otherwise. Metaphysics encase the words of God and force them through selected filters. The presence of Christ in Eucharistic participation and life remembrance reverberates through our entire bodies. Propositions about substances and essences only bounce around in our heads.

Jesus is present as dependently arisen, within our shared history, and into our shared future. So the Eucharistic meal is defined as the presence of Jesus, repeated in memory of Jesus. It is not a magic banquet where one consumes a golden elixir that renders one immortal. Its meaning flows only from remembrance, from recollection that we are dealing with the real presence of Jesus in the sacrament. Memory is so crucial to our sense of identity that when we lose our memory we lose a sense of who we are. We may find our Christian identity, on the other hand, through remembering Jesus in all he taught, in all the parables and stories he employed to upset our worlds and undermine our set ideas. We remember how he lived, healing others, helping others, going about doing good—but not just as a good man. We remember that he died and was raised from the dead, that his execution was the final defeat of his historical selfhood, and that on the point of that defeat he first redefined his being as identical with the bread and wine of the world, the source that enlivens and sustains us all.

His resurrection was not a reaffirmation of his human selfhood as though God now corrected the error of his untimely death. Rather, his risen body, as Paul insists, is a spiritual body, present among us and nurturing us. Abandoning preset notions of self, we also remember that he died because he preached justice and peace, and that he rose because he had already expanded his self-definition, identifying with the poor and marginalized, with the nobodies of his and our time. He identifies himself not just with his message, as the negators of the resurrection would have it. Rather, he identifies himself with his ongoing life in the world, again and again made concrete and local in the Eucharist, wherein we become one with Jesus and expand our definitions. Our Christian identity is never established apart from participation in that sacramental presence, for without this medicine, we have no remedy from death.

Now we too live, no longer for ourselves, but as members of the mystical, that is, the hidden, body of Christ, for that is who he truly is and that is where he is truly present. He does not take over the inner core being of the bread and wine, but just as they are they become the extended boundaries of his presence, of who he is. Neither is it that Jesus hovers above or around us, or even that, contained within the species of bread and wine, he introduces himself into our lives over and over again. Rather, personal boundaries fade and Christ and his disciples identify one with the other. It is truly a question of identity, of who Jesus is, and thus of who we are. His real presence means that we too can really become present to the world, not to withdraw from the world as with the Eucharistic piety of *The Imitation of Christ*. That—along with the Buddhist *Dharmapāda* that Pope John Paul II read and criticized—is an other-worldly book. Rather, we are sent out from the Eucharist, now identified with the Christ to go into the world. Each time, we are sent (*ita missa est*) into the world to embody the tasks of kindness, compassion, and Christian love, not in service to any cherished identity of our own that must be clung to in deluded commitment. Rather, we are sent to live transparently, openly, and ready to meet and encounter people from all cultures and all traditions.

We are not first required to determine just exactly who we are, for our true selves as Christians are always worked out in recollection of Jesus, through participation in his Eucharistic presence, by reading the scriptures, by entering into the still center of quiet prayer and meditation, and in the dependently co-arisen circumstances of our actual lives. Our identity is the final term of a long spiritual process. Let us not try to co-opt that process, jumping the gun with a deluded supernatural sense of just who we must be. That would preclude the God of surprises and steal a march on all our partners in human history and endeavor, even before we meet and engage one another.

So let us become more attuned to presence, and to the traditions of others who also practice sacramental rites. And there are many who claim that in remembering the Buddha Amida, Other Power grasps them and assures them that even as defiled beings they too are saved. Others confess that the body, voice, and mind of the primal Buddha Mahāvairocana is realized concretely in Shingon Tantric liturgies, that the primordial Buddha (*ādibuddha*) is actually experienced as present in those Tantric rituals. Hindus meet God and receive a *darśan*—God actually *looks* at them and accepts them as they are, in countless ceremonies in ancient and modern India.

If we are to be transformed from glory to glory and become with Jesus the voice of the Father from silence, let us make sure that we can and do actually engage others in our speaking, and not cut them off by insisting on cherished metaphysical structures that reduce others to lesser versions of ourselves. To meet Christ in the Eucharist is to be pried away from our canned identities and opened up to living an organic life as a community of the body of Christ, which extends beyond any institutional form and any preset encasement. Christ is present here in our very lives, not as a sometime visitor, but as the life that we all are invited to live together.

Notes

1. Jaroslav Pelikan, *The Christian Tradition: A History of the Development of Doctrine*, vol. 3. *The Growth of Medieval Theology (600-1300)* (Chicago & London: University of Chicago Press, 1975), 166.

2. Ibid., 186.

3. Ibid., 203.

4. The tale is often told, but to me the works of Étienne Gilson, such as *The Spirit of Medieval Philosophy* (New York: Charles Scribner, 1940), stand out as excellent.

5. See Alan Bloom, *The Closing of the American Mind* (New York: Simon & Schuster, 1987), which argues that the philosophies of existentialism and of suspicion that so characterize continental philosophy have indeed "trickled" down into the minds of ordinary Americans (and other modern people), rendering them far from ready to accept fixed and solid definitions of unchanging units of meaning.

6. The Dutch Catechism remarked on this tendency a number of times: "Do not such difficulties [as the apparent ineffectiveness of Communion to improve our lives] stem from the fact that we are too much inclined to regard the Eucharist as a magical device which stands apart? Communion is not magic, but food, consolation, companionship, and realization of what we are: sinners who have been called by Christ" (*A New Catechism*, 334).

7. Bernard F. Lonergan, *De constitutione Christi ontologica et psychologica* (Rome: Apud Aedes Universitatis Gregorianae, 1961), 24.

8. Paul Vanier, *Théologie Trinitaire chez Saint Thomas d'Aquin: Évolution du concept d'action notionelle* (Paris: Librairie Philosophique J. Vrin, 1953).

9. See John P. Keenan, *The Meaning of Christ: A Mahāyāna Theology* (Maryknoll, NY: Orbis Books, 1989), 45-64.

10. Pelikan, *The Christian Tradition*, 204.

11. See Dom Gregory Dix, *The Shape of the Liturgy* (New York: Seabury Press, 1982).

12. Edward Schillebeeckx, *Jesus: An Experiment in Christology* (New York: Seabury Press, 1978), 307.

13. Keenan, *The Meaning of Christ*, 221-39.

14. Bernard Cooke, *Christian Sacraments and Christian Personality* (New York: Holt, Rinehart and Winston, 1965), 131.

15. There was an extended theological discussion on "uncreated grace" in the generation immediately before Vatican II, with many books and articles by a number of thinkers: Garrigou-Lagrange, Bourassa, de Letter, Dockx, and many others. See especially Maurice de la Taille, *Created Actuation by Uncreated Act* (West Baden Press, 1952); Paul Galtier, *L'Habitation en nous des trois personnes* (Rome: Pontifica Università Gregoriana, 1950); and Karl Rahner, "Some Implications of the Scholastic Concept of Uncreated Grace" in *Theological Investigations*, vol. 1, trans. Cornelius Ernst (Baltimore: Helicon Press, 1961), 319-46. The focus of the argumentation was the nature of the indwelling of the Holy Spirit, how it came about, and how it related to the human subject—by efficient causality or perhaps by a kind of quasiformal causality, i.e., by divinizing human beings in some extended sense.

16. For a Mahāyāna meditation and discourse on the absence of presence see Malcolm David Eckel, *To See the Buddha: A Philosopher's Quest for the Meaning of*

Emptiness (San Francisco: HarperSanFrancisco, 1992). See also Gadjin Nagao, *The Foundational Standpoint of Mādhyamika Philosophy*, trans. John P. Keenan (Albany: State University of New York Press, 1989).

A Common Creation Story?
Interreligious Dialogue and Ecology

*Paul F. Knitter**

"FOR THE FIRST TIME IN OUR HISTORY, WE HAVE EMPIRICAL EVIDENCE for a common creation story." Thus declared a group of fifty representatives of various religious traditions back in the early 1990s in one of the first steps toward what eventually was to become the Earth Charter.[1] Over the past decade, that vision of a common creation story has grown in both substance and urgency, especially through the scientific research and prophetic voices of Thomas Berry and Brian Swimme.[2] The proposal—and the dream—is that science, an enterprise that is available to all cultures and religions, is now providing the religious communities of the world with something that, so far, they have not been able to find on their own: a truly common ground that will enable them to talk together and work together as never before. The creation story as science tells it is delivered in a way that all religions can, and must, hear it. Hence, science and its understanding of our earth and universe are providing the arena for a new kind of interreligious dialogue. Swimme put it this way:

> Though scientific knowledge has put lethal weapons in our hands, it has also provided the Earth with the first common story of our origins and development. . . . Precisely because this story of the universe comes to us through our investigations beginning with our eyes and ears and body, we can speak of a transcultural creation story. Members of every continent are involved in discovering and articulating this story. Members of every religious tradition are involved in its telling.[3]

What science is telling us today about the origins of the universe (especially the creative, mysterious, still-evolving Big Bang) and how the universe works (through a pervasive, on-going net of interrelationships that make humans "cousins to the stars, to the rocks and oceans, to all living creatures")[4] is a story

---

* The author teaches at Union Theological Seminary in New York, and is well-known for his many works in Christian theology relating to the religious other, including his *Introducing Theologies of Religion* (Maryknoll, NY: Orbis Books, 2002), and his most recent *Without Buddha I Could Not Be Christian* (Oxford: OneWorld, 2009).

that all religions can use to "hear again" and "deepen" their own stories of how the universe originated or how it works. As Sallie McFague has made clear, the scientific creation story is not meant to replace but to adjust and invigorate traditional myths and beliefs and relate them interreligiously:

> This common story is available to be remythologized by any and every religious tradition and hence is a place of meeting for the religions, whose conflicts in the past and present have often been the cause of immense suffering and bloodshed as belief is pitted against belief. What this common story suggests is that our primary loyalty should be not to nation or religion but to the earth and its Creator (albeit that Creator may be understood in different ways).[5]

This suggestion of a "primary loyalty" to the new creation story has been spelled out by Berry. He announced that, unless religious communities realign their traditional creeds in view of the earth as the primary revelation and context of religious experience, they will not be able to respond adequately to the sensitivities and needs of our third-millennium world. "We are . . . at a time when these earlier traditions can no longer, out of their own resources, provide adequate guidance in the task that is before us."[6] So, Berry urged the religions to open themselves to the reality of a universal revelation, or a meta-religious context, that can reanimate each and reconnect them all: "Our new sense of the universe [the new creation story] is itself a type of revelatory experience. Presently we are moving into a meta-religious age that seems to be a new comprehensive context for all religions."[7]

DANGERS AND RESERVATIONS

As I view the beauty and feel the power of Berry's "universe story," his notion of "the great work" and the possibilities of a common creation story, I find myself, with many others, both inspired and hopeful—but also hesitant and fearful. My reservations are prompted not just by what I hear from my colleagues in our thoroughly postmodern academy but also from my brothers and sisters in the interreligious dialogue. They warn me of the danger of universals, and that means the dangers of "common stories" or "meta-narratives." If I can summarize crisply the root of this danger, I think it has to do with the way universals tend to skip over the reality of language—which means the reality of how language makes all that we know and say always limited and often lethal.

The fact that language limits anything we know or say is clear from the contemporary realization that our ability to speak does not just communicate what we know; it also determines what we know. Language—or our cultural-linguistic systems—does not affect just how we speak of what we know but also how we know what we know. It determines, in other words, what we know. And, by determining, it limits. We can never see the whole picture. We can never have a universal language. Yes, languages can and must communicate with each other, but to propose a universal language will most likely mean to impose it. Hence, truth, like language, will be better served and protected when it is recognized to be inherently and ineluctably diverse. Any kind of a "common story" for humanity, therefore, will somehow also have to be diverse. Otherwise, it is dangerous.

The danger mounts when we remind ourselves, further, that language and culture not only always limit what we know; they can also render it lethal. Language is always a restriction, but it can also be a weapon. One does not have to agree fully with Michel Foucault to get his point that language is tied to power.[8] We tend to use it in a way that promotes our own well-being over others', even when we are not aware that we are doing so. So, the words we use and the stories we tell in order to know and communicate not only limit what we are saying; they can also be used to limit and control and devalue what others are saying. Language, in other words, is not only culturally conditioned; it is also politically and economically conditioned. This is why we of the so-called "first world" are told by our friends in the "two-thirds world" that the language that is used in cross-cultural conversations is usually the language of those with the most economic power. Similarly, this is why so often the "common ground" that is proposed for a universal project based on universal need turns out to be the "ground" or the "need" that is much more "common" to one group than to others—usually the group that has more money or weapons than the others.

Thus, there are critics of those of us who speak of a "common creation story" or of the way our "one earth" can provide the common ground for a new dialogue among "the many religions." I have been told that my own efforts along these lines[9] are, like all the others, nothing more than renewed and cleverly camouflaged attempts to carry on the Western-based, hegemonic project of modernity. There is a "Kantian motor" driving all this talk of a new common text—this one written by scientists—that is supposed to subsume or be the higher norm for all the earlier, disjointed, and "primitive" texts. Such proposals for a shared creation story or for a new interreligious dialogue that takes the earth as its common ground have been described as a "divinization of the earth" based on a "sacralization of science," a "new ecologism" that becomes an "eco-olatry." All this, we are told, is a "Trojan Horse" within which hide the forces of a new meta-narrative; such a narrative is not only theologically a new form of idolatry, but it can also easily become, politically, an "eco-fascism" that proclaims one unified, universal, authoritative voice—now the voice of the earth—over all other voices.[10]

In no way am I suggesting that such criticisms should derail our efforts toward a new kind of ecological dialogue of religions, which might be grounded in a shared creation myth; these criticisms, I suspect, are driven by their own motors. However, I do believe that they have to be taken seriously. They are pointing us toward real dangers that can all too easily corrupt or co-opt any efforts to call the religions of the world together around a new earth story.

In what follows, I would like to suggest ways in which we can confront and defuse these dangers, so that, if there is to be any kind of a common creation story, all religious voices will be part of telling it, and, if the earth is to be the common ground for a new dialogue, no one religion or nation will be allowed to own more stock in that ground than others. The pivotal point of what I would like to propose is simple: Where we begin and how we proceed is crucially important. I want to suggest that an interreligious dialogue that seeks to elaborate a common earth story should begin with ethics rather than with formal religion, with moral praxis rather than mystical reflection, with acting together for the earth rather than elaborating a common religious story about the earth. The first steps toward exploring common ground or a common story should be interethical more than expressly interreligious. I also hope to indicate how, if we start with ethics, we will, necessarily and happily, find ourselves closer together as religious persons. Ethical "first steps" enable and require religious "second steps." The door, or the guide, to a deep mystical ecumenicity among the religions can be found in an ethical ecumenicity. An earth ethics can be an effective key to open the door to an interfaith earth mysticism and the possibility of a common creation story. . . .

[*In two subsections not included here, the author offers the thesis that ethics or moral praxis provides the soil for religious experience, and takes this a step further to affirm that our current ecological situation is providing a shared foundation for an "earthly mysticism" that can be the basis of a common creation story.*]

Entering and Sharing the Common Creation Story

To realize that there is an ethical door through which we can pass into the mystical and revelatory splendor of nature can be a help and a safeguard, I suggest, in making more sensitive and more ecumenical use of Berry and Swimme's image of the universe story as a common creation story. As we have heard, a postmodern criticism of their proposal asks whether they run the danger of pressing the cultural-linguistic system of modern science on worldviews and cultures for which the scientific creation myth, although used in laboratories and factories, may not have validity in temples and ceremonies. Perhaps not all religious cosmologies can "hear" or relate to the scientific creation story as readily and eagerly as Berry thinks or hopes. Perhaps many religious persons, especially in the two-thirds world, will fear that the new creation myth is another example of the West's taking over, this time under the guise of science.

This is where Berry and others who urge a common universe story might profit from the ethical approach I have been suggesting. Maguire helps me formulate what I mean: "Scholars who seek out the 'common essence' [or the common creation story] of religions regularly miss the moral commons on which religions meet. This comes from introducing God-talk [or creation stories] too early." By adding the statement already cited, "Moral-talk is logically and epistemologically prior to God-talk,"[11] Maguire has helped me formulate my suggestion to Berry and others: The universe story as ethical demand may have a priority over the universe story as creation myth. In other words, rather than beginning with the beauty and the interrelatedness and the common origins of the universe story as science sees that story, we might do better to begin with the agony and the peril and the horror of the universe story as environmentalists are telling the same story.

Whereas Berry and others are taking a directly mystical view of the earth, I am suggesting another—indirect, but perhaps more readily available—mystical approach, through the ethical and the prophetic. Simply put, the sense of the sacred that Berry finds in the scientific story of the universe is even more widely at hand in the ethical practice of saving the earth. You do not have to accept the picture of the universe given by Western science, nor do you have to have the finances to go mountain climbing or to take ecological vacations, in order to feel the mystical power of nature. That same power is available by hearing the call of the impoverished earth and, especially, in acting to do something about it.

In no way am I suggesting that the two stories, the scientific-mystical and the environmentalist-ethical, are necessarily opposed. On the contrary, I am urging that, if we begin with the ethical challenge of what we all know about the earth story at the beginning of the new millennium, we are taking an epistemologically more universal and effective approach to rally the religions around the earth and its mystical, explicitly religious message.

In this regard, I suspect that Max Oelschlaeger's understanding and expectations of the creation stories of different religions are more realistic and practical than Berry's. Oelschlaeger did not find the common ingredient of all these creation stories in their ability to affirm and accept contemporary science's understanding of nature as having a common origin, as interrelated, and as evolving. Rather, for him, "Each tradition articulates its own creation story. But all find solidarity in a common core concern of caring for creation."[12] As different as creation stories or cosmologies may be in their understanding of how it all began or of how the Creator relates to creation, "Every faith . . . can articulate a compelling sacred story, based on the metaphor of caring for creation, to treat nature with respect."[13] Oelschlaeger is convinced that, when religions come together to address the ethical challenges of our environmental predicament, they will discover "that creation stories across the spectrum of belief coalesce, despite their differences, around a politically efficacious—or at least potentially useful—metaphor of caring for creation."[14]

Even if Oelschlaeger, too, is overstating the common content or potential of the many different religious creation myths, the procedure I am suggesting still remains: If the religions, whatever their creation myths and whatever their view of Western science, can respond, together, to the need for an environmental ethic, if they can share a prophetic praxis of drawing on their differing religious resources to heal the wounds and address the injustices inflicted upon the planet and its species, they might more readily experience the earth not only as an object of concern that draws them together but also as a subject that speaks to them with the voice of the Sacred. If the earth is first a common ethical story for all religions, it has greater possibilities of becoming a common religious or creation story for all religions. The prophetic experience of ethical engagement for the earth (which is also a mystical experience of the sacred call of the earth) can provide the different religious communities not only with new ears by which to hear again or to reinterpret their own creation myths and religious language; it can also provide them with personal experiences and new languages by which they might learn from and perhaps even unify their differing cosmologies and theologies. Religious persons who struggle together to save the earth can better talk together and share together about that which makes them religious.

Ecological Dialogue: A "Second Step" to Ecological Praxis

In these final reflections, I will offer some practical suggestions for realizing a "deep ecological ecumenicity" among the religious families of the world. If there is any validity to what I have said about the way an ethical common front can prepare the way for a mystical or religious common ground for dialogue among the religions, then one can say that an ecological interreligious dialogue should be a second step to an ecological interreligious praxis.

Here I speak as a Christian liberation theologian when I suggest that what is a methodological given in liberation theology might also serve an analogously similar role in an interreligious ecological dialogue. In Christian liberation theology, theology is always a "second act." It follows the *compromiso,* or ethical commitment, of liberative praxis, of actual engagement in some kind of an effort to bring justice into a world of suffering due to sociopolitical injustice. The experience of such praxis, which is both intensely individual and necessarily communitarian, enables the theologian to "hear" God's word with new ears. The kind of interpretation of the Christian tradition that takes place after praxis would not have been possible before praxis. Both at the origins of liberation theology back in the late 1960s and in its ongoing life within the Christian churches, this first step of liberative praxis and this second step of theological interpretation take place not primarily in universities but in the well-known *communidades cristianas de base*—base Christian communities.[15]

I suggest that such a methodology or procedure can vivify and direct an interreligious ecological dialogue. When persons from differing religious communities come together to "dialogue" about the sacredness of the earth and how we must care for it, they should preface (or intertwine) such explicitly religious conversations with shared engagement in some concrete environmental problem—preferably one that is facing them in their own shared ecological backyard. Let them start by looking at this problem, commit themselves jointly to doing something about it, understand and analyze it with the help of nonreligious experts, feel together what the problem seems to be demanding of them, and then propose a course of action that their religious tradition would suggest. They will be acting, analyzing, struggling, perhaps anguishing together as an interreligious community—gathered around not a common creation story but a common environmental pain. The first step in gathering together will be a shared ethical praxis to relieve environmental suffering.

As this ethical praxis moves forward, because it is the praxis not only of environmental activists but also of environmental religious activists, it will move, naturally and necessarily, toward a more explicitly religious conversation. It will become a more self-conscious religious dialogue. This movement will be propelled by two forms of energy, practical and mystical. Practically, the participants in these shared environmental efforts will want and need to explain the deeper religious reasons for the forms of action they propose; also, they will naturally feel moved to give witness to what it is that motivates and steers them in their environmental praxis, especially when that praxis might lead them to heroic acts of confronting the system and suffering the system's reaction. The environmental prophet will want to speak about his or her mystical sources. This mystical or expressly religious witnessing will also be a natural result of the shared praxis because, as I tried to lay out above, the prophetic or ethical act of responsibility toward and caring for the earth is already at least implicitly a mystical experience in which one feels the Sacred Call within the ethical commitment. Sharing in a common mystical experience, mediated through their common ethical commitment, the participants in the dialogue will want to tell each other how they "read" this mystical experience in the distinctive religious languages of their traditions. When they try to speak their different religious languages to each other, when they try to communicate to each other how they are mining or reinterpreting their sacred texts or teachings on the basis of their environmental praxis, when they enter this explicitly religious dialogue about the environment—they will, I trust, have "new ears" by which to hear each other. Having acted together, having come to know each other in the struggle for environmental justice and well-being, having felt together the mystical-religious content of their mutual prophetic commitments and actions—they will be able all the more effectively (which does not mean perfectly or fully) to understand and learn from each other's differing religious languages and stories. Shared environmental praxis will becomes what Francis Schüssler Fiorenza has called a "hermeneutical link" by which the religions will be enabled to unlock their religious treasures of experience and story for each other.[16]

What I have just described are new forms of religious communities—not Basic Christian Communities but Basic Interreligious Communities. What gathers these communities together and provides them with extraordinary capacities both to interpret and to communicate are the same two factors, analogously understood, that gather the Basic Christian Communities: (1) a commitment to justice, understood now as eco-justice, the need to address the unjust sufferings of the entire earth community; and (2) a religious commitment within a religious community and tradition, with a plural understanding of the community as a community of communities, with the door open to any religious community concerned about the environment. I expect and hope that the new millennium will see a proliferation of such Basic Interreligious Communities throughout the world.[17]

Praxis Includes a "Preferential Option" for Victims

There is another aspect of the Basic Christian Communities and their method of liberation theology that needs to inform the Basic Interreligious Communities and their ecological dialogue. Liberation theologians insist that the liberative praxis that grounds the whole hermeneutical process of their theology must be based on what they call "social" or economic analysis. In other words, one's ethical response and projects have to stem not only from one's religious experience and beliefs but also from hard-nosed examination of what is causing the blight of social and economic injustice. They use differing social analyses, of course, but common to them all is the insistence that, whatever the analysis, it must be infused with and guided by a "preferential option for the poor" or by the "epistemological privilege of victims."[18] The victims of economic and social violence, in other words, have a central, determinative role to play in doing the analysis and in determining what kind of liberative praxis is called for. The role they play is a privileged one: The experiences of the marginalized, their viewpoints, their evaluations of what might work or not are to "come before" others', and they are to carry a greater weight in the conversation and decisions about what is wrong and what is to be done. This does not mean that the victims and the poor have an absolute voice or an always decisive vote, but it does mean that their voices must be listened to first and constantly throughout the dialogue.

Liberation theologians insist on this hermeneutical privilege of victims, not just out of a sense of justice, to make up for the long exclusion or marginalization of the voices of the poor from the deliberations of political and religious leaders, but also for an epistemological reason: The victims of injustice—those who have had to live on the margins of society and who daily experience the difficulty of being heard in the halls of government, university, and church know things that the established classes do not and perhaps cannot know.[19] The voices of victims, therefore, must be given a privileged hearing in order for the liberative praxis to be based on an adequate knowledge of what is going on.

A similar "preferential option" or "hermeneutical privilege" for victims is, I believe, essential for the success or failure of the interreligious ecological praxis I have been proposing and for the interfaith religious dialogue that flows from this praxis. Such an option or privileging will require the religions to bear in mind that their analyses of whatever environmental need or suffering they are addressing must be grounded not only on the input from scientific and economic specialists but also, and especially, on the witnessed experience and assessment of those who are the primary or immediate victims of the environmental exploitation and violence. Efforts toward an interreligious environmental ethics and an interreligious ecological dialogue must include not only religious persons representing differing spiritual families; it must also, somehow, include those who, though they may not even be religious, have been the human victims of ecological injustice or have devoted their energies to speaking for the sentient beings and parts of our sentient planet that are directly suffering from the plundering of the earth. Their voices must be heard and heard within and above other voices; if they are not, we will not really understand.

This hermeneutical privileging of victims, this insistence that they occupy not only a place of honor but also a place of power within the environmental dialogues among religious communities, is one of the best safeguards, I suggest, for preventing the co-opting of the ecological dialogue by first-world powers or by the religious communities sharing in that power. Aloysius Pieris, who from his South Asian perspective has witnessed how all too often religion is used as an ideology to serve the interests of special or dominant groups (in India and Sri Lanka, that is called "communalism"), urges an effective means to offset such abuse: "The people who can truly purify a religion of communalist ideology are not the theologians . . . or the religious hierarchs, but only the conscienticized victims of that ideology."[20] By insisting that the ecological dialogue of the Basic Interreligious Communities be populated not only by "theologians" and "religious hierarchs" and leaders but also by victims—those who can speak directly out of or for the pain of the earth community—we are making sure that there will always be present someone who can keep the dialogue honest and can keep it from gliding down the slippery slopes of ideology.

The participants in our interreligious dialogues on the environment must include not just spokespersons for the religions but also spokespersons for the earth—environmentalists, whether they are religious or not. As much as possible, these environmentalists should include environmentalists from the two-thirds world, for it is they who can best alert us first-worlders to the links between social and ecological injustice and between social and ecological renewal. Larry Rasmussen has admonished that "all efforts to save the planet [must] begin with hearing the cry of the people and the cry of the earth together."[21] By making sure that the cries of people-victims and of earth-victims continue to hold a privileged place in our ecological interreligious dialogue, we can hope, more assuredly, that our dialogues will be both more effective and better protected.

A Five-Step Program

Let me try to summarize my suggestions for a deep ecumenicity—that is, for an ecological interreligious dialogue that begins with environmental ethics and leads to environmental mysticism. I recommend a five-step program for such dialogue. Each step is described with a word that bears a prefix derived from the Latin *cum*—"with"—showing that each step can and must be taken together, linking people across religious divisions.

1. Compassion: A dialogue of deep ecumenicity begins with a shared feeling—a feeling of *com-patire*, suffering with those who are suffering. This is the feeling that compels the dialogue I am talking about: not a shared feeling of the Divine, not a shared feeling of the wonder and sacrality of nature, but a shared feeling of sorrow, of concern, perhaps of horror and consternation at the plight of this planet and its inhabitants. This is the first movement of bonding between persons of differing, maybe vastly differing, religious backgrounds: They all "cannot stand to see the sufferings" of the earth.

2. Conversion: Compassion, if it is real, will not stay put. It becomes a call to do something, to change the direction of one's living in order to reach out to those for whom one feels compassion. To feel with or suffer with someone who is suffering is to be claimed by that someone. That means we can no longer live the way we did before we felt the

compassion. We are, in other words, called to some kind of conversion. This is the second step in an ecological dialogue. In being converted, or turned toward the suffering earth, we are turned toward others who feel the same conversion. We want to join ranks with them, even though, at this stage, we do not know just what we all will do. We do know that we all want to do something. We have all undergone a common conversion—not to a common God (although, as I wrote above, there is a common call and, therefore, a common caller within this conversion)—but to a common, as yet undefined, course of action: to stop or heal the suffering.

3. Collaboration: The momentum of these shared experiences moves the multiple experiences to the third step in their encounter: collaboration, or acting together. Here they enter the actual praxis that grounds and feeds their coming together. From being members of different religious communities who experienced a common call and conversion they become co-workers or co-activists, if you will. As I tried to stress earlier, they will be co-workers not only with each other as religious persons but also with the victims—or those who speak for the victims—of environmental suffering and injustice. Their collaboration with the victims will strengthen and illumine their collaboration with each other. Such collaborating is a very different way of being together than if they just gathered to study each other's religions or to pray together. Collaborating on a shared program of praxis means analyzing together, becoming frustrated and angered together, perhaps going to jail together, even dying together for the sake of the compassion and conversion they have all felt. This kind of being together creates new bondings between people, new ways of feeling about each other. It creates religious brothers and sisters among those who may know little about each other's religions.

4. Communication: Collaborating religious brothers and sisters will find themselves moved to become communicating religious brothers and sisters. With this fourth step, we enter the explicitly religious level of the dialogue—where participants will feel the need to tell each other, to witness to each other, about how their religious experience and traditions nourish and guide their ecological commitment and praxis. They will feel a need not only to witness but also to be witnessed to, for, having seen the fervor and depth of my sister's or brother's praxis, I will want to know more about the spiritual matrix of that praxis. However, they will not only feel the need to talk to each other; they will also discover an ability, which they did not have before, to talk and explain, as well as to listen and understand. The bonds that grew in their collaboration now become lines of communication. Having acted together heart-to-heart, they can now talk together heart-to-heart. In this heart-to-heart talking they will find new ways of opening their scriptures to

each other, new opportunities to "pass over" into each other's religious experiences and beliefs.

5. Communion: The passing-over will be more than communication of ideas and new insights; it will also become a passing-over to, or a recognition of, that which was already present and active in the very first steps of the encounter, that which stirred the compassion and moved the conversion and grounded the praxis. I am talking about the "mystical content" of all prophetic feeling and action. I am referring, weakly, to that in which the participants of this ecumenical ecological dialogue are communing through all the steps of their encounter—the Sacredness of the earth, or the Sacred Earth, or the Mystery housed in the universe, the Notum Ignotum (the Known Unknown) that we sense and come to know more clearly when we "suffer with," "turn to," and "work with and for" the sufferings of this earth. There comes a stage in the dialogue where the participants in this dialogue will feel both the need and the ability to give greater, clearer expression to the communion they have been experiencing all along. At this point they will certainly have to sit in silence together—but they will also have to devise new ecumenical-ecological rituals and liturgies with which they can celebrate and commemorate the Mystery that the earth has revealed to them. Such communing will clarify and strengthen the compassion, the conversion, the collaboration, and the communication.

So will turn the circle of an interfaith ecological dialogue, and the earth, with the religions, will be the better for it.

Notes

1. In a document distributed by the International Coordinating Committee on Religion and the Earth, Wainwright House, 260 Stuyvesant Ave., Rye, NY 10580.

2. See, especially, Thomas Berry and Brian Swimme, *The Universe Story* (San Francisco: HarperSanFrancisco, 1992).

3. Brian Swimme, "Science: A Partner in Creating the Vision," in *Thomas Berry and the New Cosmology*, ed. Anne Lonergan (Mystic, CT: Twenty-Third Publications, 1988), 86.

4. Sallie McFague, "Cosmology and Christianity: Implications of the Common Creation Story for Theology," in *Theology at the End of Modernity: Essays in Honor of Gordon D. Kaufman*, ed. Sheila Greeve Devaney (Philadelphia: Trinity Press International, 1991), 31.

5. Ibid., 34.

6. Thomas Berry, "The Universe Story: Its Religious Significance," in *The Greening of Faith: God, the Environment, and the Good Life*, ed. John E. Carroll, Paul Brockelman, and Mary Westfall (Hanover, NH, and London: University Press of New England, for the University of New Hampshire, 1997), 216.

7. Berry and Swimme, *The Universe Story*, 255.

8. See Michel Foucault, *Power/Knowledge: Selected Interviews and Other Writings, 1972-1977*, ed. Colin Gordon (New York: Pantheon Books, 1980); and Paul Rabinow, ed., *The Foucault Reader* (New York: Pantheon Books, 1984).

9. Paul F. Knitter, *One Earth Many Religions: Multifaith Dialogue and Global Responsibility* (Maryknoll, NY: Orbis Books, 1995).

10. John Milbank, *The World Made Strange: Theology, Language, Culture* (Oxford: Basil Blackwell, 1997), 258; Gavin D'Costa, "Critical Questions of the Pluralistic Theology of Religions with Reference to the Work of Paul Knitter," unpublished lecture delivered at a conference on pluralistic theology, Bildungshaus St. Virgil, Salzburg, Austria, May 1996, 1-5, passim. See also Gavin D'Costa, *The Meeting of Religions and the Trinity* (Maryknoll, NY: Orbis Books, 2000), 33-39.

11. Daniel C. Maguire, *The Moral Core of Judaism and Christianity: Reclaiming the Revolution* (Minneapolis, MN: Fortress, 1993), 39-40.

12. Max Oelschlaeger, *Caring for Creation: An Ecumenical Approach to the Environmental Crisis* (New Haven, CT, and London: Yale University Press, 1994), 215.

13. Ibid., 231.

14. Ibid., 119.

15. See Gustavo Gutiérrez's classic, *A Theology of Liberation: History, Politics, and Salvation*, trans. and ed. Sr. Caridad Inda and John Eagleson (Maryknoll, NY: Orbis Books, 1973).

16. Francis Schüssler Fiorenza, "Theological and Religious Studies: The Contest of the Faculties," in *Shifting Boundaries: Contextual Approaches to the Structure of Theological Education*, ed. Barbara G. Wheeler and Edward Farley (Louisville, KY: Westminster/John Knox Press, 1991), 137-42.

17. A description of such communities in India, called "Basic Gandhian Communities," can be found in Knitter, *One Earth Many Religions*, 170-72.

18. For a general review and analysis of the preferential option for the poor in liberation theology, see John O'Brien, *Theology and the Option for the Poor* (Collegeville, MN: Liturgical Press, 1992). Also see Gustavo Gutiérrez, "Option for the Poor: A Review," in *The Month*, January, 1995, 5-10.

19. Victims have "learned more about the culture of the powerful than the powerful know about those they subjugate" (Mark Kline Taylor, *Remembering Esperanza: A Cultural-Political Theology for North American Praxis* [Maryknoll, NY: Orbis Books, 1990], 65).

20. Aloysius Pieris, "Faith-Communities and Communalism," *East Asian Pastoral Review* 26, nos. 3 and 4 (1989): 308-9.

21. Larry L. Rasmussen, *Earth Community Earth Ethics* (Maryknoll, NY: Orbis Books, 1996), 291.

Towards a Pneumatological Theology of Religions

Amos Yong[*]

LOOKING AHEAD

WHAT, THEN, SHOULD A CHRISTIAN THEOLOGY THAT SUSTAINS AN intensive dialogue with the religions of the world look like? Here, let me lay out in brief what I see as the task for Christian systematic theology in the twenty-first-century global context. First, Christian theology is concerned with the truth. Truth, however, arises out of the dialectical relationship between divine revelation and human reception and interpretation. All Christians have responsibility for grappling with the truth. But wrestling with the difficult question of truth is compounded when confronted by the question of the non-Christian faiths. Since Christians in Asia, Africa, and Latin America now far outnumber Christians in Europe and North America, Christian theology should work hard to include these non-Western readings of the gospel itself in order to understand the truth of divine revelation.

This means, second, that to the extent the non-Western world is religiously infused with Hindu, Taoist, Confucian, Buddhist, and other traditions of belief and practice, the gospel will itself be read and reread through those lenses. If we naïvely push ahead with our efforts to contextualize the gospel in the non-Western world as if these non-Western religious ways are not deeply embedded in the languages and sociocultural practices of these peoples, should we be surprised if Christianity is rejected in the long run? This has certainly been the case in Japan, for instance, where after centuries of missionary activity, the church remains practically nonexistent. Of course, our ignoring other faiths could also result in an unconscious assimilation of tenets contradictory to the gospel. This is irresponsible religious syncretism, which we should rightly be cautious of and reject. The problem, however, is that of distinguishing between valid forms of contextualization and invalid ones. This process involves, as I have argued in this book, extensive interreligious and intercultural engagement and comparative religion and theology at its depths rather than on its surfaces.

Alternatively, of course, we should take the Word-made-flesh (John 1:14) and the Spirit poured-out-on-all-flesh (Acts 2:17) seriously in developing what could be called either an incarnational or a "Pentecostal" pneumatological model of contextualization (chapter 1). To do so would be to ask what the gospel

---

* The author teaches theology at Regent University, and is the author of several well-received books addressing Pentecostal Christian perspectives, including *Hospitality and the Other: Pentecost, Christian Practices and the Neighbor* (Maryknoll, NY: Orbis Books, 2008), *The Spirit Poured Out on All Flesh: Pentecostalism and the Possibility of Global Theology* (Grand Rapids, MI: Baker Academic, 2005).

might look like if its primary dialogue partners are not Plato, Aristotle, Kant, Hegel, or Whitehead, but rather the Buddha, Confucius, Lao-tzu, Chuang-tzu, Nagarjuna, Shankara, Ramanuja, Chu Hsi, Dogen, Wang Yang Ming, and so on. These thinkers are not religiously neutral, of course; but then neither are any in the so-called philosophical tradition in the West. More important, where are we able to receive divine revelation in its purity apart from all cultural-linguistic "contamination"? The truth of the matter is that theological reflection has to continuously negotiate the dialectic between revelation and enculturation since divine revelation comes always-already inculturated, even as the Word-made-flesh was a first-century carpenter who was also male, Jewish, and a Nazarene and the Spirit is poured out, not on all people in the abstract, but on real people in particular places and times.

I have argued in this book that it is a pneumatological approach to the non-Christian faiths that provides the most rigorous theological, methodological, and epistemological rationale for engaging religious otherness in a serious, in-depth, and discerning manner. Of course, the proof is in the pudding, and the value and promise of a pneumatological *theologia religionum* will need to be determined in the long run by the results this research project delivers. The long-term result of the dialogical quest for truth driven by a pneumatological theology of religions will, I believe, be a thoroughly reconstructed Christian theology that will have passed over into the other faiths and returned home transformed in such a way as to be able to speak the gospel effectively and meaningfully in a world context generally and in the context of the diversity of religions in particular.

The goal of reconstructed Christian systematic theology that takes the world religions and other non-Christian faiths seriously, however, cannot be the product of one person's reflections. I envision my own contribution to this project as one of testing the specifics of the pneumatological paradigm against the empirical reality of the world religions. In other words, I want to ask what the pneumatological categories of divine presence, divine activity, and divine absence, for example, would look like when brought into dialogue with the religious symbols of the non-Christian faiths. With regard to Buddhism, for example, these categories lead to the comparison of metaphysical and ontological visions, of soteriological analyses, and of the role and function of the demonic. Application of the pneumatological categories needs to be tested against the world religious traditions—Hinduism, Taoism-Confucianism, Islam, Judaism—as well as against the phenomenon of new religious movements.

In this book [*Beyond the Impasse: Toward a Pneumatological Theology of Religions* (Grand Rapids, MI: Baker Academic, 2003)] I have assessed the promise as well as the potential problems and pitfalls of a pneumatological theology of religions. While the turn to pneumatology certainly does not eliminate the need to grapple with christological issues, it is far too early to conclude what a renewed form of christology would look like if the pneumatological paradigm charted here is taken seriously. My purpose here, however, is motivated by my conviction that the Spirit blows wherever the Spirit wills (John 3:8). I have therefore attempted to keep the vision for a pneumatological theology of religions afloat and perhaps to blow a gentle breeze upon its sails. The entire project is still in its infancy. I maintain, however, that discerning the presence and activity of the Spirit in the religions is central to this endeavor, and we are in desperate need of more adequate categories in order to conduct more viable theological comparisons across religious lines. Is it too far-fetched to hope that a pneumatological approach to the religions will prove to be more of a conduit that advances the formation of *theologia religionum* and the interreligious dialogue and our understandings of the human condition than we have so far realized?

Readings

Spirituality in Interfaith Dialogue

Masao Abe: A Spiritual Friendship

James L. Fredericks[*]

SOME YEARS AGO, I ENJOYED A FINE JAPANESE LUNCH WITH MY
friend and teacher, Abe Masao, the great exponent of Zen Buddhism and leader
in the dialogue among Buddhists and Christians. Professor Abe has taught me
wonderful things about Buddhism for some twenty years now. I gathered with
him and his wife, Abe Ikuko, in a traditional restaurant in Kyoto. We had a
private room with a low table and sat on *tatami* mats. Abe Sensei ("Sensei" is a
term of endearment and respect for a teacher used in Japan) had been somewhat
pensive and withdrawn for most of the meal. Mrs. Abe and I had been bantering
about how late the *tsuyu* rains had been that year and the effect it was having
on Kyoto's hydrangeas. Suddenly Sensei began to speak with an unusual tone of
voice, as if saying something of great importance to no one in particular. "It is
not enough," he said. Mrs. Abe and I fell silent and attentive. He repeated himself in the same voice: "It is not enough." I knew immediately what my teacher
was talking about. In his old age and after a long and distinguished career of
teaching and lecturing about Zen in the West, Abe Sensei was talking about
a Buddhist teaching dear to his heart, "the standpoint of emptiness." Out of
politeness, I did not want to indicate that I understood his meaning so directly
and sat, wondering what I should say in response. Finally, I settled on something
like this: "I will continue to study; Sensei, please continue to teach." I spoke in
the most formal Japanese I could muster out of respect for my teacher, but also
out of friendship.

I am not sure how I should describe my relationship with Abe Masao. To
call us colleagues in the dialogue among Buddhists and Christians hardly does

---

[*] The author teaches theology at Loyola Marymount University, and is a long-time member
of the Society for Buddhist Christian Studies. He also wrote *Buddhists and Christians: Through
Comparative Theology to Solidarity* (Maryknoll, NY: Orbis Books, 2004), and has also written
other essays on the theme of interreligious friendship.

218

justice to how dear he is to me. To call me his *deshi* (disciple) does not fit the expectations this word conjures in Japan. He and I disagree professionally over many important matters. Besides, Sensei is a Buddhist and I am not. Is Abe Masao my friend? He is thirty-five years my senior and a distinguished scholar. In Japan at least, calling us friends (*tomodachi*) would be presumptuous. I will stick with friendship, however, and will try to justify the term by qualifying it. My friendship with Abe Sensei is a *spiritual* friendship. I want to write about this spiritual friendship and reflect on what my teacher meant that day in Kyoto when he said, "it is not enough."

Friendship, of course, is a familiar theme in Christian spirituality. This is hardly surprising. Friendships humanize. Friendships must therefore be related in basic ways to our spiritual lives. The one who is without friends is poor indeed. More specifically, I am interested in spiritual friendships with those who follow other religious paths. I think we should look on these "inter-religious friendships"[1] as a form of Christian spiritual practice. Friendships that reach across the boundaries of community, doctrine, scripture, asceticism, and liturgy that separate religious believers should rightly be recognized as new opportunities for exploring Christian spirituality. Certainly this is the case with my friendship with Abe Masao. Sensei's Buddhist path is central, not incidental, to our friendship. Inter-religious friendships are not common. They are not unheard of either. Gustav Weigel's friendship with Rabbi Abraham Heschel and Thomas Merton's friendship with D. T. Suzuki (one of Abe Sensei's mentors) come readily to mind.

No doubt there are Christians today who would look on my spiritual friendship with Abe Masao as a vice. I look on it as a virtue. Friendships with those who follow other religious paths contribute to human flourishing. They are a way of building-up of new forms of solidarity between religious communities. The virtue of inter-religious friendship also helps us to resist vices, like our propensity to fear those who are different. In our sinfulness, fear leads us to demonize, caricature, or simply ignore the Other. A spiritual friendship with someone who follows another religious path helps us to resist not only intolerance, but also our penchant for developing elaborate theological schemes that reduce the Other to what David Tracy calls "simply more of the same."[2] Spiritual friendships with those who follow other religious paths help us to resist vices such as these.

Every friend, no matter how good or how old a friend, was once a stranger. Therefore, every friendship, no matter how good or how old, once involved making a hospitable place in our lives for a stranger. This practice has spiritual value. Welcoming a stranger entails a de-centering of the self. We are moved off our home ground. The sovereignty of the ego is undermined. In welcoming a stranger, we have to make room for another way of imagining the world and acting within it. Sartre was unable to see the advent of the stranger as anything but a threat. Emmanuel Levinas, reflecting Jewish tradition, saw the stranger not only as threat, but also as beatitude.[3] Welcoming the stranger brings a loss of security, but also a loss of hopelessness; the ruination of autonomy, but also a liberation from self-absorption. Feminist thinkers have noted that the drama of

losing a false self in order to gain a "true self" is a male narrative that does not
serve the needs of women very well. Women do not need to be moved off their
"home ground" or lose their "autonomy." Rather, "home ground" is what patri-
archy has taken from women. Befriending the stranger is less *agon* than a discovery of *koinonia*. Therefore, inter-religious friends like Rita Gross (a Tibetan
Buddhist) and Rosemary Radford Ruether may look on their spiritual friendship
differently than I look on my friendship with Abe Masao.[4]

Every friend was once a stranger. Less obviously, friendships of lasting value
and depth retain a sense of the stranger in the friend. This is very true of my
friendship with Abe Masao. Years ago, I spent an evening with Professor and
Mrs. Abe in their home in Kyoto. Sensei was unusually gregarious and informal
that evening. He wore a summer kimono. In July, the taste of cold noodles goes
nicely with the drone of cicadas in the garden and the clean smell of the *tatami*.
Not knowing any good Japanese word for what I was trying to say, I told Mrs.
Abe that everything was *gemutlich*. Sensei laughed as he tried to translate it
into Japanese for us. In the alcove was a very simple flower arrangement and a
hanging scroll with Chinese characters painted in a spontaneous hand. I asked
Sensei about the calligraphy. The scroll contained only a few characters: form,
emptiness, emptiness, form. Now able to read the scroll, I was left with a sudden
sense of what a stranger Abe Masao remains for me.

"Form is emptiness, emptiness is form." This famous teaching comes from
the Heart Sutra and tells much about why my cherished teacher and friend is still
a stranger to me. Sensible forms, the objects we fashion out of our passions and
obsessions and call "reality," are in fact "empty." They are illusions fashioned
by what the Buddha called "the mind on fire." All our pretensions to selfhood—
our construction of racial and national identities, our preoccupation with status, our obsession with autonomy—are but fleeting forms without substance,
founded on nothing. They are empty. Clinging to such forms as if they were real
only entangles us in a world that will never be satisfactory. This is samsara, what
the Lotus Sutra calls the "burning house" of sorrow. The path of wisdom, the
path that leads to an extinguishing of the fires that inflame the mind, is a path of
renunciation. Wisdom, for a Buddhist like Abe Masao, means finding freedom
in the realization of the emptiness of all things through non-attachment.

Form is emptiness, but according to the Heart Sutra, the reverse is also the
case. Emptiness itself is merely form and has no existence apart from the fleeting and ever-changing shapes taken by the world. This means that emptiness
is not a transcendent realm beyond this world. Form is emptiness—but emptiness is simply the myriad forms themselves. Therefore, in speaking of emptiness,
Sensei likes to use phrases strange to me like, "the original naturalness of all"
(*jinen*) and the "true suchness of things" (*shin-nyo*). For my friend, things have
no "beyond." Visible forms are not symbols that speak of what is "higher." In
a way that would have been utterly foreign to the Pseudo-Dionysius, my friend
does not live in a world in which appearances open up into a redeeming transcendence. Form is emptiness and emptiness is form—nothing more.

For many years, in our discussions, Abe Masao and I have tried to find a
place for my God in those Chinese characters. Neither one of us has succeeded

to the degree we had hoped. Form is emptiness. Emptiness is nothing other than form itself. In the asymmetrical grace of a flower arrangement, in the play of textures, tastes and sounds of the tea ceremony, in the spontaneous hand of the calligrapher—there is the suggestion of a kind of intimacy at the base of things. In the "true suchness of things" and the "original naturalness of all," the perfectly ordinary finally becomes numinous in itself, without bearing the burden of pointing to a transcendence beyond it. Zen is witness to an immanence so radical and complete that the otherness of the Christian God is overcome. At the dedication of the Temple in Jerusalem, Solomon had to deal with the unimaginable otherness of God: "Even the heaven and the highest heaven cannot hold you, how much less this house that I have built!" (1 Kings 8:27). The "true suchness of things" negates this unimaginable otherness. The "original naturalness of all" deconstructs the transcendence of the God of Zion.[5] In my friend's Buddhist world, there is neither a Creator nor a creation that witnesses to the Creator. The heavens do not declare the glory of God. There is only the drone of cicadas, the clean smell of *tatami* and the taste of cold noodles, in Kyoto, in July, underneath the hanging scroll. Form is emptiness—but emptiness does not lie beyond form. Nothing lies beyond the intimacy of forms. But unlike my friend and teacher, I cannot abide contentedly in this "original naturalness" that is without transcendence. The hound of heaven will not allow me this intimacy with the ordinary. In this, Sensei is not like me. He is does not know what it means to be pursued by such a hound. For all our friendship over the years, there still are times when we look at one another in what only can be called an appalling bewilderment. This friend of mine is a stranger.

There is a paradox in all this. Our strangeness to one another is the bond that holds our friendship together. I have other friends who manage to inhabit the world of Zen and the world of Christian theism with little difficulty. No doubt, this is a grace and should be accepted as such by those to whom this grace is given. I have never prayed for such a grace. On reflection, I suppose the reason I do not pray for such grace is the fear that this might weaken my friendship with Sensei. Our strangeness to one another has brought spiritual depth and purpose to our friendship. Welcoming strangers is good spiritual practice for a Christian. Abe Masao knows how to be a stranger for a Christian like me. Buddhists call this knack for benefiting others "skillful means" (*hôben*). This too is grace.

So, as I began to discern the shape of those Chinese characters on the hanging scroll with Sensei's help, a poorly alloyed mixture of regret and gratitude began to arise within me. My dear friend and teacher, Abe Masao, for all his erudition about my God (he studied theology with Tillich and Niebuhr), does not *know* a God beyond the world of forms. He does not know the subjectivity that arises by being addressed by the Holy One of Israel, as Abraham was. Beyond the "true suchness of things," there is no One who creates and redeems, who judges but also relents. The regret arises because I recognize the goodness of the Buddhist path but cannot embrace that path as a believer and practitioner. I am not a Buddhist. To say so would be not only pretense, but harmful to Buddhism. I will not hurt my Buddhist friend. The gratitude arises in the fact that my Buddhist friend has been such a selfless and generous teacher. Through my friendship with Abe Masao, I have been changed by great Buddhist truths. I cannot be a Buddhist. I can, however, be a friend to Abe Masao. My spiritual friendship with this Buddhist is a way to embrace and honor what I cannot choose.[6]

Sitting on the *tatami* mats in that Kyoto restaurant was not the only time that Sensei has ever said "it is not enough." In April of 1942, four months after the beginning of the Pacific War, Abe Masao entered Kyoto Imperial University (now Kyoto University) to study philosophy of religion. He was twenty-seven years old, buffeted by criticism for not enlisting in the army, and fearful of the power of nihilism at work in his militarized society. In Kyoto, he was much attracted by the lectures of Tanabe Hajime, who was already filled with foreboding over Japan's impending defeat and looking to Pure Land Buddhism for guidance. Zen is focused on unflagging effort on the meditation pillow and sudden *satori*. The Pure Land path, in contrast, is a Buddhism of repentance and faith in the compassion of Amida Buddha who rescues us from our egocentricity. Tanabe's comment, "Amida is not far from here," brought Abe to weep inconsolably in the realization that it was he who was moving away from Amida even as Amida was moving toward him. Even still, Sensei would eventually find the Pure Land path "not enough" for resisting the forces of nihilism in the world and in himself.

After the war, Abe joined a Zen meditation group that met at Reiun-ji within the great temple complex of Myoshin-ji in Kyoto. The group was directed by Hisamatsu Shin'ichi, a Zen layman and lecturer on Buddhism at the University. In December, 1951, Abe had a violent encounter with Hisamatsu that people still talk about. Zen had begun to erode Abe's Pure Land faith and the threat of nihilism had returned in force. One evening, in great agitation, Abe rose from his meditation pillow and lunged toward Hisamatsu screaming, "Is this the true self?" He was restrained briefly and then left the room. Later, Abe recalled the anguish of that dark night. "Its all a lie!" he told Hisamatsu. Still later, Abe said in despair, "I cannot find any place where I can stand"; Hisamatsu answered, "Stand right at that place where there is no place to stand." Zen calls this the standpoint of emptiness.

This "place where there is no place to stand" is where my friend has stood for more than half a century. Hisamatsu introduced Abe Masao to D. T. Suzuki who was already corresponding with Thomas Merton about Zen and Christian contemplation. Abe would eventually teach at great universities in the United States and Europe and become one of the leading figures in the dialogue among Buddhists and Christians. At the heart of all of this has been Abe Sensei's unwavering commitment to expounding the standpoint of emptiness. Unwavering, that is, until that day in Kyoto over lunch when he said, "it is not enough."

Sensei's favorite passage from the New Testament is the *carmen Christi* (Phil. 2:6-11). Singing of the savior, the hymn begins, "though he was in the form of God, he did not regard equality with God something to be grasped. Rather, he emptied himself, taking the form of a slave. . . ." Abe Sensei and I discussed this passage one afternoon, drinking green tea in his office. He wanted to know what "emptied himself" meant to me. I must have said something about the Incarnation of the Word in reply—I no longer remember. Sensei spoke even more softly than usual that day. "I think it means," he began, "that Christ is a kind of bodhisattva." I was deeply touched and, after a respectful moment, I said, "Sensei, please understand that this bodhisattva-Christ who takes the form of a slave is the only God that Christians know anything about." Abe Sensei closed his eyes and made the whole room very quiet.

Of Buddhism's many impressive teachings, the bodhisattva ideal must be one of the most wondrous. A bodhisattva is one who, in the quest for enlightenment, has come to the threshold of nirvana itself. Ready to enter into bliss, the bodhisattva renounces nirvana and turns back to samsara. This return to samsara takes the form of a vow to work skillfully for the benefit of every sentient being. In the bodhisattva's vow, Buddhism teaches a great and paradoxical truth. Since attachment is the birthplace of sorrow, wisdom requires that attachment be renounced. In the quest for liberation from sorrow, however, the bodhisattva is the one who has overcome every attachment save one, the attachment to nirvana itself. If the bodhisattva is to attain enlightenment, all attachment must be renounced, even the attachment to nirvana. Herein lies the paradox: only in renouncing this last attachment, our desire to abide in nirvana, can nirvana be attained. According to the bodhisattva ideal, true enlightenment involves not an escape from samsara, but rather a return to it in order to work skillfully and compassionately for the benefit of all sentient beings. Therefore, only by turning away from nirvana does the bodhisattva become fully enlightened. In the vow, the bodhisattva uproots the last taint of egocentricity, the desire to find personal bliss by escaping samsara. Sensei sees in Christ this paradoxical truth of the bodhisattva. Christ renounces divinity and takes on the form of a slave in order to benefit sentient beings. Because of this great renunciation, Christ is raised up and exalted. The bodhisattva is truly enlightened only by renouncing nirvana. Christ is truly divine only by abandoning divinity. By entering the world of form the transcendent monarch becomes the living God.

In the restaurant in Kyoto, when my friend and teacher said "it is not enough," and I realized that he was talking about his life's work, that feeling of gratitude and regret came over me again. The regret flowed from the pathos of an old man as he realizes that this life would end before the quest was over. Abe Masao knows that he has been more creative in imagining Christianity anew with Buddhist insight than in his quest to renew Buddhism with Christian insight. The standpoint of emptiness, the place where Sensei has stood for so many years, is not enough for a world still dancing blindly over the abyss of nihilism.

I felt gratitude as well—the gratitude every Christian should feel before a bodhisattva. My teacher has had to do much renouncing over his almost ninety years of life. In his youth, the threat of nihilism drove Abe Masao to the Pure Land path of faith. But this was not enough. Only with much anguish and at great personal cost, my friend renounced his attempt to live by faith. Later, in the confrontation with Hisamatsu Shin'ichi, Abe Masao began to stand in the "place where there is no place to stand"—the standpoint of emptiness embraced by the Zen path. By standing "where there is no place to stand," Sensei has lived a Zen life that has taken him to classrooms and lecterns in the West and to friends, like myself, who follow the path of Christ. But now, in his old age, my wonderful friend has realized that even the standpoint of emptiness is "not enough." This last attachment must be renounced. The quest for true enlightenment demands it. I do not presume that Sensei will stop being a Zen Buddhist. On the contrary, his words came to me as a kind of promise that he will continue to be a good Buddhist for my benefit. I am so grateful for this. "It is not enough" was the vow of a bodhisattva, spoken to no one in particular, but for the benefit of all.

In Kyoto, sitting on the *tatami* mats, halfway through lunch, while his wife and I bantered about *tsuyu* rains and hydrangeas, my teacher took the bodhisattva path, vowing to work for the benefit of all sentient beings, including his Christian friend. Sensei is now very old—too old for dialogue meetings. His life of formal dialogue has come to an end. But his vow of compassion continues. In this, Abe Masao is a true friend, a skillful teacher and a stranger to be welcomed. What is to be said in the face of such compassion? "I will continue to study; Sensei, please continue to teach."

Notes

1. For a reflection on inter-religious friendship as a new theological virtue, see my "Inter-religious Friendship: A New Theological Virtue," *Journal of Ecumenical Studies* 35, no. 2 (Spring 1998): 159-74.

2. David Tracy, *Plurality and Ambiguity: Hermeneutics, Religion, Hope* (New York: Harper and Row, 1987), 82-114, esp. 111.

3. Jean-Paul Sartre, *Being and Nothingness*, trans. Hazel E. Barnes (New York: Philosophical Library, 1956), 259-73; Immanuel Levinas, *Totality and Infinity: An Essay on Exteriority*, trans. Alphonso Lingis (Pittsburgh: Duquesne University Press, 1969).

4. For examples of feminist thinkers taking this position, see Judith Plaskow, *Sex, Sin and Grace: Women's Experience and the Theologies of Reinhold Niebuhr and Paul Tillich* (Washington, DC: University Press of America, 1980), and the classic article by Valerie Saiving, "The Human Situation: A Feminine View," which is reprinted in *Womanspirit Rising: A Feminist Reader in Religion*, ed. Carol Christ and Judith Plaskow (San Francisco: Harper and Row, 1979), 25-42. See also Rosemary Radford Ruether and Rita Gross, *Religious Feminism and the Future of the Planet: A Buddhist-Christian Conversation* (New York: Continuum, 2001).

5. See the essay by Abe's teacher Hisamatsu Shin'ichi, "Zen as the Negation of Holiness," in *The Buddha Eye: An Anthology of the Kyoto School*, ed. Frederick Frank (New York: Crossroad, 1982).

6. For a reflection on the notion of "spiritual regret," see Lee Yearly, "New Religious Virtues and the Study of Religion," the 15th Annual University Lecture in Religion, given at Arizona State University on February 10, 1994, 6-10, 14.

How I, a Christian, Have Learned from Buddhist Practice, or "The Frog Sat on the Lily Pond, Not Waiting"

*Frances Adeney**

AS A CHRISTIAN, I HAVE PRACTICED VARIOUS FORMS OF SILENT meditation. I remember sitting under the grand piano as a child of three, watching the sun flit through white curtains during our one-hour home communion service of the Plymouth Brethren. Most of the hour was spent in communal silence, gathered around a small table upon which was placed wine and bread. My memories of these meetings are filled with a sense of awe and presence.

I practiced a different kind of silent meditation as a young adult when I spent six weeks living on a beach in Greece. I saw few people apart from my two companions and the shepherdess who brought her flock to the meadow each day. I spent hours watching the waves or studying the grains of sand at my feet. I never missed a sunset.

At certain times of my life, there were more intentional, prayer-filled kinds of silent meditation. Wordless yearnings and grievings were brought to those meditations as I sought understanding and peace during times of illness, loss, and confusion. I wouldn't call any of those experiences Buddhist meditation. They were intentionally focused on either worshiping Christ or experiencing nature. There was no attempt to leave behind desires, no longing for emptiness, no intentional focus on being in the present moment that I associate with Buddhist meditation.

The first time I joined a group of people practicing Buddhist sitting was in 1997. Yet I felt like I had been doing this kind of silent meditating for years. Here is how that convergence came about. During the early 1990s, while living in Indonesia, I frequently visited a Trappist monastery in central Java. The nuns there didn't practice Buddhism, but my spiritual director, a German priest who lived down the mountain, said to me, "Come and see." Father Hamma introduced me to sitting in a gentle non-technique-oriented way. He called it "contemplative prayer." I took up this practice daily during a difficult time of loss in my life. Spiritual retreats at the monastery up the mountain helped me learn to let go of what I could not hold onto in life. It was there that I began to experience the delight and calm that comes from a practice of meditative silence.

This silent meditation differed from other practices of silence that I had known in significant ways: (1) It was not focused on an interchange between

---

* The author teaches at the Louisville Presbyterian Theological Seminary, and has also taught and lived in several countries in Asia. Her works include *Christian Women in Indonesia: A Narrative Study of Gender and Religion* (Syracuse, NY: Syracuse University Press, 2003), and essays on aspects of mission and evangelism for various publications.

God and myself. I was not listening for God's voice. I was not bringing my concerns to God. I was simply entering a place of silence. (2) It was not predicated on specific ideas about God or thoughts from writings in the Bible. I did not need to frame this time of silence with religious meanings. (3) It was not focused on an outcome. I neither expected nor did I ask for any changes in myself or the world.

Yet there were ways in which this practice of meditative silence was framed by my Christian faith. In taking up this practice, I felt I was intentionally entering God's presence. While not looking for spiritual experiences, I was somehow seeking life, and I did believe that God met me in those silent moments. More than once I had experiences that were "sightings" if not meetings with the Divine. During the seven years that I have practiced entering silence, the space that I enter has grown larger, and the conviction that I am entering and becoming part of God's presence deepens.

The frog
Sat on the lily pond
Not waiting

This Haiku poem resulted from one such experience. I had taken the bus out from the city. It dropped me at the foot of one of hundreds of small mountains in Java covered by lush greenery. The two-and-one-half-hour trek from the main road to the monastery took me through rice fields and small villages, over streams that ran under the road, and past hens and dogs who thought the road was theirs to sleep on and explore. I stopped, as usual, across from the elementary school to buy a bottle of water and some peanuts. Children gathered around me, and a few, curious enough to put aside their shyness, asked me my name, touched my skin.

That day I arrived at the gate of Gedono during mid-morning prayers. The sound of soprano voices wafted out of the chapel above me. Rather than entering, I seated myself by a small pool at the foot of the chapel steps. The sun brightened the lily pads in the dark pool, and I noticed a green frog sitting on one of them. Just to sit like that, allowing the sun to warm my back, staying quite still, completing my journey to this place of silent retreat. I felt that I need not go further. I had come there to be in silence. I need not enter the chapel and join in the singing of the Psalms. I need not wait for the sisters to come out of the chapel. I could begin. There was nothing to wait for. I sat still with the unmoving frog. The sounds of singing became distant. The mountain faded away. The whole world became the pond and me; I and the pond became the whole world.

During the past seven years, I have continued to practice the "contemplative prayer" that I learned from Father Hamma. I call it "entering silence." I've learned that it is indeed a form of Buddhist sitting. The attention to breath, the use of a holy word, the letting-go of thoughts, the focus on the present, the importance of posture—these "techniques" prepare one for entering silence.

I use this practice alongside other forms of Christian prayer and meditation, seeing it as complementary rather than contradictory to practices of verbal prayer, meditative Bible reading, and community liturgies. As I evaluate this Buddhist practice as a Christian, I understand it as:

1. *A preparation for an encounter with the Divine.* Thomas Merton is said to have remarked that Western Christians could learn a lot about prayer from the East. This has been my experience with entering silence. I have occasionally, I believe, been taken beyond myself to a nonverbalizable encounter with what is greater and deeper, and inclusive of my own being. In more ordinary experience, entering silence deepens my faith and calls from me a compassion for others and an appreciation of their worth and ways. As a Christian, I intentionally enter God's presence each time I practice silent meditation. Because I believe that God's Spirit meets me in a concrete spiritual way in meditation, my meditative experience is full of presence. It is not that what happens differs from the Buddhist experience; the intensity of deepened consciousness, the passing of time without awareness of its passing, the stillness of little breath, and the sense of etherealness of oneself and one's surroundings are similar. But the interpretation of what happens—that God configures God's self with me in the matrix of real spatiotemporal relationship—that is different. (See Peter C. Hodgson, *God in History: Shapes of Freedom,* [Nashville, TN: Abingdon, 1989], 93.) The ontological realities of which we speak are confessionally understood from within our history and faith community, not from outside. Furthermore, respect for the Buddhist community requires that I not presume the activity of a personal God who is absent from most Buddhist theologies. But my evaluation of this practice, which I use as a Christian, leads me to conclude that encounter with God is a valued part of the process.

2. *A way of fostering self-understanding.* The experience of entering silence has allowed me to explore the deeper reaches of myself, gaining insights into areas of suppressed pain and anger and aiding me in finding direction in my life. I don't know why or how this happens, but it seems to be an experience that Buddhists and Jungians, as well as Jews and Christians, agree can spring from developing a habit of practicing silence. My way of interpreting this process as a Christian focuses on the healing power of God's love and the efficacy of prayer. Jesus, according to the Gospel of John, promised to send a Comforter, the Holy Spirit, to the community after his death. "Peace I leave with you; my peace I give to you," he said (John 14:27). I experience that peace in entering silence. In describing prayer, the apostle Paul said that when Christians don't know how to pray, "the Spirit intercedes for us with sighs too deep for words" (Rom 8:27). Meditation, for me as a Christian, sometimes feels like sinking into a deep place of peace where all suffering is wordlessly heard and compassionately soothed.

Such experiences give me rest and provide energy for life's tasks. They also enable me to extend compassion to those who are hurt or oppressed. The Christian metaphor of drinking from deep wells of living water closely describes this experience. Jesus said to the woman at the well, "Everyone who drinks of this water will thirst again, but whoever drinks of the water that I shall give will never thirst: the water that I shall give will become a spring of water in them, welling up to eternal life" (John 4:13-14). Entering silence is like drinking from a deep well of cool water. I don't think about it. I don't analyze what exactly happens or why this mystical water quenches my thirst. I come and drink.

3. *A form of discipline that puts into perspective individual transience and smallness in relation to the universe and the Divine.* Entering silence helps me to get beneath the sometimes troubled waters of my daily life and lose myself in the vastness of the universe that cradles my life, although it does not always respond to my wishes.

The times spent at Gedono were times of letting go. Facing my father's death, accepting that continents separated me from my nearly grown children, and entering midlife were situations that required relinquishing control. Eventually, I knew, I would face my own death.

My Christian faith helped me to open my hands, giving each love and life to God, accepting the inevitable losses while trusting God's wisdom. Silent meditation helped me in this process of letting go of attachments and deepening my connection with the depths of life that undergird me.

I learned the practice of Buddhist sitting at a Trappist monastery from a German Jesuit priest teaching Christian spiritual direction to Indonesian Catholics in Java. Perhaps that says something about the adaptability of the wisdom of the practice of Buddhist sitting. But the silence toward which this practice directs us does not belong to Buddhism or any tradition that adopts it. Rather, we belong to the silence and continue to search in innumerable ways for its embrace.

Bridging the World Religions:
On Being a Buddhist-Christian Woman

*Maria Reis Habito**

IN THIS ESSAY I WILL DESCRIBE STEPS IN MY PATH FROM A traditional Roman Catholic background to continuing embodiment of both the Buddhist and Christian traditions. Even though these steps are described from a basis of personal experience, they may serve to shed light on the dynamics of becoming existentially engaged, involved in, and committed to more than just one religious tradition.

---

* The author, international program director of the Museum of World Religions based in Taipei, Taiwan, is also on the board of directors of the Elijah Interfaith Institute (Israel). She is assistant Zen teacher in the Sanbo Kyodan Lineage at Maria Kannon Zen Center in Dallas, Texas, and has published books and essays on interreligious themes in German and English.

I was raised in a traditional but liberal Catholic family in Germany. Traditional in the sense that we went to church on every Sunday and on all of the feast days and prayed before meals and going to bed, liberal in the sense that there was room to criticize those people or happenings in the church that we did not agree with. When I left for my studies in Taiwan after graduating from high school, I had inherited my grandmother's and mother's firm trust in God's existence and guidance.

In 1978 in Keelung, Taiwan, at the age of eighteen, I first encountered Buddhism. Father Joseph Wang, who is now auxiliary bishop, invited my mother and me to visit a Buddhist nun who had made the vow to stay in one room for 15 years and to only eat what people would bring to support her during that time. Now she had come out of her retreat and was open to receive visitors. On the way to the monastery, my mother and I talked about how strange this nun must be to engage in such a practice. When we arrived, she greeted us with a big smile, asking: "Are you Christians?" When we answered "Yes," she smiled even more and said: "Christians or Buddhists—it does not make any difference. We are all brothers and sisters." This openness impressed me very much and made me so strongly aware of my own prejudice and ignorance that I decided to take up the study of Buddhism. Is it not often so that the initial encounter with another religion does just this: it helps us realize our own prejudice and ignorance and instills the wish to learn more about the unfamiliar religion and the people who practice it? This is the first step towards building the foundation for bridges between world religions.

My next encounter with Buddhism took place in Ilan, where I met Master Hsin Tao for the first time in 1980. It was a friend who took me to see him there in his small hermitage. Again, I was received with great friendliness. But when Master Hsin Tao told me that I had come because there existed a very deep karmic link between us, I felt rather confused. As a Christian, I was not familiar with the concept of Karma. What connection should there be between a young German woman like me and a Chinese Buddhist monk? When Master Hsin Tao invited me to come and visit him again, I felt rather hesitant at first. But after some time I mustered all my courage to see him again because, somewhere deep down, I felt that this encounter with him was existentially important. I still was not used to thinking in terms of Karma, but I believed that I had come because of God's guidance and because God wanted to give me the opportunity to learn from this exceptional Buddhist teacher. I think that this very trust or conviction that it is existentially important for us to get to know or learn from another religion is the next step towards building a bridge between religions. Our encounter and dialogue is more fruitful if we bring God or Allah or Buddha to it in our heart, rather than merely discussing about the notion of God, Buddha, or Allah in a theoretical or dogmatic manner.

Master Hsin Tao challenged many of the beliefs that I held—for example, that I was created by God and therefore an individual different from all others; that there is a big difference between God and the human being and that it is never possible for a human being other than Jesus Christ to be God; that human beings only have one existence in this world and then go on to paradise or hell;

that as a Christian and German, I could not possibly become the disciple of a Buddhist master.

One day, I saw Master Hsin Tao offering food and lighting incense in front of a white Buddhist figure that almost looked like a Madonna, and I asked him: "Master, what are you doing? Who is that figure? I thought that in Zen-Buddhism, you do not worship idols?"

He replied: "This is not an idol. This is you. This is your true nature—pure compassion and wisdom."

This answer utterly confused me at first and then launched me on a path of self-examination. "This is you." What in the world did he mean? What did he see or understand about me that I didn't? Here again, I suggest that we need to be engaged in the encounter with another religion in a way that is open to reexamining long-held beliefs about what we are, what the self is. That is another building stone for the bridge between religions.

My discussions with Master about God, the Self, or the nature of reality also made me aware of how little I really knew about my own religion and how difficult it was for me to explain the little I knew coherently. When I returned to the University of Munich in Fall 1981, I decided to enroll in Asian Studies, as well as in Philosophy to learn more about the Western notions of God and reality and about the Christian theological tradition. I think that the renewed and deepened interest in one's own tradition is almost certainly always a result of our engagement with another religion. The point of interreligious dialogue is never to give up everything and fully adopt the other religion, or to claim that basically, there is not the slightest difference, but to really understand where oneself is coming from and where the person of the other religious belief is coming from. So the renewed and deepened study of one's own tradition in order to be better able to explain it to others is another building stone of the bridges between religions.

I visited Master in 1983, when he had moved to Ling-jiu Shan where he was meditating in a cave. "This time you have come to become my disciple," he told me as a greeting. This puzzled me again—how, as a Christian, could I possibly formally become the disciple of a Buddhist master? But reading my mind, Master addressed my doubts by adding: "I know that you believe in God. This step, becoming my disciple, will not put you into any conflict with your belief in God. But it will help you to always keep a connection to the Buddhist Dharma, even if you never ever come back to see me again." This simple explanation of his helped me to overcome my inner resistance and to let go of the notion that being Catholic and taking Buddhist vows is contradictory and mutually exclusive. While I was saying the triple refuge during the ceremony, I was overcome by such deep joy and gratitude that I knew with certainty that I was meant to do just this—taking Buddhist vows; that it was the right thing to do. But here I want to emphasize that it is my very personal journey, or Karma, if you so will, that led me to this step. I do by no means want to suggest that every Buddhist person engaged in interreligious dialogue should become baptized or take steps to be formally integrated into any of the other religions. But for me, this very step—taking Buddhist vows—was a very joyful experience of non-duality that has had a deep and lasting impact on my life.

Following Master's advice that I had to really sit down and meditate if I wanted to understand what Buddhist practice is all about, and that even writing a dissertation about a Buddhist text would not bring me the understanding that comes from meditation, I started sitting on my own and then joined a weeklong Zen retreat at a Franciscan monastery. This retreat was led by Father Enomiya Lassalle, a Jesuit priest who had studied Zen meditation in Japan and was the first pioneer to introduce this practice to Christians. I continued my Zen practice with him for four years from 1983 to 1987 and then continued under the guidance of his own teacher, Yamada Koun Roshi, in Japan. The guidance of these two extraordinary teachers helped me to come to greater intimacy with God, of experiencing God not as a being outside and far away, but as a living reality right within myself. Zen meditation is a purifying process that helps us let go of dualistic concepts and notions, thereby gradually opening us up to the experience of wisdom and compassion, or, to put it in Christian terms, the love of God. It was during a retreat in 1987 that I had the first powerful glimpse into the reality that Christians call the love of God. In one grace-filled moment of pure awareness, I experienced God's pure love embracing me, the other retreatants, and the whole universe alike. This experience left me shedding tears of repentance about my former blindness and tears of infinite gratitude at the same time. It was later confirmed by Yamada Roshi as an initial Satori—or awakening experience.

No matter what religion we adhere to, the challenge is always to integrate the extraordinary moments of insight, grace, and awareness into our ordinary life, to make them transform our self-centeredness into genuine care and concern for others. I try to practice this as mother of two young sons, as a teacher, and now, as the director of international programs of the Museum of World Religions. My personal foundation in all of this is the experience of non-duality and love that I was blessed with through Zen meditation, but even this experience needs to be continually purified. So now that the children are more independent and I have a little more time, I continue in my Zen practice and Koan study, even though my progress is slow. But it seems that we are always helped on our path to grow in wisdom and compassion. In my case, the life-threatening illness of a friend and my brother's depression have transformed me into a petitionary mode of being. Now my Catholic Buddhist practices completely intermingle— I say intercessory prayers like the Hail Mary or Kyrie together with the Great Compassion Mantra in the desire to alleviate theirs and all others' suffering. A new connection to the Tibetan Tonglen practice has recently emerged in this context, and this is one further step in my own personal bridging of world religions from within.

In conclusion, let me repeat the steps and stones in the building of bridges between religions which I have found in my own personal journey and which, I believe are important in any bridge that we want to build, not only in the bridge between religions.

1. The foundation from which to start—in my case, the trust that God is guiding me in the exploration of new territory—both outside of and within myself.

2. The honesty to recognize our limitations of prejudice and ignorance vis-à-vis the other, and the sincere endeavor to overcome both.

3. The openness to self-examination, to having basic assumptions—about the self, the Other, and reality as one has known it—to be challenged.

4. The renewed study of one's own tradition in order to be better able to understand and explain it to others.

5. The renewed commitment to spiritual practice, to growing in insight, love, and compassion.

6. The integration of insight into daily life.

7. The finding of a concrete way to practice compassion—for example doing Tonglen, or social work, peace work, hospice work, etc.

Finally, we will experience that building bridges within oneself naturally leads to building bridges to every other human being. We will start to look at each other no longer as strangers, but as beloved friends and part of oneself.

Epilogue

Crossing Boundaries and Finding Common Holy Ground

Yossi Klein Halevi[*]

JERUSALEM—OUTSIDE MY WINDOW, I HEAR THE SIRENS OF ambulances transporting the dozens of victims of the latest suicide bombing, offered for the glory of God and Islam. From the Palestinian village across the road comes the muezzin's call to prayer, which for some Jews has become a reminder of violence and murder. However tempting, I resist that linkage, because I've known a different Islam.

In the year before the current intifada began, I undertook a pilgrimage of religious empathy to my Muslim neighbors, visiting mosques in Gaza, the West Bank, and Israel. Though clearly identified by my skullcap as a religious Jew, I was invited to join the Muslim prayer line. My goal wasn't to blur the borders between faiths but to test whether Muslims and Jews could share a common language of devotion and transform religion into an instrument of peace rather than holy war. The faltering Oslo process had tried to reconcile secularized Israeli and Palestinian elites, ignoring the centrality of faith among our two peoples; I was searching for a dialogue of the heart.

Despite the anti-Jewish incitement that would soon help ignite the intifada, I found eager partners—mostly among the Sufis, or Muslim mystics, on the periphery of Palestinian Islam. One sheik dismissed rival Israeli and Palestinian territorial claims by insisting that the land belongs to neither side, only to God, echoing a rabbinic teaching.

---

* The author is a journalist and researcher on Israeli culture and society who writes on current issues in the Middle East for various publications. His book *At the Entrance to the Garden of Eden: A Jew's Search for God with Christians and Muslims in the Holy Land* (2001) describes his spiritual pilgrimage as a religious Jew among Christian and Muslim communities in Israel. This essay, originally published in the *New York Times* (August 10, 2001) as "An Islam Much Forgotten," is offered as a concluding message for this entire volume.

In showing reverence for Islam, I was able to elicit a reciprocal gesture from some Muslims, who acknowledged that the return of the Jews to Israel wasn't a colonialist imposition but in accord with the will of God.

The culmination of my journey occurred during the festival of Lailat al-Miraj, the night Muslims believe that Muhammad ascended to heaven from Jerusalem. I was invited to join services in a little Sufi mosque located in Gaza's Nuseirat refugee camp. The building was so forlorn that it lacked a minaret; its narrow prayer room could barely hold 50 worshipers. Eight years earlier, during the Israeli occupation, I'd served as a reservist soldier in Nuseirat, the heartland of Islamic extremism, and had been hit in the head with a rock while on patrol near the mosque.

Now, together with the mosque's devotees, I participated in the Sufi service known as *zikr,* or remembrance of God's presence. For perhaps an hour we chanted, leapt, and rapidly exhaled in a dance of controlled ecstasy, celebrating God's oneness and the mystic's transcendence over human fragmentation.

Since the violence intensified last September, the conciliatory—and sadly marginal—voices within Palestinian Islam have been intimidated into silence. Clergy on Palestinian television urge the faithful to kill Jews, while children in white shrouds, with simulated bombs, march in processions of martyrdom. My Muslim friends are unable to publicly express their shame as their faith is sullied.

Today, my forays into Palestinian Islam seem like fantasies. Islam has once again become untouchable, pervasive, and elusive as air. Many Arab Muslims, encouraged by official media and leading clergy, now embrace a medieval kind of hatred of Jews. While religious extremists are hardly lacking among Jews, Israeli society has repudiated their theology and their actions; not so with the Palestinian mainstream. And while no Israeli leader denies the sanctity of Jerusalem for Islam, Palestinian leaders have repudiated the historical connection between Jerusalem and the Jewish people.

Still, my religious journey taught me that Islam contains those qualities necessary for peacemaking—humility before God and an acute and fearless awareness of mortality. I know that Jews and Muslims can share wisdom, if not doctrine. Even as suicide bombers explode in our streets, and as Israel confronts a war that is being forced upon it, I recall the Muslim mystics who opened their doors and their hearts to me, and I refuse to despair.

List of Sources

Part I

Early Christian Voices

Justin Martyr. *The Apostolic Fathers with Justin Martyr and Irenaeus*, ed. Philip Schaff. Christian Classics Ethereal Library. http://www.ccel.org/ccel/schaff/anf01.doc., chapters I, II, V, VI, IX, XX, XLVI.

Clement of Alexandria. *Fathers of the Second Century: Hermas, Tatian, Athenagoras, Theophilus, and Clement of Alexandria (Entire)*, ed. Philip Schaff. Christian Classics Ethereal Library. http://www.ccel.org/ccel/schaff/anf02.doc., "Exhortation to the Heathen," chapter VI; *Stromata*, Sections 1.2, 1.5, 1.9, 1.13, 1.19, 5.13.

Tertullian. *Latin Christianity: Its Founder, Tertullian*, ed. Philip Schaff. Christian Classics Ethereal Library. http://www.ccel.org/ccel/schaff/anf03.doc., "Prescriptions against Heretics," chapters VII, XII, XVI.

Cyprian. *Fathers of the Third Century: Hippolytus, Cyprian, Caius, Novatian, Appendix*, ed. Philip Schaff. Christian Classics Ethereal Library. http://www.ccel.org/ccel/schaff/anf05.doc., "To Jubaianus, Concerning the Baptism of Heretics," sections 1 and 21.

Augustine. *The Confessions and Letters of St. Augustine, with a Sketch of His Life and Work*, ed. Philip Schaff. Christian Classics Ethereal Library. http://www.ccel.org/ccel/schaff/npnf101.doc., "Letter to Deogratias," 8, 9, 11, 12, 15.

The Christendom Synthesis

Thomas Aquinas. *Summa Theologica*, trans. Fathers of the English Dominican Province. Benziger Brothers edition, 1947. Christian Classics Ethereal Library. http://www.ccel.org/ccel/aquinas/summa.doc., 2-2, Q.2, Art 7; 2-2, Q. 10, Art. 4; III, Q. 69, Art. 4.

Nicholas of Cusa. *De Pace Fidei and Cribratio Alkorani*, 2nd ed., trans. Jasper Hopkins. Minneapolis, MN: Arthur J. Banning Press, 1994. http://cla.umn.edu/sites/jhopkins/CAI-12-2000.pdf.

Bartolomé de Las Casas. *History of the Indies*, trans. and ed. Andrée Collard. New York: Harper & Row, 1971, 5-6, 14, 281-82, copyright © 1971 by Andrée M. Collard, renewed © 1999 by Joyce J. Contrucci, reprinted by permission of Joyce J. Contrucci; *The Only Way*, ed. Helen Rand Parish, trans. Francis Patrick Sullivan. Mahwah, NJ: Paulist, 1992, 63, 68-69, 164. Reprinted with permission of Paulist Press.

Modern and Postmodern Voices

Friedrich Schleiermacher. *The Christian Faith*, ed. H. R. Macintosh and J. S. Stewart. Edinburgh: T&T Clark, 1999, 12, 17-18, 26, 31, 33-35, 37-38. By kind permission of Continuum International Publishing Group.

Ernst Troeltsch. *Christian Thought, Its History and Application*, trans. Mary E. Clarke. New York: Meridian Books, 1957, 53-63.

Karl Barth. *Church Dogmatics*, I/2, 2nd ed., trans. G. W. Bromiley; ed. G. W. Bromiley and T. F. Torrance. New York: T&T Clark International, 2004, 280-81, 294-95, 297-301, 302-3, 314, 325-27, and 344. By kind permission of Continuum International Publishing Group.

Karl Rahner. *Theological Investigations. Vol. V: Later Writings*, trans. Karl-H. Kruger. Baltimore, MD: Helicon, 1966, 118-23, 125, 128, 131-34. Copyright 1966 by Darton Longman and Todd Ltd, London, and used by permission of the publishers.

John Hick. "Religious Pluralism and Salvation." Pp. 54-63 in *The Philosophical Challenge of Religious Diversity*, ed. Philip L. Quinn and Kevin Meeker. New York: Oxford University Press, 2000; reprinted with permission of the original publisher *Faith and Philosophy*.

Rosemary Radford Ruether. "Feminism and Jewish-Christian Dialogue: Particularism and Universalism in the Search for Religious Truth." Pp. 137-42 in *The Myth of Christian Uniqueness*, ed. John Hick and Paul F. Knitter. Maryknoll, NY: Orbis Books, 1987.

Marjorie Hewitt Suchocki. "In Search of Justice: Religious Pluralism from a Feminist Perspective." Pp. 149-60 in *The Myth of Christian Uniqueness*, ed. John Hick and Paul F. Knitter. Maryknoll, NY: Orbis Books, 1987.

Aloysius Pieris. *An Asian Theology of Liberation*. Maryknoll, NY: Orbis Books, 1988, 87-88, 107-10.

Engelbert Mveng. "African Liberation Theology." Pp. 17-34 (26-29) in *Theologies of the Third World: Convergences and Differences*, ed. Leonardo Boff and Virgil Elizondo. Concilium 199. Edinburgh: T&T Clark, 1988. By kind permission of Continuum International Publishing Group.

Chung Hyun Kyung. "'*Han-pu-ri*': Doing Theology from Korean Women's Perspective." Pp. 52-63 (59-61) in *Frontiers in Asian Christian Theology: Emerging Trends*, ed. R. S. Sugirtharajah. Maryknoll, NY: Orbis Books, 1994.

S. Mark Heim. *Salvations: Truth and Difference in Religion*. Maryknoll, NY: Orbis Books, 1995, 129-30, 144-47, 149, 158, 160-63, and 165-66.

Michael Amaladoss. "Interreligious Dialogue: A View from Asia." *International Bulletin of Missionary Research* (19 January 1995): 2-5.

James Fredericks. *Buddhists and Christians: Through Comparative Theology to Solidarity*. Maryknoll, NY: Orbis Books, 2004, 25-27, 97, 103-4.

Part II

Andrew Wingate. "Mission as Dialogue: A Contextual Study from Leicester, UK." *Swedish Missiological Themes* (*Svensk missionstidskrift*) 92, no. 3 (2004): 463-88.

Jeanne Matthew Sommers. "Jesus Loves Me This I Know, for the Buddha Tells Me So." Pp. 158-67 in *A Socially Engaged Spirituality: Essays in Honor of Sulak Sivaraksa on His 70th Birthday*, ed. David Chappell. Bangkok: Sathirakoses-Nagapradipa Foundation, 2003.

Joseph Stamer. "Can Christians and Muslims Pray Together?" *Theology Digest* 46, no. 3 (Fall 1999): 209-15. Originally published as "Praying with Muslims?" *Encounter: Documents for Muslim-Christian Understanding* 243 (1998).

Timothy Tennent. "Trinity and Sacchidananda in the Writings of Brahmabandav Upadhyaya." *Dharma Deepika* (January-June 2003): 61-75.

John Keenan. "A Mahayana Theology of the Real Presence of Christ in the Eucharist." *Buddhist Christian Studies* 24, no. 1 (2004): 89-100.

Paul Knitter. "A Common Creation Story? Interreligious Dialogue and Ecology." *Journal of Ecumenical Studies* 37, no. 3/4 (Summer/Fall 2000): 285-300.

Amos Yong. "Toward a Pneumatological Theology of Religions," final segment of the concluding chapter, entitled "Transitions: Pneumatological Imagination and Discernment in the World Religions." Pp. 184-92 in *Beyond the Impasse: Toward a Pneumatological Theology of Religions*, ed. Amos Young. Grand Rapids: Baker Academic, 2003. The excerpt for this volume does not include the footnotes of the original publication; used with permission of the Baker Publishing Group.

James Fredericks. "Masao Abe: A Spiritual Friendship." *Spiritus* 3, no. 2 (Fall 2003): 219-30.

Frances Adeney. "How I, a Christian, Have Learned from Buddhist Practice, or A Frog Sat on a Lily Pad, Not Waiting." *Buddhist Christian Studies* 21, no. 1 (2001): 33-36.

Maria Reis Habito. "Bridging the World Religions: On Being a Buddhist Christian Woman." Pp. 81-86 in *A Socially Engaged Spirituality: Essays in Honor of Sulak Sivaraksa on His 70th Birthday*, ed. David Chappell. Bangkok: Sathirakoses-Nagapradipa Foundation, 2003.

Yossi Klein Halevi. "An Islam Much Forgotten," *New York Times*, August 10, 2001 (retitled for this volume).

Suggested Readings

Global Society and the Multireligious Arena

Berthrong, John H. *The Divine Deli: Religious Identity in the North American Cultural Mosaic*. Maryknoll, NY: Orbis Books, 1999.

Eck, Diana L. *A New Religious America: How a "Christian Country" Has Become the World's Most Religiously Diverse Nation*. San Francisco: HarperSanFrancisco, 2001.

Ehrlich, Paul R., and Anne H. Ehrlich. *One with Nineveh: Politics, Consumption and the Human Future*. Washington, DC: Island Press, Shearwater Books, 2004.

Korten, David C. *The Great Turning: From Empire to Earth Community*. Bloomfield, CT: Kumarian Press, and San Francisco: Berrett-Koehler, 2006.

Singer, Peter. *One World: The Ethics of Globalization*. New Haven: Yale University Press, 2002.

Wuthnow, Robert. *America and the Challenges to Religious Diversity*. Princeton, NJ: Princeton University Press, 2005.

Relating to Religious Others: Theology of Religions

Cobb, John B., Jr. *Beyond Dialogue: Toward a Mutual Transformation of Christianity and Buddhism*. Philadelphia: Fortress, 1982.

Cohn-Sherbok, Dan, ed. *Interfaith Theology: A Reader*. Oxford: Oneworld, 2001.

Cracknell, Kenneth. *In Good and Generous Faith: Christian Responses to Religious Pluralism*. Peterborough, UK: Epworth, 2005. Cleveland, OH: Pilgrim Press, 2006.

Dupuis, Jacques, S.J. *Toward a Christian Theology of Religious Pluralism*. Maryknoll, NY: Orbis Books, 2001.

Heim, S. Mark. *Salvations: Truth and Difference in Religion*. Maryknoll, NY: Orbis Books, 1995.

Knitter, Paul F. *Introducing Theologies of Religions*. Maryknoll, NY: Orbis Books, 2002.

———. *No Other Name: A Critical Survey of Christian Attitudes toward the World Religions*. Maryknoll, NY: Orbis Books, 1985.

Lochhead, David. *The Dialogical Imperative: A Christian Reflection on Interfaith Encounter*. Maryknoll, NY: Orbis Books, 1988.

Martey, Emmanuel. *African Theology: Inculturation and Liberation*. Maryknoll, NY: Orbis Books, 1993.

Panikkar, Raimundo. *The Cosmotheandric Experience: Emerging Religious Consciousness*. Maryknoll, NY: Orbis Books, 1993.

———. *The Intrareligious Dialogue*. Rev. ed. New York: Paulist, 1999.

Pieris, Aloysius. *An Asian Theology of Liberation*. Maryknoll, NY: Orbis Books, 1988.

Race, Alan. *Christians and Religious Pluralism: Patterns in the Christian Theology of Religions*. Maryknoll, NY: Orbis Books, 1983.

Yong, Amos. *Beyond the Impasse: Toward a Pneumatological Theology of Religions*. Grand Rapids, MI: Baker Academic, 2003.

Listening to, Learning from and with Religious Others: Comparative Theology

Amaladoss, Michael. *Making All Things New: Dialogue, Pluralism, and Evangelization in Asia*. Maryknoll, NY: Orbis Books, 1990.

Cobb, Jr., John B., and Christopher Ives, eds. *The Emptying God: A Buddhist-Jewish-Christian Conversation*. Maryknoll, NY: Orbis Books, 1990.

Clooney, Francis X. *Hindu God, Christian God: How Reason Helps Break Down the Boundaries between Religions*. New York: Oxford University Press, 2001.

Fredericks, James L. *Buddhists and Christians: From Comparative Theology to Solidarity*. Maryknoll, NY: Orbis Books, 2004.

————. *Faith among Faiths: Christian Theology and Non-Christian Religions*. Mahwah, NJ: Paulist, 1999.

Heim, S. Mark. *The Depth of the Riches: A Trinitarian Theology of Religious Ends*. Grand Rapids, MI: Eerdmans, 2001.

Keenan, John P. *The Meaning of Christ: A Mahāyāna Christology*. Maryknoll, NY: Orbis Books, 1989.

Tracy, David. *Dialogue with the Other: The Inter-Religious Dialogue*. Grand Rapids, MI: Eerdmans, 1990.

Spirituality in Interreligious Dialogue

Abhishiktananda. *Saccidānanda: A Christian Approach to Advaitic Experience*. Delhi: ISPCK, 1984.

Arai, Tosh, and Wesley Ariarajah, eds. *Spirituality in Interfaith Dialogue*. Geneva: World Council of Churches, 1989.

Boykin, Kim. *Zen for Christians: A Beginner's Guide*. San Francisco: Jossey-Bass, 2003.

D'Costa, Gavin. *The Meeting of Religions and the Trinity*. Maryknoll, NY: Orbis Books, 2000.

De Mello, Anthony. *Sadhana, a Way to God: Christian Exercises in Eastern Form*. New York: Image Books, 1984.

Griffiths, Bede. *A New Vision of Reality: Western Science, Eastern Mysticism, and Christian Faith*. Templegate, 1990.

Habito, Ruben L. F. *Healing Breath: Zen for Christians and Buddhists in a Wounded World*. Boston: Wisdom Publications, 2006.

————. *Living Zen, Loving God*. Boston: Wisdom Publications, 2004.

Halevi, Yossi Klein. *At the Entrance to the Garden of Eden: A Jew's Search for Hope with Christians and Muslims in the Holy Land*. New York: HarperCollins, 2002.

Healy, Katherine. *Entering the Cave of the Heart: Eastern Ways of Prayer for Western Christians*. New York: Paulist, 1986.

Kasimow, Harold, John Keenan, and Linda Klepinger Keenan, eds. *Beside Still Waters: Jews, Christians, and the Way of the Buddha*. Boston: Wisdom Publications, 2003.

Kennedy, Robert. *Zen Mind, Christian Mind*. New York: Continuum, 1995.

————. *Zen Gifts to Christians: The Place of Zen in Christian Life*. New York: Continuum, 2004.

Lefebure, Leo. *Life Transformed: Meditations on the Christian Scriptures in the Light of Buddhist Perspectives*. Chicago: ACTA Publications, 1989.

Paul, Russill. *Jesus in the Lotus: The Mystical Doorway between Christianity and Yogic Spirituality*. Novato, CA: New World Library, 2009.

Teasdale, Wayne. *Mystic Heart: Discovering a Universal Spirituality in the World's Religions*. Novato, CA: New World Library, 2001.

Tasks for Interreligious Cooperation

Hao, Yap Kim. *Doing Theology in a Pluralistic World*. Singapore: Kin Keong Printing, 1990.

Knitter, Paul F. *Jesus and the Other Names: Christian Mission and Global Responsibility*. Maryknoll, NY: Orbis Books, 1996.

————. *One Earth Many Religions*. Maryknoll, NY: Orbis Books, 1995.

————, and Chandra Muzaffar, eds. *Subverting Greed: Religious Perspectives on the Global Economy*. Maryknoll, NY: Orbis Books, in association with the Boston Research Center for the 21st Century, 2002.

Küng, Hans, and Helmut Schmidt, eds. *A Global Ethic and Global Responsibilities: Two Declarations*. London: SCM Press, 1998.

Smith-Christopher, Daniel L., ed. *Subverting Hatred: The Challenge of Nonviolence in Religious Traditions*. Maryknoll, NY: Orbis Books, in association with the Boston Research Center for the 21st Century, 1998.

Veitch, James, ed. *Can Humanity Survive? The World's Religions and the Environment*. Auckland: Awareness Book Co., 1996.

Wingate, Andrew. *Celebrating Difference, Staying Faithful: How to Live in a Multi-Faith World*. London: Darton, Longman & Todd, 2005.

CPSIA information can be obtained
at www.ICGtesting.com
Printed in the USA
LVHW091320230621
690948LV00012B/126